VULNERABLE ADULTS AND THE LAW

Vulnerable Adults and the Law

JONATHAN HERRING

Professor of Law, Faculty of Law, University of Oxford;
Fellow in Law, Exeter College, University of Oxford

OXFORD
UNIVERSITY PRESS

OXFORD

UNIVERSITY PRESS

Great Clarendon Street, Oxford, OX2 6DP,
United Kingdom

Oxford University Press is a department of the University of Oxford.
It furthers the University's objective of excellence in research, scholarship,
and education by publishing worldwide. Oxford is a registered trade mark of
Oxford University Press in the UK and in certain other countries

Published in the United States of America by Oxford University Press
198 Madison Avenue, New York, NY 10016, United States of America

British Library Cataloguing in Publication Data
Data available

Library of Congress Control Number: 2015959834

ISBN 978-0-19-873727-8

To Kirsten

Acknowledgements

I am grateful to many friends and colleagues for their support, encouragement, and inspiration during the writing of this book. In particular, Alan Bogg, Shazia Choudhry, Charles Foster, Stephen Gilmore, Michelle Madden Dempsey, Imogen Goold, Mary Neal, Rachel Taylor, and Julie Wallbank deserve particular gratitude.

I am much obliged to the team at OUP. In particular, Anne-Marie Forker and Paul Tompsett did excellent work in the editing process, and Natasha Flemming was supportive from the very start.

Above all I owe everything to my children, Laurel, Joanna, and Darcy, who inspire this book in many ways, and my dear partner Kirsten, who cares so much.

Table of Contents

Table of Cases

Table of Legislation

1

Introducing Vulnerability

Let us rejoice in our vulnerability. That is, in short, the message of this book. It is a startling statement because vulnerability comes with so many negative connotations in our society. Vulnerability, we are told, is something to be avoided. We are encouraged to be independent, self-sufficient, autonomous, and free from reliance on others. The ideal that politicians urge us to aspire to is a person not dependent on state benefits, a burden to others, but to be self-reliant.[1] We are to save now so that we can fund our old age and do not become a drain on our children or the rest of our society. The response to changing demographics from the Government is to urge older people to be independent and exercise choice.[2]

The law, unsurprisingly, reflects these attitudes. The law is built around the ideal of legal personhood: a man who is autonomous, self-sufficient, in control, capacitous, and independent. For such a man the law gives the legal tools he needs to maintain his status: the rights of autonomy, privacy, liberty, and freedom from state interference. For him, legal rights are designed to keep him free from intrusion. Rights are designed to keep people apart, to give people their space.

This book will claim that this is all a dangerous fiction. In our nature we are deeply vulnerable. We are profoundly dependent on others and social provision to meet our bodily, emotional, and cultural needs. Our relationships are essential to our well-being; our sense of self; and our understanding of the world around us. We need a legal system that acknowledges our responsibilities to those we are in relationships with and others in our society, one which encourages and promotes caring relationships. A legal system that is designed around relational people, dependent on others to meet their needs and one whose key values are not autonomy, freedom, and privacy but mutuality, interdependence, and relational responsibilities.

---

[1] David Cameron, *Speech on Welfare Reform* (25 June, 2012).
[2] Department of Health, *Independence, Wellbeing and Choice* (Department of Health, 2005).

This book is designed to explore how the current law responds to the notion of vulnerability. It should not be read as an authoritative guide on everything the law has to say about vulnerable adults, but rather as an exploration of how the law uses vulnerability in a range of contexts and what a law which took the approach advocated above might look like.

In Chapter 2 I explore the concept of vulnerability and the difficulties in defining it. At the heart of the disputes is a disagreement between those who claim that vulnerability is universal and is an inevitable part of the human experience; and those who argue that it is more profitable to recognize that there are particular individuals or groups of individuals who suffer particular vulnerabilities. This book takes a middle path between these two options. It agrees that vulnerability is a universal condition. This is significant because it has profound effects on how we understand ourselves and what the values that underpin our legal system should be. It also agrees that there are particular groups of individuals who are rendered especially vulnerable by the lack of provision of social support and services. I put the argument that way to indicate the especial vulnerability that should be seen to result from social provision, rather than factors inherent in the individual. That indicates that the cause of, and therefore the response to, the vulnerability needs to be focused on the social support. This chapter also highlights the dangers that are associated with vulnerability. At the moment in political and legal discourse it is used as a concept to identify groups who can be a source of paternalistic interventions. Ironically this can operate to increase the vulnerability of these groups, by promoting individualistic interventions which promote values such as independence. It also fails to protect those who are vulnerable but do not fall within one of the recognized categories.

Chapter 3 examines the law's understanding of capacity. This is a central plank in the law's response to vulnerable adults. It draws a sharp distinction between those who have capacity and whose decisions require complete respect; and those who lack capacity and for whom decisions can be made by others based on an assessment of what is in their best interests. This chapter seeks to problematize that distinction. While capacity claims to be used to protect autonomy, I suggest six ways in which a person might have capacity under the current law, but, in fact, lacks autonomy. The chapter claims autonomy should be understood as scalar. It is not an all-or-nothing concept; rather we possess autonomy to a greater or lesser extent. The requirements for a richly autonomous decision are strict and few of us are able to reach them. The chapter advocates a more nuanced approach that enables the court to weigh up the harm that might result from a decision and the extent to which the decision is richly autonomous.

That last point is picked up in Chapter 4 and is used to justify the courts' use of the inherent jurisdiction to protect vulnerable adults. The chapter explores the history behind this jurisdiction and the current state of the case law. It promotes the use of this jurisdiction, even in cases where a person has been found to retain capacity. This is an important acknowledgement of the point argued in Chapter 3 that simply because a person has capacity for the purposes of the Mental Capacity Act 2005 does not mean they are able to act autonomously. Further, this jurisdiction is justified by the Human Rights Act 1998 which places obligations on the state to protect vulnerable adults from abuse.

Chapter 5 expounds on the duties on the state to protect vulnerable adults in the European Convention on Human Rights, given effect in England and Wales through the Human Rights Act. The chapter explores the case law of the European Court of Human Rights and explains that Articles 2, 3, and 8 not only require the state not to infringe those rights directly, but also require the state to take reasonable steps to ensure that one citizen does not infringe the rights of another. What can be reasonably expected of a state is discussed in this chapter.

The next chapter looks at the responsibilities public authorities have towards those who may be considered vulnerable. It focuses on the impact of the Care Act 2014 which has transformed this area of the law. The Act receives a mixed response in the chapter. There are some aspects which are positive: in particular the emphasis on ensuring that services are tailored to the needs of the individual, rather than being a set package which is offered regardless of the individual circumstances of the case. It is also welcome to see, for the first time, a duty to make enquiries in cases where an adult is at risk of abuse or neglect. There are, however, serious issues for concern. While the duties to make enquiries and to assess individuals are clearly set out, there are effectively no obligations on the local authority to then provide services or make an intervention. The Human Rights Act 1998 might provide some teeth to the legislation here. The issue is particularly concerning given the serious cutbacks in the financial provision for local authorities, meaning there will be plenty of cases where provision will be at the minimum the local authority considers necessary. In the light of that the use of personal budgets is particularly concerning because it may provide too easy a way for the council to deflect blame for an inadequacy in the provision of services. A person whose needs are not met can be blamed for their inefficient use of the budget, rather than the council being blamed for failing to provide the services. Further, the ever tightening requirement of when social services can be provided for free means the significance of the legislation will in practice be severely curtailed.

Chapter 7 explores the concept of vulnerability as it is understood in criminal law. Two themes in particular are explored. The first is the claim that when the criminal law seeks to protect vulnerable groups it does so in a way which undermines autonomy. One example discussed in the chapter is prostitution, which analyses the claim that laws prohibiting prostitute-use undermine the autonomy of those prostituted women who freely choose to enter 'the profession'. That argument is challenged in this chapter. The autonomy of one person cannot be so easily separate from the autonomy of others. It is also noted that not intervening in prostitution leaves trafficked women who are acting non-autonomously without protection. The autonomy argument does not clearly point in one direction on this issue. The chapter also explores the way that sometimes, when the criminal law is designed to protect one set of vulnerable adults, it can end up penalizing another set. It looks at the offences of gross negligence manslaughter and familial homicide to show how these have been used to prosecute victims of domestic violence and those with limited capacities.

Chapter 8 moves on to the law on contract. It is argued there that the law is based around a particular understanding of a contractor who is well-informed, able to stand up for themselves, free from pressure, and materialistically minded. That is the very opposite of the image of the norm I argue we should use to build our law around in Chapter 2. Contract law is an interesting example of where the law favours the contractor who does not reach out to the other party and is self-contained; is suspicious of the contractor who lives in relationships with others; and sees relationships as reducible to a single moment of time (the entering of the contract). Contract law notably does take account of vulnerable contractors and does use a range of devices (such as the law on unconscionable bargains and the doctrine of undue influence) to protect them. However, it is argued that these are inadequate and do not disrupt the norm around which the law is based. The chapter advocates a new vision for contract law, which is based around the parties looking out for each other; where the law is designed to recognize the responsibilities the parties have towards each other; and where the aim of contracts is to provide a framework for an ongoing relationship which promotes the interests of both parties.

Chapter 9 concludes, bringing out some of the key themes in this book. We need a rethinking of the norms that underpin our legal system. A move away from the isolated, self-contained, self-sufficient man to the relational, interdependent woman. A law that is based not on the image of the be-suited businessman armed with his briefcase, but the mother changing a nappy at three in the morning.

2

Defining Vulnerability

Introduction

Vulnerability has become a major theme in political and social discourse. Charities, politicians, social commentators, and lawyers commonly refer to vulnerability in their publications. To give some examples: David Cameron has stated '[t]he test of a good society is you look after the elderly, the frail, the vulnerable, the poorest in our society';[1] Action for Children say they support 'the UK's most vulnerable and neglected children and young people';[2] and the guiding principle under the influential Family Justice Review was said to be 'the court's role should be focused on protecting the vulnerable from abuse, victimisation and exploitation and should avoid intervening in family life except where there is a clear benefit to children or the vulnerable in doing so'.[3] In politics the notion of vulnerability has come to play a significant role in debates over welfare reform and the extent to which someone can be expected to find work and/or is entitled to claim benefits. Some of the recent cases involving widespread 'grooming' and sexual exploitation of young women involved claims that social workers had failed to appreciate that the abusers had exploited 'vulnerable victims'.[4] All of this suggests that vulnerability has become one of the words of the age.

In this chapter I will seek to explore the meanings of vulnerability. As will soon become apparent, there is no single definition of vulnerability, and indeed the term is used in different contexts with different meanings.

---

[1] <http://news.bbc.co.uk/1/hi/programmes/andrew_marr_show/8656998.stm>
[2] <https://www.actionforchildren.org.uk>
[3] HM Government, *The Government Response to the Family Justice Review* (Stationery Office, 2012), para. 45.
[4] Rochdale Borough Safeguarding Children Board, *Review of Multi-agency Responses to the Sexual Exploitation of Children* (Rochdale BC, 2012), 9.

The meaning of vulnerability

Vulnerability is a notoriously vague term.[5] One of the reasons for this is that it is used in so many disciplines,[6] including biology, ecology, psychiatry, law, and politics. Unsurprisingly in each of these contexts it is used to perform a particular role and therefore has a particular understanding. It might be designed to designate a person who is in need of especial attention; or a group who are entitled to protection; or to define those who may not participate in certain activities. The purpose to which the term is put will, to a significant extent, determine its meaning. Indeed, vulnerability cannot really be defined unless we know the purpose the definition is to be used for and the context of its use. Nevertheless vulnerability has become such a persistent theme in public discourse and in a range of literature. It seems, therefore, undesirable, not to make some attempt to identify its features. Even if a single dictionary definition cannot be produced, there are certain common themes that connect the use of the notion.

Official definitions

Vulnerability has its origin in the Latin word 'vulnerare', meaning 'to wound'. According to the *New Oxford Dictionary of English*, to be vulnerable means 'to be exposed to the possibility of being attacked or harmed, either physically or emotionally'.[7] That is a very broad definition. Indeed it is hard to imagine anyone who is not exposed to that possibility. That is not necessarily a reason for rejecting the definition. As we shall see, many legitimately claim that, in fact, we need to recognize our universal vulnerability.

The well-known *No Secrets* definition of a vulnerable adult is as follows:

[A vulnerable adult is a person] who is or may be in need of community care services by reason of mental or other disability, age or illness; and who is or may be unable to take care of him or herself, or unable to protect him or herself against significant harm or exploitation.[8]

---

[5]   B. Fawcett, 'Vulnerability. Questioning the Certainties in Social Work and Health', (2009) 52 *International Social Work* 473; S. Hurst, 'Vulnerability in Research and Health Care; Describing the Elephant in the Room?', (2004) 7 *Medicine, Health Care and Philosophy* 281; M. Kottow, 'Vulnerability: What Kind of Principle is It?', (2004) 7 *Medicine, Healthcare and Philosophy* 281.

[6]   M. Dunn, I. Clare, and A. Holland, 'To Empower or to Protect? Constructing the "Vulnerable Adult" in English Law and Public Policy', (2008) 28 *Legal Studies* 234.

[7]   *Oxford English Dictionary* (Oxford University Press 2010).

[8]   Department of Health, *No Secrets* (Department of Health 2000), 8.

This definition notably ties the understanding of being vulnerable with being a person who is need of services by the state. A similar approach can be found in the Safeguarding Vulnerable Groups Act 2006, which views a person to be a vulnerable adult if they have attained the age of eighteen and he or she:

(a) is in residential accommodation
(b) is in sheltered housing
(c) receives domiciliary care
(d) receives any form of health care
(e) is detained in lawful custody
(f) is by virtue of an order of a court under supervision by a person exercising functions for the purposes of Part 1 of the Criminal Justice and Court Services Act 2000 (c. 43)
(g) receives a welfare service of a prescribed description
(h) receives any service or participates in any activity provided specifically for persons who fall within subsection (9)
(i) payments are made to him (or to another on his behalf) in pursuance of arrangements under section 57 of the Health and Social Care Act 2001 (c. 15), or
(j) requires assistance in the conduct of his affairs (s. 59(1)).

This is a very broad definition. Sub-section (d)'s reference to 'receives any form of health care' is defined as receiving 'treatment, therapy or palliative care of any description' (s. 59(5)). Taking an aspirin seems to fall within that definition. We are back again to a definition which seems to capture nearly everyone in the population. Certainly it seems to assume that a disabled person is automatically vulnerable: something that may not be objectionable if it is claimed that everyone is vulnerable, but may well be if the definition is seeking to identify those who have a weakness of some kind.

Looking at the academic literature on the definition of vulnerable, there are two major schools of thought. The first emphasizes our universal vulnerability. Our vulnerability is seen as an essential aspect of our humanity. The second is that there are some people, or groups of people, who should be seen as vulnerable. Although these are often presented as two competing understandings, I argue there is no contradiction between them once it is recognized that the second understanding is seeking to identify a category of people who are vulnerable in a way above and beyond the way we are all vulnerable. I will explore the two aspects of vulnerability next.

All are vulnerable

Everyone is vulnerable. That is a central claim of this book. This section will start by establishing that argument. It will then examine its significance.

Vulnerability is an inherent part of being human.[9] As Lévinas put it: 'The I, from head to foot and to the bone-marrow, is vulnerability.'[10] Or as Mackenzie, Rogers, and Dodds explain, 'To be vulnerable is to be fragile, to be susceptible to wounding and to suffering; this susceptibility is an ontological conditional of our humanity.'[11] Admittedly, this is not how people generally understand themselves. We emphasize our capacity, independence, and autonomy. But we puff ourselves up with such talk.

Even if we take a standard approach towards vulnerability and seek to list characteristics that render a person vulnerable, it is apparent that very many people fall under such a list.[12] Samia Hurst, for example, after looking at existing international guidelines on research ethics, has produced a list of vulnerable groups. This includes the following:

- Racial minorities
- The economically disadvantaged
- The very sick
- The institutionalized
- Children
- Prisoners
- Pregnant women and foetuses
- Incompetent persons
- Persons susceptible to coercion
- Persons who will not derive direct benefits from participation
- Persons for whom research is mixed with clinical care
- Junior or subordinate members of a hierarchical group … [such as] medical and nursing students, subordinate hospital and laboratory personnel, employees of pharmaceutical companies, and members of the armed forces or police
- Elderly persons
- Residents of nursing homes
- Patients in emergency rooms
- Homeless persons
- Refugees or displaced persons
- Individuals who are politically powerless
- Members of communities unfamiliar with modern medical concepts
- Patients with incurable diseases

---

[9] M. Shildrick, *Embodying the Monster: Encounters with the Vulnerable Self* (London, Sage 2002); A. Beckett, *Citizenship and Vulnerability* (Basingstoke, Palgrave 2006).

[10] E. Lévinas, *Humanismo Del Otro Hombre* (Mexico, Siglo 1993), 123.

[11] C. Mackenzie, W. Rogers, and S. Dodds, 'Introduction' in C. Mackenzie, W. Rogers, and S. Dodds (eds), *Vulnerability* (New York, Oxford Unversity Press 2014), 4.

[12] E. Gilson, 'Vulnerability, Ignorance, and Oppression', (2011) 36 *Hypatia* 281.

She acknowledges that more could be added to that list.[13] But there can be few people who do not fall into one category or another.

Consider further the following statistics. I list these simply to indicate that the hyper-autonomous, non-vulnerable man as the norm around which the law is developed is a fiction. I do not mean to suggest any of these characteristics necessarily imply especial vulnerability:

- 75 per cent of the population have an IQ of less than 110.[14]

- One in four people will experience some kind of mental health problem in the course of a year.[15]

- In 2012 in England, among adults who had drunk alcohol in the last week, 55 per cent of men and 53 per cent of women drank more than the recommended daily amounts, including 31 per cent of men and 24 per cent of women who drank more than twice the recommended amounts.[16]

- In 2012, almost a quarter of adults (24 per cent of men and 25 per cent of women aged sixteen or over) in England were classified as obese (BMI 30kg/m2 or over).[17]

- For 2013/14 around one in eleven adults aged sixteen to fifty-nine (8.8 per cent) had taken an illicit drug in the last year. However, this proportion more than doubled when looking at the age subgroup of sixteen to twenty-four-year-olds (18.9 per cent).[18]

- In England in 2013/14 there were 82.1 million people who attended outpatient appointments at hospitals.[19]

- Total unemployment stood at 1.83 million for the three months to March 2015.[20]

- The population of the United Kingdom is ageing. There were over half a million people aged ninety and over living in the United Kingdom in 2013.[21]

- From a population of 64.1 million, over 11 million people have a limiting long term illness, impairment, or disability.[22]

[13] C. Coleman 'Vulnerability as a Regulatory Category in Human Subject Research', (2009) 37(1) *Journal of Law, Medicine and Ethics* 12. For another list see World Medical Association, *Declaration of Helsinki* (Ferney-Voltaire 2008), A(9).

[14] G. Boeree, *Intelligence and IQ* (Shippensburg, PA: Shippensburg University Press).

[15] Mental Health Foundation, *Statistics on Mental Health* (London, 2015).

[16] NHS, *Statistics on Alcohol, England 2014* (London, 2015).

[17] NHS, *Statistics on Obesity, Physical Activity and Diet, England* (London, 2014).

[18] NHS, *Statistics on Drug Misuse: England* (London, 2015).

[19] NHS, *Hospital Outpatient Activity, 2013–14* (London, 2015).

[20] Office of National Statistics, *Employment* (London, 2015).

[21] Office of National Statistics, *Estimates of the Very Old* (London, 2014).

[22] MPH, *Disability Statistics* (London, 2015).

- In 2013/14, 23 per cent of people in the United Kingdom were living in absolute low income (after housing costs) according to official government statistics.[23]

But the argument is not simply to suggest that vulnerability is more common than is often presented. Rather, it suggests that we are all vulnerable.[24]

We are all vulnerable because we are all profoundly dependent on others for our physical and psychological well-being. Our society has built up a wide range of structures and forms of assistance which disguise our vulnerability. Indeed we are forced by a wide range of societal pressures to disguise or mitigate our vulnerability so that we can behave in an acceptable way in the public realm. In a powerful article Kate Lindemann contrasts the emphasis that is paid to the accommodations provided for disabled people so as to minimize the impact of their disability, with the lack of appreciation of the accommodations for the able-bodied:

Colleagues, professional staff members, and other adults are unconscious of the numerous accommodations that society provides to make their work and life style possible. ATMs, extended hours in banks, shopping centres and medical offices, EZpass, newspaper kiosks, and elevators are all accommodations that make contemporary working life possible. There are entire industries devoted to accommodating the needs of adult working people. Fast food, office lunch delivery, day time child care, respite care, car washing, personal care attendants, interpreters, house cleaning, and yard and lawn services are all occupations that provide services that make it possible for adults to hold full time jobs.[25]

We thus highlight the facilities used to deal with the vulnerabilities of others, while overlooking the accommodations 'we' need to deal with our own vulnerabilities. We are all deeply dependent on others to meet our needs.[26] As Rogers, Mackenzie, and Dodds put it, 'all human life is conditioned by vulnerability, as a result of our embodied, finite, and socially contingent existence. Vulnerability is thus an ontological condition of our humanity.'[27] Any personal achievements are in reality the product of many people's efforts.[28] Any academic will readily acknowledge their debt to the writings of earlier

---

[23] DWP, *Households Below Average Income* (London, 2014).

[24] B. Fawcett, 'Vulnerability', (n. 5).

[25] K. Lindemann, 'The Ethics of Receiving', (2003) 24 *Theoretical Medicine and Bioethics* 501.

[26] S. Dodds, 'Gender, Ageing, and Injustice: Social and Political Contexts of Bioethics' (2005) 31 *Journal of Medical Ethics* 295.

[27] W. Rogers, C. Mackenzie, and S. Dodds, 'Why Bioethics Needs a Concept of Vulnerability', (2012) 5 *International Journal of Feminist Approaches to Bioethics* 11.

[28] M. Fine and C. Glendinning, 'Dependence, Independence or Interdependence? Revisiting the Concepts of "Care" and "Dependency"', (2005) *Ageing and Society* 601, 601.

academics and discussions with others in the production of research. The skills we have are passed to us by teachers and given to us by others. We are normally dependent on others to provide us with the equipment, support, and help to exercise skills. We all need others to provide the services we cannot provide ourselves: from electricity to food; from emotional support to transport. Few of us could, and fewer seek to, live utterly independent lives. Yet with interdependence comes vulnerability. Others might let us down in the provision of what we need, we might let others down and fail to provide them with what they need.[29]

Mary Neal puts it this way:

I am vulnerable because I am penetrable; I am permanently open and exposed to hurts and harms of various kinds. These two sources of vulnerability—reliance on others for co-operation, and openness to positive harm—are simply two means by which I might come to experience suffering; thus, it is suffering, and the capacity for suffering, that is definitive of this negative aspect of vulnerability. The extent and intensity of my vulnerability at a particular moment, or with regard to a particular need or harm, may be affected by my age, my sex, my degree of capacity, my health, my social status, my wealth, and a variety of other factors. Nevertheless, even the least vulnerable human being is still fundamentally, and inescapably, vulnerable in the negative sense, since none of us can meet her basic needs and satisfy her core desires without the co-operation of others; and even the most capable adult is vulnerable to hurt and harm, both physical and emotional.[30]

I will now explain more precisely why it is that we are in our nature vulnerable.

The body

We are corporeal beings. This corporality creates vulnerability. Experiences teach us that our bodies are vulnerable to sickness, illness, and accidents.[31] Our health is frail. As Fineman puts it: '[W]e are born, live, and die within a fragile materiality that renders all of us constantly susceptible to destructive external forces and internal disintegration?'[32] Death itself is the ultimate sign of that, but more can be said. Our bodies are 'profoundly leaky'.[33] They are

---

[29] S. Whitney, 'Dependency Relations: Corporeal Vulnerability and Norms of Personhood in Hobbes and Kittay' (2011) 26 *Hypatia* 554.

[30] M. Neal, '"Not Gods but Animals": Human Dignity and Vulnerable Subjecthood', (2012) 33 *Liverpool Law Review* 177.

[31] S. Matambanadzo, 'Embodying Vulnerability: A Feminist Theory of the Person', (2012) 20 *Duke Journal of Gender Law & Policy* 45.

[32] M. Fineman, 'Feminism, Masculinities and Multiple Identities', (2013) 13 *Nevada Law Review* 619.

[33] M. Shildrick, *Leaky Bodies and Boundaries* (London, Routledge 1997).

constantly changing with new material being added to them and old material being discarded. Inside our bodies we are dependent on a wide range of non-human material to survive and outside it is constantly interacting with the environment.[34]

We should notice, however, that these vulnerabilities affect not only us, but also those we are in relationships with. Not only are we at risk of harm to our own bodies, the bodies of those with whom we are in relationships are at risk of harm, and injuries to their bodies can impact on ours.

We are in our nature embodied people. Academics are, perhaps, particularly prone to elevate the cerebral above the physical, but there is no denying that the frailty of our bodies catches up with us all. We hide the vulnerabilities created by our bodies by emphasizing the enclosed, controlled, bounded body.[35] This is most powerfully reflected, I would argue, in the claim that we own our bodies.[36] The truth is our bodies are in constant flux; profoundly leaky; deeply dependent on other bodies and the broader environment.[37] They are programmed to wear down and tire.[38]

The self

In a radical sense our relationships constitute our selves.[39] At its heart is the belief that people are relational and so all intelligible action is relations and all psychological processes are relational. Society is not made up of individual atoms, perusing their own view of the self. Our emotions exist and we understand them from our relational traditions.[40] This is even more radical than it might at first sound. It is not that we have selves that join together to form relationships, but it is out of our relationships that the self exists.

We only understand ourselves in terms of how we relate to and are understood by others. We define ourselves in terms of how others understand us. It

---

[34] P.-L. Chau and J. Herring, 'My Body, Your Body, Our Bodies', (2007) 15 *Medical Law Review* 34.

[35] D. Perpich, 'Vulnerability and the Ethics of Facial Tissue Transplantation', (2010) 7 *Bioethical Inquiry* 173.

[36] J. Herring, 'Why We Need a Statute Regime to Regulate Bodily Material' in I. Goold, J. Herring, L. Skene, and K. Greasley (eds), *Persons, Parts and Property: How Should We Regulate Human Tissue in the 21st Century?* (Oxford, Hart Publishing 2014).

[37] M. Neal '"Not Gods but Animals": Human Dignity and Vulnerable Subjecthood', (2012) 33 *Liverpool Law Review* 177.

[38] A. Carse, 'Vulnerability, Agency and Human Flourishing'; in C. Taylor and R. Dell'Oro (eds), *Health and Human Flourishing* (Washington, Georgetown University Press 2006).

[39] K. Gergen, *Relational Being* (Oxford, Oxford University Press 2009); K. McLaughlin, *Surviving Identity: Vulnerability and the Psychology of Recognition* (London, Routledge 2012).

[40] J. Sugarman and K. Martin, 'Theorizing Relational Agency', (2011) 24 *Journal of Constructivist Psychology* 283.

is only in response to others that our selves have meaning. From our beginnings we are in relationships. Pregnancy is the most intimate relationship between two beings. From birth the child comes to interpret themselves and the world through their interactions with their parents. That is why neglect of children is a serious wrong. It is not just that the child does not develop, it is that the child has no sense of self. Babies are taught a sense of self through relationships with parents and carers. They then develop their understanding of self and their goals in terms of relationships with others. The language we use; the way we look at the world; and the sense of self in the world is generated through these early relationships and develops and changes through subsequent relationships. This understanding of the self means we are in constant danger of our self being challenged by others rejecting us; not accepting us as members of a group; not providing the support we expect; or using our relationships to harm us.

The claim that people are relational in their being is complex and requires much more argumentation than is possible here.[41] However, the claim is important and its significance is important for this book. If people are constituted through their relationships with others, then we are dependent on others and our trust is given to them.[42] That makes the self inherently vulnerable. Judith Butler explains why: 'Loss and vulnerability seem to follow from our being socially constituted bodies, attached to others, at risk of losing those attachments, exposed to others, at risk of violence by virtue of that exposure.'[43]

Care

Dependency is an inevitable facet of human life.[44] There will be times during our lives, in a very obvious way, when we will be dependent on others for our most basic needs. In early years and in times of sickness, perhaps particularly towards the end of life, we will need care. In such a dependency we must rely on others to survive and this inevitably creates vulnerability. That care may cease or may be inadequate. Of course for most people there will be times when this overt kind of dependency will not be apparent. However, often then others will be dependent on us to meet their needs, be that as parents or carers for others. This itself creates a vulnerability.[45] Our responsibilities to meet the needs of others in one sense limit our lives. We are on constant call

---

[41] J. Herring, *Caring and the Law* (Oxford, Hart 2013).

[42] A. Baier, *Moral Prejudices: Essays on Ethics* (Cambridge, Harvard University Press 1994).

[43] J. Butler, *Precarious Life* (London & New York, Verso 2004), 20.

[44] J. Herring, *Caring and the Law* (n. 41).

[45] S. Dodds, 'Dependence, Care and Vulnerability' in C. Mackenzie, W. Rogers, and S. Dodds (eds), *Vulnerability* (n. 11), 3.

to meet others. Their vulnerabilities become a feature of the relationship. Eva Feder Kittay wrote of our interdependence:

My point is that this interdependence begins with dependence. It begins with the dependency of an infant, and often ends with the dependency of a very ill or frail person close to dying. The infant may develop into a person who can reciprocate, an individual upon whom another can be dependent and whose continuing needs make her interdependent with others. The frail elderly person … may herself have been involved in a series of interdependent relations. But at some point there is a dependency that is not yet or no longer an interdependency. By excluding *this* dependency from social and political concerns, we have been able to fashion the pretense that we are *independent*—that the cooperation between persons that some insist is *inter*dependence is simply the mutual (often voluntary) cooperation between essentially independent persons.[46]

The picture of interdependency painted in the discussion so far demonstrates that an inevitable part of a life is care of others.[47] As Fiona Williams argues, we need to recognize 'us all as interdependent and as having the potential and responsibility to be caring and cared for'.[48] If care is an essential part of what it is to be a person and care produces vulnerability then vulnerability is an essential part of being a person.

Mutual care is essential for the functioning society.[49] As Joan Tronto writes: 'Care is not a parochial concern of women, a type of secondary moral question, or the work of the least well off in society. Care is a central concern of human life. It is time we began to change our political and social institutions to reflect this truth.'[50] Care work therefore needs to be recognized and valued within the legal system.[51] The legal and social response to caring provides a challenge to the way legal rights and responsibilities are understood.[52] Much of the law is based on the assumption that we are competent, detached, independent people who are entitled to have our rights of self-determination and autonomy fiercely protected.[53] However, the reality is

---

[46] E. Feder Kittay, *Love's Labor: Essays on Women, Equality and Dependency* (New York, Routledge 1999), xii.

[47] T. Kröger, 'Care Research and Disability Studies: Nothing in Common?', (2009) 29 *Critical Social Policy* 398.

[48] F. Williams, 'The Presence of Feminism in the Future of Welfare', (2002) 31 *Economy and Society* 502, 503.

[49] M. Fineman, *The Autonomy Myth* (New York, New Press 2004), xvii; S. Levy, 'The Relational Self and the Right to Give Care', (2006) 28 *New Political Science* 547, 548.

[50] J. Tronto, *Moral Boundaries: A Political Argument for an Ethic of Care* (Abingdon, Routledge, 1993), 180.

[51] F. Williams, 'The Presence of Feminism', (n. 49), 509.

[52] R. Tong, 'The Ethics of Care: A Feminist Virtue Ethics of Care for Healthcare Practitioners', (1998) 23 *Journal of Medicine and Philosophy* 131.

[53] L. Lloyd, 'Mortality and Morality: Ageing and the Ethics of Care', (2004) 24 *Ageing and Society* 235.

that we are ignorant, vulnerable, interdependent individuals, whose strength and reality is not in our autonomy, but in our relationships with others.[54]

Much of the writing on the ethics of care offers alternatives to individualistic approaches.[55] There is extensive literature on this and only a very brief summary will be offered here. Ethics of care regard the role of law as to promote caring relationships, rather than the pursuit of individual rights. Rights have been misused as tools 'to keep other people out of my life'. They need not be so understood. They can be used in progressive ways to protect and promote values of community and mutuality. In failing to properly acknowledge care work, the law misses an important and inevitable aspect of life.

In relationships of caring and dependency our interests become intermingled.[56] We do not break down into 'me' and 'you'. To harm a caregiver is to harm the person cared for; to harm the person cared for is to harm the caregiver. There should be no talk of balancing the interests of the caregiver and the person cared for: the question rather should be emphasizing the responsibilities they owe to each other in the context of a mutually supporting relationship.[57]

Indeed, it is simplistic to imagine we can identify in a caring relationship who is the caregiver and who is the cared-for; their relationship is marked by interdependency. The 'cared-for' provides the 'caregiver' with gratitude, love, acknowledgement, and emotional support, which will be of great emotional value to him. Indeed, often a 'caregiver' will be the 'cared-for' in another relationship. As Diane Gibson noted, our society is made up of overlapping networks of dependency.[58]

Caring relations often involve a complex interplay of dependencies and vulnerabilities.[59] Michael Fine and Caroline Glendinning have argued:

Recent studies of care suggest that qualities of reciprocal dependence underlie much of what is termed 'care'. Rather than being a unidirectional activity in which an active care-giver does something to a passive and dependent recipient, these accounts

[54] C. Meyers, 'Cruel Choices: Autonomy and Critical Care Decision-making', (2004) 18 *Bioethics* 104.

[55] For example S. Sevenhuijsen, *Citizenship and the Ethics of Care* (London & New York, Sage 1998); V. Held, *The Ethics of Care* (Oxford, Oxford University Press 2006); D. Engster, *The Heart of Justice: Care Ethics and Political Theory* (Oxford: Oxford University Press 2007); J. Herring, *Caring and the Law* (n. 41).

[56] T. Shakespeare, *Help* (Birmingham, Venture Press 2000).

[57] V. Held, *The Ethics of Care* (n. 55), chapter 1.

[58] D. Gibson, *Aged Care: Old Policies, New Solutions* (Melbourne, Cambridge University Press 2005), 185.

[59] C. Chorn Dunham and J. Harms Cannon '"They're Still in Control Enough to be in Control": Paradox of Power in Dementia Caregiving', (2008) 22 *Journal of Aging Studies* 45.

suggest that care is best understood as the product or outcome of the relationship between two or more people.[60]

When assessing the rights of any individual or the medical needs of an individual, such a person should be considered in a situational context. Never should it be a matter of assessing a person in isolation. Rather, each person's needs and rights must be considered in the context of their relationships.

An approach based on an ethic of care is one that recognizes our mutual vulnerabilities that makes care a necessary, and rewarding, part of life. Without a recognition of our common vulnerability there is a danger, as some critics have complained, that 'care ethics' can be seen to valourize the carer, and devalue the 'cared for'.[61] Once our common vulnerability and the mutuality of care is recognized this criticism to a large extent is greatly reduced.[62]

Care and vulnerability are, therefore, closely linked. Once we accept that we all are, to some extent, in relationships of care, then we see that we are all, to some extent, vulnerable. Once we accept that we are all vulnerable, then we need relationships of care to survive.

All the time or some?

Martha Fineman has argued that looking at a typical lifespan, there will be times of different capacity and strengths. The typical 'adult liberal subject' focuses on just one part of that life span and essentializes this as the norm of people. Martha Fineman argues:

> Throughout our lives we may be subject to external and internal negative, potentially devastating, events over which we have little control—disease, pandemics, environmental and climate deterioration, terrorism and crime, crumbling infrastructure, failing institutions, recession, corruption, decay, and decline. We are situated beings who live with the ever-present possibility of changing needs and circumstances in our individual and collective lives. We are also accumulative beings and have different qualities and quantities of resources with which to meet these needs of circumstances, both over the course of our lifetime and as measured at the time of crisis or opportunity.[63]

But the recognition that at different times in our lives we may be more overtly in use of societal resources should not disguise the fact that we are in

---

[60] M. Fine and C. Glendinning, 'Dependence, Independence or Inter-dependence? Revisiting the Concepts of Care and Dependency', (2005) 25 *Ageing and Society* 601, 616.
[61] See for example T. Shakespeare, *Help* (n. 56).
[62] J. Herring, 'The Disability Critique of Care', (2014) 8 *Elder Law Review* 1.
[63] M. Fineman, 'Feminism, Masculinities and Multiple Identities', (n. 32).

need of communal and relational support for all our lives.[64] Alison Diduck[65] argues that even if we see everyone as vulnerable it is still possible to recognize that we are positioned differently within a web of economic and social relationships and these will impact on our vulnerabilities differently. That may be vulnerability caused through caring for others. As Martha Fineman argues:

Like vulnerability, dependency is universal: all of us have been dependent as infants and many will in the future become dependent on others for resources, care, and support. I am not talking about the idea of interdependence here, but about a physical or developmental aspect of the human condition. This form of dependence I have labelled 'inevitable.' All of us were dependent as children and many will become so as we age, fall ill, or become disabled. This biological or developmental dependency is often thought of as the basis for denying agency or decision making autonomy to an individual and therefore is profoundly stigmatizing for adults and the basis for denying them, as well as children more generally, of certain liberties or rights. This embodied dependency has been assumed to attach to the elderly as a group, although many within that category are physically and mentally able.[66]

Fineman is not arguing simply that we are all vulnerable at some point in our lives. She is claiming that there is universal vulnerability, but that at a particular time in people's lives this vulnerability becomes particularly apparent. But she sees the recognition of universal vulnerability as what should be at the heart of the approach of the law.[67]

The significance of the claim that we are all vulnerable

It might legitimately be asked whether vulnerability is a particularly helpful concept if it is simply an aspect of the human condition. If we are all vulnerable then it is not a very helpful factor for lawyers to take into account in determining the correct legal response to individuals or situations. As we have seen, many supporters of the view that we are all vulnerable would want to go on to say that although we have a shared vulnerability there may be particular situations where individuals are super-vulnerable; or our inherent

---

[64] B. Daniel and A. Bowes, 'Re-thinking Harm and Abuse: Insights from a Lifespan Perspective', (2011) 41 *British Journal of Social Work* 820.

[65] A. Diduck, 'Autonomy and Vulnerability in Family Law: The Missing Link' in J. Wallbank and J. Herring (eds), *Vulnerabilities, Care and Family Law* (London, Routledge 2013).

[66] M. Fineman, ' "Elderly" as Vulnerable: Rethinking the Nature of Individual and Societal Responsibility', (2012) 17 *Elder Law Review* 23.

[67] Ibid.

vulnerability has particular significance. But if so, we should be seeking to define these and the observation that we are all vulnerable is not particularly helpful. I disagree. I think the view that we are all vulnerable has significant repercussions in a range of ways.

Our image of the legal self

The legal conception of the self profoundly affects the kinds of legal rights we have. As adults we like to emphasize our independence, capacity for rational thought, and autonomy. Hence in our legal system autonomy and liberty are emphasized as key rights, whose interference requires strong justification. Our right to be able to make our own choices over how to act, to only be subject to those responsibilities we choose to take, is seen as a central pillar of the economic, social, and legal structures. The law's role is, under that image of the self, to protect the individual from unwanted intrusions and to protect liberty to pursue one's goal for one's life. We are portrayed as independent self-interested people.[68] Those who most obviously fall outside the paradigm are described as 'vulnerable' and that terminology is used to monitor, supervise, and discipline them.[69] They lack those essential skills to direct their own lives and protect themselves and so need others to do that for them.

If, however, we start with a norm of vulnerable, interdependent, caring people then the nature of legal intervention becomes different. The importance of upholding and maintaining those relationships becomes key. The law does not emphasize independence, liberty, and autonomy; but rather seeks to uphold relationships and care.

Rethinking the law from this fundamentally different starting point has profound impacts on the legal approaches. To take one example, rather than starting from the assumption that each person is free to negotiate their own contracts and that the law should respect liberty of contract, in fact we should start from the image of vulnerable contractors liable to manipulation and exploitation. We shall explore that further in Chapter 8. Bryan Turner[70] has used universal vulnerability as the starting point for his understanding of human rights, arguing that it provides a 'a norm for the assertion of a human bond across generations and culture'. Susan Dodds argues: 'Attention to vulnerability ... changes citizens' ethical relations from those of independent actors carving out realms of rights against each other and the state, to those of mutually-dependent and vulnerability-exposed beings whose capacities to

[68] S. Sevenhuijsen, 'Too Good to be True', (1999) 34 *Focaal* 207.

[69] M. Fineman, ' "Elderly" as Vulnerable' (n. 66).

[70] B. Turner, *Vulnerability and Human Rights* (Pennsylvania, Pennsylvania State University Press 2006), 35.

develop as subjects are directly and indirectly mediated by the conditions around them.'[71] The acknowledgement of universal vulnerability also creates a different image of the legal relationship between the individual and the state. Rather than seeing the obligations of the state as owed towards a few particularly vulnerable citizens to meet their needs, it acknowledges that the institutions and provision of the state are used to meet the needs of all.[72] The question then becomes the extent to which the state meets all of our needs and which needs it chooses not to meet.

Martha Fineman argues the role of institutions is important:

This focus on institutions is to my mind one of the most significant aspects of the vulnerability analysis. Societal institutions are theorized as having grown up around vulnerability. They are seen as interlocking and overlapping, creating layered possibilities of opportunities and support but also containing gaps and potential pitfalls. These institutions collectively form systems that play an important role in lessening, ameliorating, and compensating for vulnerability. Together and independently they provide us with resources in the form of advantages or coping mechanisms that cushion us when we are facing misfortune, disaster, and violence. Cumulatively, these assets provide individuals with resilience in the face of our shared vulnerability.

The argument here is that while a person or group may be identified as vulnerable as a result of a particular characteristic or body, it may in fact be the way institutional, economic, and social support is distributed that generates the vulnerability. In the face of universal vulnerability the needs of some are better met than the needs of others, and so it may be if a particular group are disadvantaged that is not due to any vulnerability resting in them, but rather the allocation of social support. The response may not therefore be in seeking to address their 'weaknesses' but rather in re-examining the distribution of support. Vast sums of money are spend on ensuring there are adequate sewerage and toileting provision for most people, but if an individual has particular toileting needs, this can be seen as a special burden on the state, which might not be affordable.[73]

Divisions

One of the major advantages of the universal vulnerability claim is that it challenges the divisions that can be created between 'them and us'; 'the competent and the not competent'; the 'vulnerable and the non-vulnerable'. It

---

[71] S. Dodds, 'Depending on Care: Recognition of Vulnerability and the Social Contribution of Care Provision', (2007) 21 *Bioethics* 500, 501.

[72] M. Fineman, 'The Vulnerable Subject and the Responsive State', (2010) 60 *Emory Law Journal* 251.

[73] *R (McDonald) v Kensington and Chelsea RBC* [2011] UKSC 33.

means that in seeking intervention or protection we need to recognize our own fallibility, weakness, and vulnerability to influence in determining what is the correct response. Given the stigma that can attach to being labelled 'vulnerable', some people will exaggerate their own abilities. The 'vulnerable' become stigmatized and something to eschew.[74] This will cause people to exaggerate their own understandings and abilities or protect their own interest.[75] Tom Shakespeare has noted that non-disabled people 'project their fear of death, their unease at their physicality and mortality onto disabled people, who represent all these difficult aspects of human existence'. I suspect some of the negative associations with vulnerability can be analysed in the same way. Erinn Gilson[76] writes of 'the production of invulnerability' to capture the idea that if the distinction between the vulnerable and non-vulnerable is emphasized then this encourages people to disavow their own vulnerability and to emphasize the vulnerability of others.[77] As Fineman puts it:

The designation of vulnerable (inferior) populations reinforces and valorizes the ideal liberal subject, who is positioned as the polar opposite of the vulnerable population. This liberal subject is thus constructed as invulnerable, or at least differently vulnerable, and represents the desirable and achievable ideals of autonomy, independence, and self-sufficiency.[78]

One of the dangers in seeking to separate the vulnerable and non-vulnerable is that it leads to an exaggeration. An example of this can be shown with children. There are a mass of social structures which push children towards a passive, non-autonomous role, and a mass of social structures which enable adults to live apparently independent and autonomous lives. These often go unnoticed and assumed as normal.[79] The division between the adults and children becomes reinforced and ignored.

It also means that the division between carer and cared for is less emphasized. Vulnerability is often tied up with concepts of dependence and care receiving. A person who is vulnerable is seen as in need of dependence from another and needs their care. However, in dividing the 'carer' from the person receiving care we overlook the interdependence between the two and the ways that caring creates vulnerabilities for both parties.[80] In caring

---

[74] E. Gilson, 'Vulnerability, Ignorance, and Oppression', (2011) 26 *Hypatia* 308.

[75] Ibid.   [76] Ibid.

[77] A. Satz, 'Overcoming Fragmentation in Disability and Health Law', (2010) 69 *Emory Law Journal* 277.

[78] M. Fineman, '"Elderly" as Vulnerable', (n. 66).

[79] A. Peterson and I. Wilkinson, *Health, Risk and Vulnerability* (London, Routledge 2007).

[80] B. Hughes, L. McKie, D. Hopkins, and N. Watson, 'Love's Labours Lost? Feminism, the Disabled People's Movement and an Ethic of Care', (2005) 39 *Sociology* 259.

relationships the division between bodies and selves becomes blurred, so that a harm to one body is a harm to another.

Vulnerability and care as private

Many writers on care have demonstrated that care of the 'vulnerable' is downgraded in modern legal and social thought.[81] It is seen as a private matter for individuals and their families to organize. Care is largely ignored or undervalued by the state and legal system. This is challenged by an acknowledgement that vulnerability is universal. To quote Fineman again:

Privatization of dependency masks it, along with the other implications of human vulnerability and allows us to indulge in fantasies of independence, self-sufficiency, and autonomous agency. In an autonomous liberal subject analysis, if individuals or their private institutions fail, it is perceived as reflecting their weakness and incapacity, because the divide between public and private leaves them outside of general public or state responsibility—they occur in a separate sphere.[82]

An acknowledgement of our universal vulnerability should go hand in hand with an acknowledgement of the importance of care work.

Autonomy

There are strong links between autonomy and vulnerability. Alison Diduck[83] argues that 'autonomy cannot exist without its "other", which in current rhetoric has become vulnerability. In the same way that autonomy may be the "friendly face" of individual responsibility, vulnerability may be the friendly face of dependence.' She argues that autonomy, the argument that people should be free to develop and live out their own version of the good life, is closely linked to the claim that people are responsible for the choices that they make. Vulnerability is seen as the antithesis of this. Vulnerability is a state for which an individual is not to be blamed and is not accountable. Diduck argues that vulnerability 'implies disability, lack of capacity, of competence or victimhood, rather than the irresponsibility which tended to pervade dependency discourse'.[84] The vulnerable person in this regard is to be treated as grateful for the protection and services of the state, which an autonomous person is normally spared.

---

[81] J. Herring, *Caring and the Law* (n. 41).
[82] M. Fineman, ' "Elderly" as Vulnerable', (n. 66).
[83] A. Diduck, 'Autonomy and Vulnerability in Family Law', (n. 66), 97.
[84] Ibid., 97.

Diduck, in support of her claims about the use of vulnerability, refers to a speech by David Cameron, which she suggests exemplifies the link between the concepts:[85] 'We will look after the most vulnerable and needy. We will make the system simple. We'll make work pay. We'll help those who want to work, find work. But in return we expect people to take their responsibilities seriously too.' Diduck is however clear that she is suspicious of the elevation of autonomy that the vulnerability discourse permits. She argues autonomy is 'premised on the myth of a pre-existing equal playing field on which each individual has equal freedom, power and capacity to express it'.[86] Her argument is that this claim is only plausible if an account can be provided for those who undoubtedly are unable to protect themselves. Vulnerability provides the language to account for the blatantly unautonomous, and leaves the norm of autonomy possible.

I suggest that Diduck is entirely right to question the extent to which we are autonomous. In fact, we are all too aware of our own limitations in decision-making. Very few people consenting to medical treatment or people making financial decisions are in fact able to make a fully informed decision or to act on the basis of a rational decision-making process.[87] Unsurprisingly, we often delegate such decisions to others or at least involve others in our decision-making.[88] Further, an exploration of how decisions are made suggests that people are typically influenced by forces and motivations of which they are unaware. The typical presentation of an unencumbered, free, rational decision maker is simply a fiction.

Criticisms of the claim

Rogers, Mackenzie, and Dodds[89] have mounted a powerful argument against the claim that everyone is vulnerable:

The 'everyone is vulnerable' approach dulls our responses to particular vulnerabilities, fails to account for context-specific harms, and can lead to discrimination and stereotyping of whole groups as incapable of caring for their own needs or of being self-determining. This finding in turn can then be used to justify unwarranted and unjust paternalistic responses.

---

[85] Ibid., 109.   [86] Ibid., 101.

[87] For a discussion of the non-rational dimension to much decision making, see D. Redelmeier, P. Rozin, and D. Kahneman, 'Understanding Patients' Decisions: Cognitive and Emotional Perspectives', (1993) 270 *Journal of the American Medical Association* 72.

[88] S. Adler Channick, 'The Myth of Autonomy at the End-of-life: Questioning the Paradigm of Rights', (1999) 44 *Villanova Law Review* 577.

[89] W. Rogers, C. Mackenzie, and S. Dodds, 'Why Bioethics Needs a Concept of Vulnerability', (n. 27).

This is a serious criticism, but the claim that everyone is vulnerable is different from a claim that everyone is equally vulnerable. It seems few are arguing in favour of the latter claim. One can sensibly claim that we are all vulnerable, while at the same time accepting that some are in particularly vulnerable situations and therefore deserve especial attention. This is particularly true given the unequal allocation of state resources in response to human vulnerability, meaning that the impact of some people's vulnerabilities is more mitigated than others. A recognition that we are all vulnerable means that there is no stereotyping of groups as incapable of caring for their own needs. Their enhanced vulnerability is as a result of the allocation of state resources, not any inherent feature.

Some commentators are concerned that universal vulnerability may lead to the genuine disadvantages suffered by some being overlooked. Kittay has argued that it is important to recognize that corporal vulnerability is not equally shared. Not to recognize the differences people have is to ignore reality. To say everyone is vulnerable 'masks inequitable dependencies, those of infancy and childhood, old age, illness, and disability'.[90] While she accepts it is true to say that everyone will experience utter dependency at some point in their life, it would be wrong to say that we all do equally all the time. The concern is that if we are all regarded as vulnerable, then the claims of disabled people that they are particularly excluded or disadvantaged become harder to make. We are all disabled, the universalist position may claim, but Bill Hughes argues that it ignores the particularities of disabled lives and downplays disability.[91]

The danger is summarized by three points from Hughes:

Firstly, in treating the body as a limit it fails to recognize that disabled bodies embody potential and possibility and thus leaves unchallenged the profoundly invalidating vision of disability that haunts the non-disabled imaginary. Secondly, it fails to treat the body as a body subject. As a consequence of the loss of the 'lived body', the materialist ontology proposed by our main protagonists as they labour to map out an anthropology of frailty ends up mechanistic and mired in reductionism. Thirdly, in appealing to a universal human subject the approach taken by Turner and Shakespeare and Watson annihilates disability as an identity and conceals the discrimination and exclusion that is the ubiquitous experience of people who embrace disability as a subject position. The argument is Rousseauesque. We are all the same. There is no room for difference and diversity.

---

[90] Kittay, (n. 46), xi.
[91] B. Hughes, 'Being Disabled: Towards a Critical Social Ontology for Disability Studies', (2007) 22 *Disability & Society* 673.

What this quote suggests is that there is a tension in the claim we are all vulnerable and the claim that some particular vulnerabilities need especial attention. The more the first is emphasized, the weaker the emphasis is placed on the real experiences of disadvantages faced by some. The more the second is emphasized, the less significant the first claim is. However, this is not necessarily an impasse, in part because the claims are addressing essentially different kinds of questions. The first is the legal norms and expectations around which we build legal systems. The second responds to particular individuals and groups who may be identified as being at a particular or increased risk beyond the norm.[92] Further, I would emphasize the point made earlier. The manifestations and impact of our vulnerabilities depends on the responses of society to them. As Fineman writes:

> Vulnerability, therefore, is both universal and particular; it is experienced uniquely by each of us. Important in regard to this particular[] point is the fact that our individual experience of vulnerability varies according to the quality and quantity of resources we possess or can command. While society cannot eradicate our vulnerability, it can and does mediate, compensate, and lessen our vulnerability through programs, institutions, and structures. Therefore, a vulnerability analysis must consider both individual position and institutional relationships.[93]

Jennifer Collins[94] also sees the claim that we are all vulnerable as unhelpful. She argues it undermines the use of vulnerability to highlight groups which should be entitled to especial protection from the state and to whom especial obligations are owed. However, as already acknowledged, these goals are not incompatible. We can recognize that the allocation of social provision has been unequal, leaving some people's vulnerabilities more acute than others, and requiring attention.

A more challenging response is that the claim of universal vulnerability opens the gates to paternalistic intervention. If people are all vulnerable and unable to look after themselves or make decisions for themselves then the state is entitled to offer protection. The concept of vulnerability is typically used by the state to justify protective coercive measures to avoid the vulnerability being exploited. Feminists in particular might have reasons to be concerned at an approach which seeks to justify state intervention.[95] As Munro and Scoular[96] argue, 'the merits and demerits of state involvement

---

[92] S. Hurst, 'Vulnerability in Research and Health Care', (n. 5).

[93] M. Fineman, ' "Elderly" as Vulnerable', (n. 66), 80.

[94] J. Collins, 'The Contours of Vulnerability' in J. Wallbank and J. Herring (eds), *Vulnerabilities, Care and Family Law* (Abingdon, Routledge 2013).

[95] V. Munro and J. Scoular, 'Abusing Vulnerability? Contemporary Law and Policy Responses to Sex Work in the UK', (2012) 20 *Feminist Legal Studies* 189.

[96] Ibid.

have long been debated within feminist theory and the extent to which it is progressive both to increase the scale of state intervention and to legitimate that encroachment as presumptively in the service of redressing vulnerability is contentious'. I would argue that such comments are in danger of underplaying the extent to which the state is already meeting people's needs and intervening in people's lives in a way which is uncontroversial. Whether it be the provision of sewerage, electricity, transportation, or security, the state is already meeting our needs and few would question it doing so.

Defining the particularly vulnerable

A claim that we are all vulnerable does not preclude that there is an equality in the vulnerability we all face. As Wallbank and I have argued:

Vulnerabilities are not distributed equally among human beings. Although we share the commonality of being born, living lives and dying, the ways we live a vulnerable life are likely to be highly differentiated and affected by factors such as ethnicity, sexuality, gender, age, health, social class, employment status and care responsibilities. Indeed the range of factors impacting upon vulnerabilities is limitless.[97]

I suggest that the literature on vulnerability typically takes three unifying elements which capture a core notion of vulnerability. P is vulnerable if the following three factors are present:[98]

1. P faces a risk of harm.
2. P does not have the resources to be able to avoid the risk of harm materializing.
3. P would not be able to adequately respond to the harm if the risk materialized.

The first requirement is that P faces a risk of harm. Clearly if the risk is of something that is not harmful there is no vulnerability. The risk of winning the lottery does not make one vulnerable! Similarly in Britain we would not say a person is vulnerable because they are at risk of harm from a tornado, because tornadoes are so rare that it is not a meaningful risk.

---

[97] J. Wallbank and J. Herring, 'Introduction' in J. Wallbank and J. Herring (eds), *Vulnerability Care and Family Law* (Aldershot, Ashgate 2014), 8.

[98] J. Alwang, P. Siegel Steen, and S. Jørgensen, *Vulnerability: A View From Different Disciplines* (World Bank Social Protection Discussion Paper 115, 2001). Even limiting the concept to these three factors is controversial: F. Sherwood-Johnson, 'Constructions of "Vulnerability" in Comparative Perspective: Scottish Protection Policies and the Trouble with "Adults at Risk"', (2013) 28 *Disability & Society* 908.

The second requirement to consider is whether a person is easily able to avoid the risk materializing. It may be that there is a serious risk of harm, but P can easily be expected to avoid it by taking steps to avoid it. For example, P is at risk of an infection, but by being inoculated can avoid it.

The third point recognizes that some people will be easily able to mitigate the harm, while others will not. For example, a damage to a piece of property may be of little problem to P if she has insurance and can quickly obtain a replacement; but may be a significant problem to a person with no insurance and limited economic resources. It is here that the state provision may be particularly significant. Our society provides extensive protection against some harms, but not others. The opportunity to mitigate the loss through insurance is only available to the wealthy.

As this demonstrates, although all people may face the same risk, it may be that opportunities to avoid the risk materializing, or responding to it if it does materialize, may differ from person to person. Doris Schroeder and Eugenijus Gefenas[99] suggest that vulnerability is to be exposed to the possibility of harm (what they describe as the external element of vulnerability) *and* to be substantially unable to protect oneself from that possibility (what they describe as the internal element). They therefore define vulnerability in this way: 'To be vulnerable means to face a significant probability of incurring an identifiable harm while substantially lacking ability and/or means to protect oneself.' The Council for International Organizations of Medical Sciences' (CIOMS) guidelines capture this in their definition of vulnerable people as 'those who are relatively or (absolutely) incapable of protecting their own interests because they may have insufficient power, intelligence, education, resources, strength, or other needed attributes to protect their own interests'.[100] The differences can be related to the differences in the physical, emotional, and intellectual variances in humanity making people more or less at risk of harm.[101] As already mentioned, the distinction between these two can be exaggerated. Societal provision and attitudes can render some personal characteristics a source of vulnerability, when they may not be. Race and gender, for example, have been re-created in our society as a hierarchy of power. It would be possible to imagine societies where that is not so.

It is important to notice there can be layers of vulnerability. Florencia Luna and Sheryl Vanderpoel explain:[102]

---

[99] D. Schroeder and E. Gefenas, 'Vulnerability too Vague and too Broad', (2009) 18 *Cambridge Quarterly of Healthcare Ethics* 113.

[100] Council for International Organizations of Medical Sciences, *Guidance* (CIOMS 2002).

[101] M. Fineman, 'Feminism, Masculinities and Multiple Identities', (n. 32).

[102] F. Luna and S. Vanderpoel, 'Not the Usual Suspects: Addressing Layers of Vulnerability', (2013) 17 *Bioethics* 325.

For example, being a woman does not *per se* entail vulnerability. However, a woman living in a country that does not recognize or is intolerant of *reproductive rights* would acquire a layer of vulnerability. In turn, an educated and resourceful woman in that same country can overcome some of the consequences of the denial of reproductive rights; however, a *poor woman* in that country acquires another layer of vulnerability. Moreover, an *illiterate* poor woman in that situation acquires yet another layer. And, if this woman is an *immigrant, undocumented* or belongs to an *aboriginal community*, she will acquire increasing layers of vulnerabilities and would suffer proportionately under these overlapping layers.

The source of vulnerability

Some commentators draw a distinction between sources of vulnerability.[103] Vulnerability, it is suggested, should not be seen as an external state of affairs, but is one's ability to protect oneself. Hence, if there is a natural disaster, say a flood, some people will not be vulnerable: they will have the resources they need to ensure their well-being. Others will be vulnerable because they lack the resources they need to respond to the emergency.[104] However, the distinction between an external threat and an internal vulnerability is not straightforward. An individual characteristic can only be a source of vulnerability in the context of particular social circumstances. Being unable to walk might, or might not, render one at greater risk of being mugged depending on a wide range of social circumstances. It is better, therefore, not to rely on a distinction between inherent characteristics and external circumstances, but rather to simply focus on the risk of harm being faced and abilities to avoid the threat.[105]

Dunn, Clare, and Holland, exploring the concept of the vulnerable adult in the law, have expressed concern at the shift from including within the concept those whose vulnerability includes situational factors, such as being in abusive relationships,[106] as well as those for whom the source of vulnerability is innate (e.g. someone with learning disabilities). Those authors are concerned that this extension is 'potentially infinite in scope and application'.[107] Of course, for those who, like me, would emphasize universal vulnerability, the width of the vulnerable concept is of less concern. However, where

---

[103] See the discussion in S. Hurst, 'Vulnerability in Research and Health Care', (n. 5).

[104] Ibid.   [105] Ibid.

[106] C. Mackenzie, W. Rogers, and S. Dodds (eds), *Vulnerability: New Essays in Ethics and Feminist Philosophy* (Oxford, Oxford University Press 2014), separates situational factors from pathogenic. Pathogenic factors arise from relational abuse or socio-political oppression; whereas situational factors arise from environmental or material circumstances.

[107] M. Dunn, I. Clare, and A. Holland, 'To Empower or to Protect?', (n. 6), 241.

I would depart from Dunn, Clare, and Holland is the argument that we can separate out the innate and situational values.

To explore why it is worth thinking more about how the distinction is drawn. Kipnis,[108] in a much quoted analysis, suggests there are seven types of vulnerability. Before listing these it is important to note that these were in the context of medical research and so primarily focused on impediments to giving consent:

(1) cognitive: the ability to understand information and make decisions;
(2) jurisdictional: being under the legal authority of someone such as a prison warden;
(3) deferential: customary obedience to medical or other authority;
(4) medical: having an illness for which there is no treatment;
(5) allocational: poverty, educational deprivation;
(6) infrastructure: limits of the research setting to carry out the protocol; and
(7) social: belonging to a socially undervalued group.[109]

Under Dunn et al.'s distinction we might see the first and fourth of these as innate and the rest as situational. However, such a distinction is not readily drawn. Take, for example, the category of an illness. Historically we can see what were regarded as illnesses (e.g. homosexuality) would now be regarded as simply a construction by those particular societies. Similarly, what constitutes an ability to understand information is a product of a particular mind and assessment of that by social forces. What might today constitute a learning disability, due to its impact on reading or maths, might not even have been recognized as such several hundred years ago when there was less formal education. The distinction between social and personal sources of vulnerability, therefore, collapses.

Subjective vulnerability

A more helpful distinction can be drawn between the sense of vulnerability as understood by the individual themselves (a subjective understanding) and that assessed by outsiders (an objective understanding). Dunn, Clare, and Holland[110] are concerned that considering vulnerability from an objective

---

[108] K. Kipnis, 'Vulnerability in Research Subjects: A Bioethical Taxonomy' in *Ethical and Policy Issues in Research Involving Human Research Participants* (National Bioethics Advisory Commission, 2001).

[109] Ibid.

[110] M. Dunn, I. Clare, and A. Holland, 'To Empower or to Protect? Constructing the 'Vulnerable Adult' in English Law and Public Policy', (2008) 28 *Legal Studies* 234.

perspective will mean that the individual will not be at the heart of the intervention. They distinguish 'etic' and 'emic' understandings of vulnerability:

'Etic' approaches equate vulnerability with risk, and assess an individual's vulnerability in terms of the risk facing that person, justifying intervention as a means of managing that risk with regard to objectively determined standards. 'Emic' approaches, in contrast, are based on the experiential perception of 'exposure to harm through challenges to one's integrity ... [It] places vulnerability in a psycho-social cultural context',[111] and focus on the subjective reality of a person's everyday life ... [V]ulnerability exists as lived experience. The individual's perception of self and challenges to self, and of resources to withstand such challenges, define vulnerability.[112]

That seems a reasonable approach. There are some matters whose meaning depends on the perspective. John Williams uses the example of an elderly couple who live with their son.[113] Every now and then the son takes money from their wallet without asking them and uses it to buy a drink. That might look like a clear case of financial abuse. However, imagine the couple are aware of this. They are aware that their care imposes a burden on their son, but he would never ask for money for fear that would make them feel awkward. They leave their wallet out in an open place so the money can be taken. To them the removal of the money is a convenient way of providing him treats, which would be awkward if done more openly. One of the benefits of this distinction is that it recognizes that it encourages listening to the person said to be vulnerable and understanding their perspective, as well as encouraging an objective assessment of risk.

Labelling groups

In practice and legal regulation it is common to label a particular group of people as a vulnerable group. For example, if a medical researcher has a volunteer from a member of a vulnerable group, this will automatically trigger a set of mechanisms to ensure that the volunteer is protected and freely consenting, or may indeed prohibit a member of that group. As we have already seen, and will be developed in this book, various legal provisions are directed towards 'vulnerable adults'.

---

[111] J. Spiers, 'New Perspectives on Vulnerability Using Emic and Etic Approaches', (2000) 31 *Journal of Advanced Nursing* 715, 718.

[112] M. Dunn, I. Clare, and A. Holland, 'To Empower or to Protect?', (n. 6).

[113] J. Williams, 'State Responsibility and the Abuse of Vulnerable Older People: Is There a Case for a Public Law to Protect Vulnerable Older People From Abuse?' In J. Bridgeman, H. Keating, and C. Lind (eds), *Responsibility, Law and Family* (Aldershot, Ashgate 2008).

Such labelling has benefits. It certainly assists bodies dealing with the general public, who do not have the time to make individual assessments, to be alerted to groups of vulnerable people. It also avoids infringement of privacy that might be required if individual assessments are made for every adult who is dealt with by an organization. It also ensures all members of the group receive the enhanced protection, even if their vulnerability would not have been apparent on a more cursory individualized basis. For example, a woman who has just given birth will be visited by a health worker and assessed for signs of post-natal depression. That is because depression is particularly linked with post-birth life. If new mothers were not identified as such a vulnerable group, it may well be that many cases would not be identified. The groups that are typically identified as vulnerable include those of doubtful capacity; those who are susceptible to coercion or exploitation; and those who are at increased risk of harm (e.g. through illness).[114]

The problem with the group approach is that it contains false positives and false negatives. A person may fall into one of these groups but not in fact be particularly vulnerable and someone may fall outside a group and yet be especially vulnerable. That argument is a fair one, but there is no denying its bureaucratic benefits in some contexts.

The concerns with group vulnerability are summarized in this way:

[T]he concept of vulnerability stereotypes whole categories of individuals, without distinguishing between individuals in the group who indeed might have special characteristics that need to be taken into account and those who do not. Particular concerns have been raised about considering all poor people, all pregnant women, all members of ethnic or racial minorities, and all people with terminal illness as inherently vulnerable.[115]

Several things are notable about such a viewpoint. First, it assumes that being labelled as vulnerable is something negative. As already mentioned, it reflects a false elevation of autonomy and independence as desirable states. Second, it is perhaps an unfair characterization of how such labelling can be used. It may not be being used as a way of saying that every member of that group is especially vulnerable. It may just be alerting an organization or decision-maker to the fact that people in that group may need particular services or help. This issue is raised in the next issue we need to discuss, the political use of vulnerability.

---

[114] W. Rogers, C. Mackenzie, and S. Dodds, (n. 27).

[115] C. Levine, R. Faden, C. Grady, D. Hammerschmidt, L. Eckenwiler, and J. Sugarman, 'The Limitations of "Vulnerability" as a Protection for Human Research Participants', (2004) 4 *American Journal of Bioethics* 44.

Politics and vulnerability

Politicians regularly talk about the vulnerable. It has become a cliché, although with considerable merit, that 'the mark of any civilised society is how it protects the most vulnerable'.[116]

Since the New Labour government's attitudes towards welfare changed there has been a shift towards the notion that welfare is conditional. There may be a right to welfare support, but that comes with responsibilities.[117] The goal and expectation is for everyone to be self-sufficient and independent. State support may be needed as a safety net and a last resort, but should not be misused. Even that is questioned, with claiming benefits being suggested as a 'wrong thing' to do in this quote from George Osborne:[118]

We are simply asking people to make the same choices as working families traditionally do. These are the realities of life for working people and they should be the realities for everyone else too … For too long, we have had a system where people who do the right thing, get up in the morning and work hard, get penalised for it while others who do the wrong thing get rewarded.

The 'vulnerable' are seen as not fitting into the general discourse about personal responsibility and independence, which are promoted by discourse of this kind. No doubt George Osborne, if questioned, would not apply his comments to people who are unable to work. There is generally an acceptance that vulnerable people are not to be expected to become dependent. In some ways it used to reflect the difference between what used to be called the deserving and the undeserving poor. Kate Brown suggests that the word 'vulnerable' can be a 'get out of jail free' card for those said to be responsible for their position or for getting themselves out of it.[119] Vulnerability in this discourse becomes linked and associated with a lack of agency and responsibility.

Kate Brown draws out three themes from the political use of vulnerability:

i) links between 'vulnerability', state power, and professional 'discretion';
ii) the relationship of 'vulnerability' to citizenship; and
iii) the vulnerable as 'deserving' of resources.

---

[116] Jacqui Smith, [Hansard HC vol 486 col 524 (19 January 2009)].

[117] K. Brown, 'Re-moralising "Vulnerability"', (2012) 6 *People, Place & Policy Online* 41.

[118] Quoted in J. Wallbank and J. Herring, 'Introduction' in J. Wallbank and J. Herring (eds), *Vulnerability Care and Family Law* (n. 97), 8.

[119] K. Brown, 'Re-moralising "Vulnerability"', (n. 117).

As to state power, she sees vulnerability as a moral justification for 'social control mechanisms'. Professionals have the power to determine who is vulnerable and so what decisions should be made for them. Children, by being deemed vulnerable, require extra surveillance and restrictions. Some feminist writers claim that intervention in prostitution has been justified by deeming them to be vulnerable.[120] Ironically, complying with an approved image of a vulnerable person can be a source of power. Brown claims that 'people who conform to commonly held notions of how 'vulnerable' people behave may find their entitlement to be more secure'.[121] Hence, in terms of housing and mental health service provision the 'servile vulnerable person', who is grateful for help, will find themselves in a better position to access services, while those who resist the role and are 'difficult' will lose out on services.

In relation to citizenship, some claim that vulnerability can operate in a patronizing and oppressive way. It fails to acknowledge the extent to which society as a whole contributes to the perception of especial vulnerability or disability.[122] The 'vulnerable citizen' is promoted as in part justifying the state's existence, but also as lacking full citizenship by not being able to fully take up the responsibilities of a self-sufficient citizen.

The third theme, that vulnerability can be used to show who is deserving of resources, has already been discussed. The vulnerable are seen as unable to look after themselves and so having a justified claim on benefits. This distinguishes them from the lazy or those lacking 'aspiration' who need to work harder.

An important part of focusing on vulnerability is that it highlights the importance of how social provision can ameliorate or magnify our vulnerability. That means our focus can shift from calling some people vulnerable to recognizing that some people have more power. As Jenny Kitzinger suggests, it means we can move from vulnerability to look at oppression.[123] The danger is that use of power not only creates vulnerability, it justifies it. To take one example, the corporal punishment of children is justified in the name of enabling parents to exercise control over children in order to protect them from risk. Yet the practice and acceptance of corporal punishment reveals a diminished acceptance of children's rights and personhood. It creates its own range of vulnerabilities. An appreciation of the common and interlocking

---

[120] V. Munro and J. Scoular, 'Abusing Vulnerability?', (n. 95).
[121] K. Brown, 'Re-moralising "Vulnerability"', (n. 117).
[122] F. Sherwood-Johnson, 'Constructions of "Vulnerability"', (n. 98).
[123] J. Kitzinger, 'Who are You Kidding? Children, Power and the Struggle Against Sexual Abuse' in A. James and A. Prout (eds), *Constructing and Reconstructing Childhood* (Abingdon, Routledge 1997).

vulnerabilities of adults and children can reveal what can otherwise be an unrecognized use of power.

Duties to the vulnerable

In Robert Goodin's significant work, *Protecting the Vulnerable: A Reanalysis of our Social Responsibilities*,[124] he argues that the vulnerability of other people is the source of our responsibility to them.[125] To him the extent of these duties depends on the details of our relationship with the person.[126] We have especial responsibility towards the vulnerability of friends and families, but also have a duty towards vulnerable people at large.[127] He argues 'we have an obligation to act so as to prevent harm to, or protect the interests of, those who are especially vulnerable to our actions and choices'.[128] The greater the needs a person has and the better position the other is in to meet those needs, the greater the responsibility.[129] Hence a parent has especially strong responsibilities to a baby, but less so as the child matures.

An important aspect of his thinking is that it rejects the traditional liberal approach which suggests that obligations must be agreed or chosen. Indeed for Goodin, 'duties and responsibilities are not necessarily (or even characteristically) things that you deserve. More often than not, they are things that just happen to you.'[130]

Notably, Goodin's obligation is not limited to cases where someone has caused another's vulnerable state. Rogers, McKenzie, and Dodds are not convinced by that last point:

How or why we find ourselves in a position where another is vulnerable to us is often crucial in determining not only whether or not the allocation of responsibility for that vulnerability is morally warranted or just, but also what kind of response to the other's vulnerability is morally appropriate.[131]

The issue that point highlights is a difficulty with Goodin's argument, and that is that a person may find themselves with a range of people vulnerable towards them. How are the competing arising obligations to be weighed? Goodin explains that 'the principle of protecting the vulnerable is first and

---

[124] R. Goodin, *Protecting the Vulnerable: A Reanalysis of Our Social Responsibilities* (Chicago IL, University of Chicago Press 1985).
[125] Ibid.   [126] Ibid., 112.   [127] W. Rogers, C. Mackenzie, and S. Dodds, (n. 27).
[128] As defined in W. Rogers, C. Mackenzie, and S. Dodds, (n. 27).
[129] S. Miller, *The Ethics of Need* (Abingdon, Routledge 2012).
[130] R. Goodin, *Protecting the Vulnerable*, (n. 124), 133.
[131] W. Rogers, C. Mackenzie, and S. Dodds, (n. 27).

foremost an argument for aiding those in dire need'.[132] We must meet, he explains, the vital needs first. Vital needs are those which the person will be seriously harmed or fail to flourish without. That is not as straightforward as it sounds. Is a deeply depressed person needing comfort in greater need than the hungry person needing a nourishing meal? It is even harder in practice when a person is unclear of the needs of the other. Our weighing of needs can depend on a range of social, cultural, and political issues and meeting those in a particular context is difficult. Imagine X's neighbour is entitled to regular care from her local authority social services. They are facing cutbacks and so decide not to visit as they know X keeps an eye on the neighbour. Should X 'connive' in the failure to provide the required services or assist the cash strapped authority?

A gap in Goodin's analysis identified by Rogers et al. is that he does not explain how autonomy and protection might be balanced. He appears to prioritize protection, and gives little weight to autonomy. What if the vulnerable person does not want their needs met? Or what if they have other needs that are less vital that they wish addressed first? Two possible, not inconsistent, responses could be made.

First, we could take the balancing of autonomy and protection literally and imagine a scale with weights for autonomy on one side, reflecting the extent to which the decision is richly autonomous (see Chapter 3) and the extent of the harm on the other. The more richly autonomous the decision the more likely the scale will win out, even over serious harm. However, the more weakly the autonomous decision the more likely the harm, if more than negligible, will win out. We will explore this further in Chapter 3.

Second, we could reimagine autonomy in a way which is premised on vulnerability and the importance of relationships. Relational autonomy may be seen as one such approach. Rogers et al. explain how such an approach may help:

Relational theorists argue that autonomy is a socially constituted capacity, which is developed, sustained, and exercised only with extensive social scaffolding and support. Further, because autonomy is a socially constituted capacity, its development can be impaired and its exercise thwarted by exploitative or oppressive interpersonal relationships, and by repressive or unjust social and political institutions. This approach to autonomy is thus premised on the fact of our inescapable dependency on, and hence vulnerability to, others. Moreover, because relational theorists regard agency and some degree of autonomy as important for a flourishing human life, a relational approach is committed to the view that the obligations arising from vulnerability extend beyond protection from harm to the provision of the social

---

[132] R. Goodin, *Protecting the Vulnerable*, (n. 124), 111.

support necessary to promote the autonomy of persons who are more than ordinarily vulnerable.

The aim then of intervention to protect is to restore or support autonomy. The interventions should not be designed to increase powerlessness, but to put the person in the position where they can make the decision.[133] This is likely to mean that a person must have their basic needs met before they are fully in a position to exercise autonomy.

Critiques of vulnerability

The concept of vulnerability has received criticism.

First, there are those who are concerned with its practical applications, in particular that it is a mask for paternalism. Those who are labelled vulnerable are treated as appropriate subjects of paternalistic state intervention. In particular there is a concern when the intervention is designed to impose 'order' on the chaotic lives of individuals. Munro and Scoular put it this way:

> For current purposes, what is particularly problematic about this approach is that it tends to generate a rather 'flat' notion of vulnerability. Not only does it conflate too many different experiences and positions under the header of 'vulnerability', but it fails to dissect and interrogate the multiple and complex causes (both inter-personal and social) of that vulnerable condition, and pays insufficient attention to the voice and narrative of the individual sex worker. What is more, it tends to attach the condition too firmly to the individual herself and accepts uncritically the appropriateness of criminal law as a mechanism by which to seek its eradication, or at least its recompense.[134]

However, as we have seen, the legal response to vulnerability need not be of that nature. It can be designed to enable a person to be able to fully exercise autonomy. Alternatively we can balance protection and autonomy to ensure that the intervention is proportionate to meeting their needs. So, although a misuse of the notion of vulnerability can lead to inappropriate paternalism, it is not clear it necessarily needs to.

A second powerful critique comes from disability studies. By describing disabled people as vulnerable this downplays their voice in decision making and deprives them of full equality with the 'able-bodied'.[135] The

---

[133] E. Ziarek, 'Feminist Reflections on Vulnerability: Disrespect, Obligation, Action', (2013) 132 *SubStance* 67.

[134] V. Munro and J. Scoular, 'Abusing Vulnerability?', (n. 95).

[135] B. Fawcett, 'Vulnerability', (n. 5).

label vulnerability, it is said, emphasizes the idea that disabled people lack something and the dangers they face, generating a need for protection, rather than highlighting all disabled people can do.[136] However, the concept of universal vulnerability, supported in this chapter, provides a powerful tool for disability advocates. The arguments made here, that it is provision or absence of social supports that can render some vulnerability more visible or potent, echo and indeed support the social model critique of disability.

It is, for example, entirely consistent with the following summary of a feminist critique of disability promoted by Rosemarie Garland-Thomson:[137]

Disability ... is a cultural interpretation of human variation rather than an inherent inferiority, a pathology to cure, or an undesirable trait to eliminate. In other words, it finds disability's significance in interactions between bodies and their social and material environments. By probing the cultural meanings attributed to bodies that societies deem disabled, feminist disability studies does vast critical cultural work. First, it understands disability as a system of exclusions that stigmatizes human differences. Second, it uncovers communities and identities that the bodies we consider disabled have produced. Third, it reveals discriminatory attitudes and practices directed at those bodies. Fourth, it exposes disability as a social category of analysis. Fifth, it frames disability as an effect of power relations. Feminist disability studies show that disability—similar to race and gender—is a system of representation that marks bodies as subordinate, rather than an essential property of bodies that supposedly have something wrong with them.

Further, the arguments to be brought together shortly, that vulnerability should be seen as a good thing, counter the negative associations sometimes attached to impairment.

A third concern is that abuse can occur within dependency relationships. Shiloh Whitney has written about the importance of not assuming dependency is always good: 'Dependencies may be enabling, nourishing, and caring. But surely dependency is not wholly without danger: dominating, exploitative responses to vulnerability are still possible.'[138] We will return to this point in Chapter 7. However, in brief my response is that a vulnerability centred approach means that we are able to recognize both the benefits and the dangers attached to vulnerability. It urges us to ensure that our universal vulnerability is a source of the good things mentioned above, and is not manipulated for the exploitation of others. Only a vulnerability centred

---

[136] F. Sherwood-Johnson, 'Constructions of "Vulnerability"', (n. 98).

[137] R. Garland-Thomson, 'Feminist Disability Studies', (2005) 30 *Signs* 1557.

[138] S. Whitney, 'Dependency Relations: Corporeal Vulnerability and Norms of Personhood in Hobbes and Kittay', (2011) 26 *Hypatia* 554.

approach will have a full appreciation of the ways that vulnerabilities can be exploited and the incentive for ensuring an effective legal response.

Vulnerability is good

Vulnerability is often seen in a negative light. David Archard, writing about childhood, has written:

There may be features of childhood but not of adulthood which are valuable, such as innocence, wonder and trust. There may, correspondingly be features of adulthood but not childhood which are valuable, such as experience and independence. It is also evident that there may be features of childhood but not of adulthood which are not valuable, such as dependence and vulnerability.[139]

This dislike of dependence and vulnerability is not restricted to philosophers. Self-reliance has become a dominant theme in social policy.[140] John Moore, then the Secretary of State for Social Security, once claimed: 'A climate of dependence can in time corrupt the human spirit. Everyone knows the sullen apathy of dependence and can compare it with the sheer delight of personal achievement.'[141] I think such views are profoundly mistaken. Vulnerability and dependence are not only inevitable parts of humanity, as argued above, they are to be greatly welcomed. They are often virtues, not vices.

In our society independence and self-sufficiency are seen as goals and vulnerability is something to be avoided. To become 'dependent on welfare'; a 'burden to others'; to 'lose independence' is seen as a disaster. Be it terms of policies towards lone parents, disabled people, or care in the community, autonomy and independence has become a key policy goal. As Margrit Shildrick noted, 'in western modernity at least, vulnerability is figured as a shortcoming, an impending failure'.[142] As Shildrick goes on to argue, such views are bizarre: if vulnerability is an inherent aspect of the human condition it is hard to seek to avoid it.

---

[139] D. Archard, 'Philosophical Perspectives on Childhood' in J. Fiona (ed.), *Legal Concepts of Childhood* (Oxford, Oxford University Press 2001), 52.

[140] K. Halvorsen, 'Symbolic Purposes and Factual Consequences of the Concepts "Self-Reliance" and "Dependency" in Contemporary Discourses on Welfare', (1998) 7 *Scandinavian Journal of Social Welfare* 56.

[141] J. Moore, UK Secretary of State for Social Security, 1987, quoted in M. Fine and C. Glendinning, 'Dependence, Independence or Interdependence? Revisiting the Concepts of "Care" and "Dependency"', (2005) *Ageing and Society* 601, 601.

[142] M. Shildrick, *Embodying the Monster: Encounters with the Vulnerable Self* (London, Sage 2002); A. Beckett, *Citizenship and Vulnerability* (Basingstoke, Palgrave 2006), 71.

But more positive things can be said about vulnerability than that it is simply an inevitable part of the human condition. Our mutual vulnerability requires us to reach out to others to offer and receive help from them. The virtues of beneficence and compassion are encouraged and necessary. We have to become open to others and our own and others' needs. A recognition of our mutual vulnerability leads to empathy and understanding.[143] It creates intimacy and trust. It compels us to focus on interactive, co-operative solutions to the issues we address. It encourages creativity in finding new ways of overcoming our human limitations and requires a desire to accept others as they are. As Carse puts it: 'Our vulnerability is inextricably tied to our capacity to give of ourselves to others, to treasure and aspire, to commit to endeavors, to care about justice and about our own and other's dignity.'[144]

The political use of vulnerability narratives tends to promote disablist approaches to the issue.[145] As many writers of disabilities studies have written, there is great pressure to be perceived as independent and lacking vulnerability. Success for a person with a disability is measured by the extent to which they may be able to be (or present themselves as being) independent and autonomous: in short, to be 'normal'.[146] But that is a completely wrong use of the concept. The vulnerability approach promoted in this chapter recognizes the disability in all of us. It recognizes that all of us need social provision; we all need help. It can only be in our joining together and co-operation that human flourishing can be found. We may have different needs and different strengths. Our vulnerabilities may be manifest in different ways.

Vulnerability is essential to relationships. In entering a relationship with others this creates an understanding of trust, the assumptions of responsibility, and obligations of care. These things create a vulnerability: we are in danger of not meeting our obligations; we are at risk of others not meeting theirs to us. Our trust might be misplaced. The opening up of our natures creates a risk we will be taken advantage of,[147] that private information will be used to harm us, and the risk of grief and loss. Yet relationships are good and beneficial. Indeed they may well be described as one of the basic goods. Relationships, intimacy, care; all of these things in their nature render us

---

[143] E. Feder Kittay, 'The Ethics of Care, Dependence, and Disability', (2011) 44 *Ratio Juris* 49.

[144] A Carse, (2006) 'Vulnerability, Agency and Human Flourishing' in C. Taylor and R. Dell'Oro (eds), *Health and Human Flourishing* (Washington DC, Georgetown University Press 2006), 48.

[145] M. Fine and C. Glendinning, 'Dependence, Independence or Interdependence? Revisiting the Concepts of "Care" and "Dependency"', (2005) *Ageing and Society* 601, 601.

[146] T. Shakespeare, *Help*, (n. 56).

[147] S. Sevenhuijsen, *Too Good to be True?* (IWM Working Paper No. 3/1998).

vulnerable.[148] Exclusion of the other to achieve invulnerability is anathema to relationships. As Phillips puts it:

Helplessness is the precondition for human bonds, for exchange; you have to be a helpless subject in order to be helped, in order to be understood, in order to become a moral creature. And so, by the same token, if you can't experience helplessness you are precluded from these fundamental human experiences.[149]

For those who see the self in a relational way, then the separation of the 'Other', with the rejection of vulnerability that goes with that, leads to a denial of the self. As Butler puts it:

It is not as if an 'I' exists independently over here and then simply loses a 'you' over there, especially if the attachment to 'you' is part of what composes who 'I' am. If I lose you, under these conditions, then I not only mourn the loss, but I become inscrutable to myself. Who 'am' I, without you? When we lose some of these ties by which we are constituted, we do not know who we are or what to do. On one level, I think that I have lost 'you' only to discover that 'I' have gone missing as well. At another level, perhaps what I have lost 'in' you, that for which I have no ready vocabulary, is a relationality that is composed neither exclusively of myself nor you, but is to be conceived as *the tie* by which those terms are differentiated and related.[150]

Imagine the life of a Stoic, who renders himself invulnerable to the blow of fortune and safe from the 'slings and arrows' of life. That would not be a life we expect to be marked by virtue;[151] it would lack empathy. The ability to provide deep care for others and a lack of investment in the well-being of others. No love. If relations with others are what produces identity then identity is inherently vulnerable, but not in a bad way.[152] To quote Butler again:

One does not always stay intact. One may want to, or manage to for a while, but despite one's best efforts, one is undone, in the face of the other, by the touch, by the scent, by the feel, by the prospect of the touch, by the memory of the feel.[153]

Our vulnerability, further, requires us to reach out to others to meet their needs and to have our needs met. These interactions are fulfilling and creative. Our very vulnerability provides us with the seeds for our growth through relationships with others.[154]

---

[148] G.W. Harris, *Dignity and Vulnerability* (Berkeley CA, University of California Press 1997).
[149] A. Phillips, 'Freud's Helplessness' in G. Levine (ed) The Joy of Secularism (Princeton University Press, Princeton NJ, 2011), 139.
[150] J. Butler, *Precarious Life*, (n. 43), 22, emphasis in original.
[151] C. Card, 'Stoicism, Evil and the Possibility of Morality', (1998) 29 *Metaphilosophy* 245.
[152] S. Drichel, 'Reframing Vulnerability: "So Obviously the Problem…?"', (2013) 42 *SubStance* 3.
[153] J. Butler, *Precarious Life*, (n. 43), 23–4.
[154] M. Fineman, ' "Elderly" as Vulnerable', (n. 66).

Further, the emphasis on vulnerability promotes a particular set of values which are relevant when discussing which characteristics generate the high moral status of personhood in ethical discourse. To some commentators it is our rationality and our intellectual capabilities which generate personhood. However, doing so can exclude those with severe cognitive impairments from the status. The mistakes of such an approach are revealed in the writing of Eva Feder Kittay,[155] who has written movingly of the attitudes displayed towards her severely disabled daughter, Sesha:

Sesha's life is a human life, but a tragic one because her situation is such that she can never achieve functioning of all the capabilities to some satisfactory degree. I believe that were Sesha capable of replying, she would remind us that people with disabilities have worked hard to insist that life with impairments, even serious impairments need not be 'tragic'. What is tragic is the failure of the larger society to include people with variant bodies and modes of functioning. Yes, when Sesha was born I had envisioned a different future for her. Yes, when I learned of her very significant impairments I saw a human tragedy. But I have since learned— from her, from the disability community and from my own observations —that she is capable of having a very good life, one full of joy, of love, of laughter: a life that includes the appreciation of some of the best of human culture, great music and fine food, and the delights of nature, water, the scent of flowers, the singing of birds. No, she cannot participate in political life, she cannot marry and have children, she cannot read a book or engage in moral reasoning, but her life is richly human and full of dignity. We need to work hard to see that her life is not tragic . . .

Feder Kittay in this passage shows how the disabled can be branded 'non-persons' and defined by their lack of abilities in accordance with the norm. Kittay concludes her discussion of dignity with a central point: 'I urge that we not look for the basis of dignity in attributions we have as individuals, but in the relationships we bear to one another. Relationships of caring serve as conduits of worth—the worth of the caregiver is conferred on the one to whom she devotes herself.' I would want to add that in relationships of care it is hard to separate out who is the cared for and who is the carer.[156] There is often an interdependency and interchange which means the obvious categories of care and cared for break down. If our source of value, dignity, and humanity is not our intellect but our feelings, relationships, care, and love, then separation between children as the vulnerable and the non-vulnerable collapses.

---

[155] E. Kittay, 'Equality, Dignity and Disability' in M. Lyons and F. Waldron (eds), *Perspectives on Equality* (Dublin, Liffey Press 2005), 95.

[156] J. Herring, 'Caregivers in Medical Law and Ethics', (2008) 25 *Journal of Contemporary Health Law and Policy* 1.

As Mary Neal argues:

We are beings who strive for—and achieve—the sublime, the awe-inspiring, and the transcendent. We aspire to be, not just animals, but moral beings: to pursue second order preferences and desires; to hold ourselves and others to standards of behaviour that surpass those we tolerate from other animals and would settle for from ourselves if we were content to fulfil only the animal side of our nature; and we characteristically hope for immortality, either in the literal sense of 'life after death', or in a secular sense through the legacies of our work (art, invention, discovery) and the personal marks we leave on those whose lives have intersected with our own (we wish not to be forgotten).

Earlier I argued that vulnerability is inevitably part of life. In this section I have taken that further and argued it is a part of a good life. It is what makes life valuable. It urges us to reach beyond ourselves and to co-operate. It is essential to what makes life fine.

Conclusion

The law tends to assume that adults have capacity, are autonomous, and are able to make decisions for their life which are worthy of respect. The general law's rules apply to such people. There are then special areas of the law which are marked off for those lacking capacity. For example, there are special exceptions to the rules of contract which apply to minors, those under undue influence, or those lacking mental capacity. These vulnerable groups are seen as falling within one of these exceptional cases deserving of special rules. We can see this in the very structure of the law syllabuses at most UK law schools, where the subjects of contract, land, and tort dominate, and the subjects of child law, mental health law, welfare law, and elder law are very much to the side, if visible at all. They are seen as exceptional cases. Indeed an undergraduate could work through their law degree reading but only a tiny number of cases in which a child or a person lacking capacity is involved. It may be the world of a select group of law firms, but it is not the real world, as any high street solicitor or social worker will be aware. Something has gone terribly wrong that our law graduates are well able to advise the business person planning an aggressive take-over of a rival firm, but unable to advise an anorexic teenager fleeing an abusive relationship.

We could, and should, present a rather different legal system, which starts with an acknowledgement of everyone's vulnerability.[157] Law degrees would

---

[157] P. Blaikie, T. Cannon, I. Davis, and B. Wisner, *At Risk: Natural Hazards, People's Vulnerability, and Disasters* (Abingdon, Routledge 2003).

have the law on mental health, child law, carer law, elder law, and undue influence at their heart. This would produce a rather different way of looking at the world. Gone would be the special 'concessions' involved in protecting especially disadvantaged groups such as the disabled or children. Rather, they would be regarded as the norm and the focus would be on the special privileges that are given to the able-bodied or some adults.[158]

As Fineman argues, law tends to emphasize and presume actors are marked by autonomy, self-sufficiency, and self-determinacy. She spells out the significance of this approach:

When we only study the poor, the rich remain hidden and their advantages remain relatively unexamined, nestled in secure and private spaces, where there is no need for them or the state to justify or explain why they deserve the privilege of state protection. We need to excavate these privileged lives. While sometimes this will be a difficult and complex undertaking, there are certainly abundant records and instruments of privilege all around us that can be accessed relatively easily. These archives are located in corporate boardrooms and in the rules setting up or limiting state and national regulatory regimes. They can be gleaned from tax and probate codes, history books, literature, political theories, and of course, from the language and logic of the law.[159]

It is not just the 'subjects' that make up the law degree that is the problem; it is the norm of independence, autonomy, and non-vulnerability that is perpetuated.

The law focuses on adults and independent adults as the norm, and children and other 'vulnerable adults' as departures from that norm requiring special protections or privileges. The power exercised by some is lost with these assumptions and the emphasis placed on vulnerability. The role of the law could shift to restricting and reducing the power of the powerful, rather than seeking to protect the vulnerable from an exercise of power.[160] Those labelled 'vulnerable' are not some pre-existing category but better seen as having been labelled as such in order to legitimate political ends and to justify current inequalities. A recognition of our mutual vulnerability and the reliance we all have on the provision of help from the state and others must be at the heart of our political and legal response.[161]

---

[158] M. Fineman, 'The Vulnerable Subject: Anchoring Equality in the Human Condition', (2008) 20 *Yale Journal of Law and Feminism* 1.

[159] M. Fineman, 'Equality: Still Illusive After All These Years' in J. Grossman and L. McClain (eds), *Social Citizenship and Gender* (Cambridge, Cambridge University Press 2010).

[160] S. Bray, 'Power Rules', (2010) 110 *Columbia Law Review* 1172.

[161] C. Beasley and C. Bacchi, 'Envisaging a New Politics for an Ethical Future', (2007) 8 *Feminist Theory* 279.

But, perhaps more importantly, an understanding of our mutual vulnerability is important for us to be good and have good lives. It requires us to acknowledge and embrace our helplessness on our own.[162] It is by reaching out, breaking down the barriers between selves, embarking on co-operative projects, and finding ways of enabling each other to flourish that our lives will go well. We need to rejoice in our vulnerability, for it is that which is central to our humanity.

---

[162] A. Phillips, *On Balance* (London, Picador 2011).

3

Vulnerable Adults and Capacity

Introduction

One of the most fundamental distinctions in the law is drawn between people with capacity and those without.[1] Those found to lack capacity are not
able to make legally effective decisions for themselves: they cannot consent
to medical treatment; consent to sexual relations; or enter binding contracts;
and even lack the authority to decide where they will live. For those deemed
to lack capacity, decisions are made on their behalf by others based on an
assessment of their best interests.

The notion of capacity is, therefore, key as it is pre-requisite to the right to
bodily integrity and autonomy, which are foundational human rights. It is a
key concept for this book, because those who lack capacity are seen as vulnerable and need protection from themselves and for others. Capacity is used
by the law as a key marker between the vulnerable and the non-vulnerable.

The basic legal structure

Underpinning the doctrine of capacity is a commitment to autonomy. At its
heart this is the belief that individuals should be able to determine for themselves how they wish to live their life. Others may find a person (P)'s decisions
about what they want to eat, what they spend their time doing, or whom they
have sex with unwise or even immoral, but as long as the decision is made by
P with capacity to make the decision and it does not cause harm to others it
should be respected.

The protection for autonomy is reinforced by the right to bodily integrity.
This is a powerful principle which states that except in a few situations, one
person cannot touch another person. In the medical context this was made

---

[1] In this chapter I draw on J. Herring and J. Wall, 'Autonomy, Capacity and Vulnerable
Adults: Filling the Gaps in the Mental Capacity Act' *Legal Studies* forthcoming.

clear by the Court of Appeal in *R (Burke) v GMC*: 'Where a competent patient makes it clear that he does not wish to receive treatment which is, objectively, in his medical best interests, it is unlawful for doctors to administer that treatment. Personal autonomy or the right of self determination prevails.'[2] This is so even if there is strong evidence that the operation is in the best interests of the patient.[3] A dramatic example of the weight attached to the principle was made in *St George's Healthcare NHS Trust v S*[4] where a woman in labour was told that she needed a Caesarean section and that without such an operation she and the foetus she was carrying would die. Despite her refusal to consent, the operation was carried out. The Court of Appeal held this to be unlawful. Her right to bodily integrity prevailed and the fact that she and the foetus would die without the operation did not provide a good enough reason to justify carrying out the Caesarean without her consent.

There are, of course, exceptions to the right to autonomy. It is essentially a liberty right: a right to be left alone. Simply because you choose to go on holiday to Spain does not give a right to demand you are given the resources to do so. It is simply that you should not be prevented from going. There are a few cases where there are rights to be given positive resources (e.g. the right to education), but these tend to be limited to the most fundamental of rights.

The right to bodily integrity is especially strongly protected, but there is a notable exception to it in the Mental Health Act 1983. This authorizes the treatment of mental disorder in certain circumstances, even where the patient is not consenting. The Mental Health Act 1983 cannot be used to authorize treatment for conditions which are not mental disorders, so it could not be used to authorize an abortion on a person with a mental disorder. Much more could be said about the scope of these rights and they are discussed elsewhere.[5]

Mental capacity

In this section I will summarize the law's approach to defining mental capacity. A critique of the law's approach will follow. The governing legislation is the Mental Capacity Act 2005 (MCA).

[2] *R (Burke) v GMC* [2005] 3 FCR 169, para 30.
[3] *Williamson v East London and City HA* (1998) 41 BMLR 85.
[4] [1998] 3 All ER 673.
[5] J. Herring, *Medical Law and Ethics* (Oxford, Oxford University Press 2014), ch 3.

The presumption of capacity

Section 1(2) of the MCA makes it clear that the law presumes that a person (P) is competent, unless there is evidence that they are not.[6] If the case comes to court the burden is on the person who treated P as lacking capacity to demonstrate that P indeed lacked capacity on the balance of probabilities.[7] Understandably when the court is determining whether P has capacity, the views of the medical experts carry 'very considerable importance'.[8]

Issue specific

A central aspect of the MCA's approach to capacity is that it is 'issue specific'. So the question is always whether a person has capacity to decide a particular question. Someone may have the capacity to decide some issues, but not others. For example, they may be able to decide whether they would like a cup of hot chocolate or not, but lack the capacity to be able to execute a will. In other words, a person should not be dismissed as 'simply incompetent'. Except in the most extreme cases, there are likely to be at least some issues which any person is able to decide for themselves. The thinking behind this stance is that we should maximize the opportunity for people to make decisions for themselves.

Diagnostic and functional test

Section 2(1) MCA states: '[A] person lacks capacity in relation to a matter if at the material time he is unable to make a decision for himself in relation to the matter because of an impairment of, or a disturbance in the functioning of, the mind or brain.' There are two elements to the capacity test.[9] First, under the 'diagnostic test' it must be found that P has an impairment or a disturbance in the functioning of the brain. Under the 'functional test' it must be determined whether as a result of the disturbance P is unable to make the decision. Importantly, it must be shown that the inability to make the decision results from the impairment. So, if P has a mental disorder, but it is their recalcitrance that is preventing them making a decision, they will not lack capacity for the purposes of the Act.

---

[6] *R v Sullivan* [1984] AC 156, 170–1.
[7] *R (N) v Dr M, A NHS Trust* [2002] EWHC 1911 (Admin). The Act in section 5 offers a legal protection to those who treat a patient based on a reasonable but incorrect assessment that they lack capacity.
[8] *A NHS Trust v Dr A* [2013] EWHC 2442 (COP).
[9] *A Local Authority v TZ* [2013] EWHC 2322 (COP).

The Code of Practice lists the following as examples of conditions which might involve an impairment or disturbance of the functioning of the brain:

- conditions associated with some forms of mental illness;
- dementia;
- significant learning disabilities;
- the long-term effects of brain damage;
- physical or medical conditions that cause confusion, drowsiness, or loss of consciousness;
- delirium;
- concussion following a head injury; and
- the symptoms of alcohol or drug use.[10]

This is a very important aspect of the test. It means that a person with a mental disorder is not automatically treated as lacking capacity. If the disorder has not impaired their decision making ability they will retain capacity. It also means that even if a person is unable to make a decision, but not as a result of a mental impairment, then they will not lack capacity under the MCA. For example, a person who is hopelessly in love and unable to weigh issues up in the balance will still retain capacity. Similarly, a person who has unusual religious beliefs and so understands the world in a very different way from everyone else will not, as a result, lack capacity.

Understanding the relevant information

People lack capacity if they are unable to make a decision for themselves. Section 3(1) explains:

[A] person is unable to make a decision for himself if he is unable—
(a) to understand the information relevant to the decision,
(b) to retain that information,
(c) to use or weigh that information as part of the process of making the decision, or
(d) to communicate his decision (whether by talking, using sign language or any other means).

As this indicates, there are a number of ways P may be said to be unable to make a decision. It may be a case of lack of comprehension: P is not capable of understanding their condition or the proposed treatment or the consequences of not receiving treatment.[11] However, P should not be treated as

[10] Department of Constitutional Affairs, *Mental Capacity Act: Code of Practice* (DCA, 2007: para. 4.12).
[11] Mental Capacity Act 2005, s. 2(4).

lacking capacity 'unless all practical steps to help him' reach capacity 'have been taken without success'.[12] Further, under section 2(2): 'A person is not to be regarded as unable to understand the information relevant to a decision if he is able to understand an explanation of it given to him in a way that is appropriate to his circumstances (using simple language, visual aids or any other means).' A fundamental question is what is meant by the 'information relevant to the decision' which a person must understand if they are to have capacity. There is a difficulty here. If we are too strict and require an understanding of every single aspect of the decision then few people would have capacity to make a decision and autonomy could be greatly restricted. On the other hand, if we are too loose with what capacity means we might claim to be respecting P's choice to do A, but they have so misunderstood what A involves that they are not really selecting A at all. In such a case, especially where A will result in harm, we might be causing harm to P and saying we are respecting their choice, when that was not what their choice was at all.

This is clearly not a straightforward issue. The courts have avoided issuing general guidance. The law in England and Wales does not recognize the so-called 'doctrine of informed consent' which states that a patient can only provide effective consent if given the relevant and necessary information to make a proper decision. All that is required is that the patient must understand 'in broad terms the nature of the procedure which is intended'.[13] Macur J in *LBL v RYJ*[14] explained that 'it is not necessary for the person to comprehend every detail of the issue ... it is not always necessary for a person to comprehend all peripheral details'. An easy example of this is *A NHS Trust v K*,[15] where a woman needed to have an operation because she suffered from cancer. She suffered from a mental disorder and refused to consent because she did not accept that she had cancer. Her choice, in her mind, was to remain healthy and not have the operation. However, that choice was not one available on the facts. She lacked understanding of an essential fact necessary to making the decision.

A less straightforward case was *PC v City of York Council*,[16] where PC was a forty-eight-year-old woman with significant learning disabilities who married NC whilst he was imprisoned for serious sexual offences. He was due for release and they intended to cohabit. It was accepted that NC posed a risk to PC if they were to live together, given his history of violence against women.

---

[12] See Department of Constitutional Affairs, *Mental Capacity Act: Code of Practice* (DCA, 2007: para. 2.6) for a further discussion.
[13] *Chatterton v Gerson* [1981] 1 All ER 257, 265.
[14] [2010] EWHC 2664 (Fam), at para. 24.   [15] [2012] EWHC 2922 (COP).
[16] [2013] EWCA Civ 478.

The local authority sought an order that PC lacked capacity to agree to cohabit with NC. The Court of Appeal held it had to be shown she understood what cohabitation with NC would be like. In this case PC refused to believe that NC had been violent in the past and that he posed a risk to her. She, therefore, lacked understanding of a crucial piece of evidence in making the decision. However, the Court of Appeal concluded that she did not lack capacity under the Mental Capacity Act because it had not been shown that she did not accept his violent past because of her mental disorder.[17] The Court of Appeal were also critical of the expert witness who gave evidence that PC lacked capacity because they felt he had focused on the decision reached, rather than the process of the decision making. The fact the decision she had made would be seen by some as foolish was not a reason for finding a lack of capacity. As it could not be shown she lacked capacity the court could not interfere.

This case sits slightly uneasily with a set of other decisions, where the courts have drawn a distinction between 'person specific' decisions and 'act specific' decisions. Sometimes the courts have taken an 'act specific approach'. Then the court determines that the person understands the nature of the act, even though they do not need to understand the nature of the person they are doing it with or the circumstances in which they are doing it. This is the approach the courts have taken in relation to marriage: the question is does P understand what marriage is like, not does P understand what marriage to X is like? In other situations a 'person specific approach' is taken, so the question is whether P understands the decision in terms of the particular context they are dealing with. Interestingly, in *York* they thought capacity to cohabit had to be person specific, so PC had to understand what living with NC was like, not just what cohabitation in general was like. Commentators have struggled to find a coherent basis for how the courts determine whether an act specific or person specific test is used.

Unwise decision

MCA, s. 1(4) states that '[a] person is not to be treated as unable to make a decision merely because he makes an unwise decision'. So this line of reasoning is not permitted: this decision is irrational therefore the patient lacks capacity. However, the use of the word 'merely' is significant as it means that the fact the decision is unwise can be a factor to take into account.[18]

---

[17] The court was not explicit about this but the point was presumably that her lack of belief in his violent past may have been as a result of her being besotted with him.

[18] See J. Savulescu and R. Momeyer, 'Should Informed Consent be Based on Rational Beliefs?' (2007) 23 *Journal of Medical Ethics* 282, who insist that a patient's decision must be based on rational belief if it is to be respected.

As was emphasized in *Re B*: 'The doctors must not allow their emotional reaction to or strong disagreement with the decision of the patient to cloud their judgment in answering the primary question whether the patient has the mental capacity to make the decision.'[19] As that case goes on to explain, a decision may appear irrational to others and yet make perfect sense given P's religious or personal beliefs. In such a case P can be found to have capacity. However, as the Code of Practice indicates, there will inevitably be concerns that a person lacks capacity if they repeatedly make 'unwise decisions that put them at significant risk of harm or exploitation' or make 'a particular unwise decision that is obviously irrational or out of character'.[20] That might be evidence that they lack capacity.

Weighing the information

To have capacity P must also be able to use the information, weigh it, and be able to make a decision.[21] Again it should be clear that it is not enough to show that others think that P attached too much weight to one factor or failed to weigh the appropriate factors. It must be shown that P's mental disorder meant they were unable to weigh the factors at all.

A controversial example concerns anorexia nervosa. In *A Local Authority v E*[22] a thirty-two-year-old woman suffered from anorexia nervosa and alcohol dependency and was refusing to eat. Jackson J concluded that E lacked capacity to refuse treatment in relation to forcible feeding:

[T]here is strong evidence that E's obsessive fear of weight gain makes her incapable of weighing the advantages and disadvantages of eating in any meaningful way. For E, the compulsion to prevent calories entering her system has become the card that trumps all others. The need not to gain weight overpowers all other thoughts.

This inability to weigh the relevant factors meant she lacked capacity. A similar point was made in *F v F* deciding a vegan fifteen-year-old girl lacked capacity to refuse the MMR vaccine because it contained animal products.[23] Her very strong vegan views meant she had not weighed up the competing arguments and so lacked capacity. This is less straightforward. Many people have absolute moral principles which mean they object to

---

[19] *Re B (Consent to Treatment: Capacity)* [2002] EWHC 429 (Fam), [2002] 1 FLR 1090. See also *A NHS Trust v Dr A* [2013] EWHC 2442 (COP).

[20] Department of Constitutional Affairs, *Mental Capacity Act Code of Practice* (TSO, 2007), para. 2.11.

[21] *Bolton Hospitals NHS Trust v O* [2003] 1 FLR 824.

[22] [2012] EWHC 1639 (COP).   [23] *F v F* [2013] EWHC 2783 (Fam).

things and no factors can justify them. For example, some people believe abortion is always wrong. There is no weighing up of competing arguments to be done because they simply follow that rule. One way of analysing *A Local Authority v E*[24] is to say that the disease of anorexia had changed her reasoning process. The 'real' E would want to live and we should take that into account.[25] That might lead one to distinguish the *F v F* case as the 'real F' was a vegan.

The patient must be free from coercion or undue influence

Even if P is competent and is aware of the crucial issues, if their consent is not given freely it will not be legally valid consent. It is rare for this issue to arise and it is difficult to demonstrate that an apparent consent was only given under coercion or undue influence.[26] In *Mrs U v Centre for Reproductive Medicine*[27] a man amended a form dealing with the infertility treatment he was receiving with his wife to read that his sperm could not be used after his death. When he died his wife sought to claim that her husband had only amended the form because he was under pressure from a nurse. It was held by the Court of Appeal that this was not a case where it was believable that he had signed the form under undue influence. The following comment of Butler-Sloss P was approved:

[W]hen one stands back and looks at the facts of this case, it seems to me that it is difficult to say that an able, intelligent, educated man of 47, with a responsible job and in good health, could have his will overborne so that the act of altering the form and initialing the alterations was done in circumstances in which Mr U no longer thought and decided for himself.

That case might be contrasted with *A Local Authority v Mr and Mrs A.*[28] There a woman had low mental functioning and had proved unable to look after two children who had been removed into care. Since then she had used a monthly depot injection to provide long-lasting contraception. However, on her marriage to Mr A she stopped using the contraception. When asked to explain her decision she simply said Mr A did not like it. Her social workers were concerned that Mr A dominated Mrs A and the decision was not genuinely hers, but simply a reflection of his viewpoint.

---

[24] [2012] EWHC 1639 (COP).

[25] T. Hope, J. Tan, A. Stewart, and J. McMillan, 'Agency, Ambivalence and Authenticity: The Many Ways in Which Anorexia Nervosa Can Affect Autonomy', (2013) *International Journal of Law in Context* 20.

[26] *PS v LP* [2013] EWHC 1106 (COP).   [27] [2002] Lloyd's Rep Med 259.

[28] [2010] EWHC 1549 (Fam). See also *MCC v WMA* [2013] EWHC 2580 (COP).

The importance of autonomy

I have already mentioned that underpinning the law on capacity is an attachment to the principle of autonomy. Many people will agree with Isaiah Berlin, who stated:

I wish my life and decisions to depend on myself, not on external forces of whatever kind. I wish to be the instrument of my own, not of other men's act of will. I wish to be a subject, not an object; to be moved by reasons, by conscious purposes, which are my own, not by causes which affect me, as it were from outside.[29]

However, many others might believe that P's decision is harmful or immoral and that an alternative course of action would be better. For them P's right to autonomy allows them to decide for themselves how they wish to live their life. The idea of someone else coming along and telling you what to do with your life, and how to live, is repellent to most people.

Ronald Dworkin explains:

[A]utonomy makes each of us responsible for shaping his own life according to some coherent and distinctive sense of character, conviction, and interest. It allows us to lead our own lives rather than being led along them, so that each of us can be, to the extent a scheme of rights can make this possible, what he has made himself. This view of autonomy focuses not on individual decisions one by one, but the place of each decision in a more general program or picture of life the agent is creating and constructing, a conception of character and achievement that must be allowed its own distinctive integrity.[30]

It is also perhaps notable that the rise of autonomy has been matched by a lack of confidence about declaring what is or is not in a person's best interests.[31] With an increasing lack of trust in medical expertise and a breakdown in agreed moral values it has become highly controversial to declare what is or is not in a patient's interests. To replace such paternalism with an assessment of what the patient wants avoids controversial judgements.[32] Hence we have the 'triumph of autonomy'.[33]

Despite the significance given to autonomy, I will present two main challenges to it in the current law. The first will question the development of

---

[29] I. Berlin, *Four Essays on Liberty* (Oxford, Clarendon Press 1961), 131.

[30] R. Dworkin, 'Autonomy and the Demented Self', (1986) 64 *The Milbank Quarterly* 4, at 5.

[31] T. Tännsjö, 'Utilitarianism and Informed Consent', (2014) 40 *Journal of Medical Ethics* 445.

[32] R. Bailey-Harris, 'Patient Autonomy—A Turn in the Tide?' in M. Freeman and A. Lewis (eds), *Law and Medicine* (Oxford, Oxford University Press 2000).

[33] C. Foster, *Choosing Life, Choosing Death: The Tyranny of Autonomy in Medical Ethics and Law* (Oxford, Hart 2009).

the law on capacity as the marker for protecting autonomy. I will argue that the law as set out in the MCA fails to adequately ensure effective protection for the right of autonomy. Second, and more briefly, I will go on to question whether in any event autonomy deserves as much weight as it should in the law.

The failure of MCA and capacity to protect autonomy

As Genevra Richardson explains:

The law currently employs mental capacity to define the line between legally effective and legally ineffective decisions. It does this because it regards mental capacity as an essential ingredient of individual autonomy, and the law in the UK (and many other comparable jurisdictions) has been designed to respect individual autonomy and self-determination.[34]

In this section I will seek to explore the gaps between the definition of capacity in the MCA and the nature of autonomy. In other words I will be arguing that the MCA's definition of capacity is leaving some people being found to have capacity, even though in fact they are not autonomous.

To be clear, there are two terrible things that can go wrong in an assessment of capacity. First, you could be assessed to lack capacity when you do not. Others will make decisions on your behalf and set aside your own wishes based on what they think is in your best interests. You lose control over your life. You are no longer in charge of your destiny. But second, you could be assessed to have capacity when you do not have it. You could suffer harms and injuries and you would be told that that was your choice, even though in fact that was not what you were choosing at all. I will argue that current law is guilty of making both of these errors. I will highlight six circumstances in which the law's use of capacity fails to properly correlate with a proper understanding of the principle of respect for autonomy.

1. The two box problem

As those familiar with the writing on autonomy realize, there is no single understanding of what it means to be autonomous and therefore what it means to have capacity. John Coggon has listed three versions of autonomy:

[34] G. Richardson, 'Mental Disabilities and the Law From Substitute to Supported Decision-making', (2012) 65(1) *Current Legal Problems* 333, 334.

1. Ideal desire autonomy—leads to an action decided upon because it reflects what a person should want, measured by reference to some purportedly universal or objective standard of values.

2. Best desire autonomy—leads to an action decided upon because it reflects a person's overall desire given his own values, even if this runs contrary to his immediate desire.

3. Current desire autonomy—leads to an action decided upon because it reflects a person's immediate inclinations, i.e. what he thinks he wants in a given moment without further reflection.[35]

Makenzie and Rogers argue to be able to exercise autonomy we need the following:[36]

- self-determining: being 'able to determine one's own beliefs, values, goals and wants, and to make choices regarding matters of practical import to one's life free from undue interference. The obverse of self-determination is determination by other persons, or by external forces or constraints.' [37]

- Self-governing: being 'able to make choices and enact decisions that express, or are consistent with, one's values, beliefs and commitments. Whereas the threats to self-determination are typically external, the threats to self-governance are typically internal, and often involve volitional or cognitive failings. Weakness of will and failures of self-control are common volitional failings that interfere with self-governance'.[38]

- Having authenticity: 'a person's decisions, values, beliefs and commitments must be her "own" in some relevant sense; that is, she must identify herself with them and they must cohere with her "practical identity", her sense of who she is and what matters to her. Actions or decisions that a person feels were foisted on her, which do not cohere with her sense of herself, or from which she feels alienated, are not autonomous'.[39]

One might question how often, if ever, anyone can meet all of these and so be richly autonomous.[40]

Much more could be said about these understandings of autonomy, but as will already be clear, it is wrong to regard autonomy or capacity as an

---

[35] J. Coggon, 'Varied and Principled Understandings of Autonomy in English Law: Justifiable Inconsistency or Blinkered Moralism?', (2007) 15 *Health Care Analysis* 235.

[36] C. Makenzie and W. Rogers, 'Autonomy, Vulnerability and Capacity: A Philosophical Appraisal of the Mental Capacity Act', (2013) *International Journal of the Law in Context* 37.

[37] Ibid., 43.   [38] Ibid.   [39] Ibid.

[40] For further discussion see F. Freyenhagen and T. O'Shea, 'Hidden Substance: Mental Disorder as a Challenge to Normatively Neutral Accounts Of Autonomy', (2013) *International Journal of Law in Context* 66.

'all or nothing' thing. It is much better to regard capacity as on a scale. A considered autonomous decision, based on full knowledge of the facts and reflecting a person's underlying and enduring values, might be thought to be deserving of greater moral weight than the decision based on mistakes or which is inconsistent with the values they live their life by.[41] In short, not all autonomous decisions deserve the same level of protection.[42]

Yet under the approach traditionally adopted by the Mental Capacity Act 2005 there is no room for giving different weights to autonomy. Once a person is found to have capacity their decision is respected as much whether they are close to the borderline of incapacity or the decision is as richly autonomous as a person may wish.

2. Capacity and conflicting wishes

The MCA fails to provide an adequate response to cases of conflicting wishes. A good example is provided by *Re MB*[43] where, due to a needle phobia, a woman refused to consent to a Caesarean section which she wanted and was necessary in order to save her life and that of the foetus. The Court of Appeal stated that to force the injection on her against her wishes would be to infringe her autonomy, although it was permissible in that case because she lacked capacity to refuse the injection and it would be in her best interests to receive it. But was this a correct classification of her autonomous wishes?

A better analysis is that MB had contradictory wishes: to have the Caesarean section operation, but not to have the injection. To not give her the injection would respect one decision, but thwart the other. In such a case if we are seeking to protect the principle of autonomy the court should seek to ascertain, between the two conflicting decisions, which is closer to the individual's sense of identity. In *Re MB* if such an approach was taken, surely the desire to remain alive and give birth to a healthy baby was more important to her than the wish to avoid the prick of a needle.[44] The issue could be put in these terms: should her wishes and beliefs as experienced over a considerable time be given less weight than the momentary decision to reject the injection

---

[41] J. Craigie, 'Capacity, Value Neutrality and the Ability to Consider the Future', (2013) *International Journal of Law in Context* 4.

[42] S. Gilmore and J. Herring, '"No" is the Hardest Word: Consent and Children's Autonomy', (2011) 23 *Child and Family Law Quarterly* 3; J. Coggon and J. Miola, 'Autonomy, Liberty and Medical Decision-making', (2011) *Cambridge Law Journal* 523.

[43] [1997] 2 FCR 541.

[44] J. Herring, 'The Caesarean Section Cases and the Supremacy of Autonomy' in M. Freeman and A. Lewis (eds), *Law and Medicine* (Oxford, Oxford University Press 2000).

in a moment of anguish? A similar issue arises in relation to addicted patients who may wish to use a substance and not wish to be addicted.[45]

Where there are conflicting wishes it can help to distinguish between a person's first-order desires and their second-order appropriation of, or identification with, the desires. The problem is that the MCA is effectively unable to account for circumstances where a person's decision may not be motivated by their authentic own values, wishes, or desires.

Catriona Mackenzie and Wendy Rogers explain that to have autonomy, one must be 'able to determine one's own beliefs, values, goals and wants, and to make choices regarding matters of practical import to one's life free from undue interference. The obverse of self-determination is determination by other persons, or by external forces or constraints.'[46] Not only that, but a person must have authenticity:

> [A] person's decisions, values, beliefs and commitments must be her 'own' in some relevant sense; that is, she must identify herself with them and they must cohere with her 'practical identity', her sense of who she is and what matters to her. Actions or decisions that a person feels were foisted on her, which do not cohere with her sense of herself, or from which she feels alienated, are not autonomous.[47]

To give an extreme example, a person who has been 'brainwashed' into adopting a belief may be acting on a value, but it will not be their value. We need to identify with our values, preferences, and commitments. In short, we have to want the things we want.

Under the MCA it is sufficient for P to understand the information and use it to make a decision. It provides no mechanism for determining whether their values or preferences are those that have been adopted by the decision maker. An obvious case could be someone in an abusive relationship where the abuser has come to have utter control over their victim. Less dramatically, P has values and has reached a decision which is consistent with some of their values and not others. This is of course common. The best known scenario is where a person satisfies their short term desire over a longer term goal. Dieters or those trying to quit smoking, for example, will inevitably experience a clash between a carefully thought out decision, to diet or quit smoking, and an immediate desire to eat or smoke.

Identifying these cases, however, can be extremely difficult. We are all inevitably influenced by our family and broader society. How we view

---

[45] A. Andreou, 'Making a Clean Break: Addiction and Ulysses Contracts', (2008) 22 *Bioethics* 25.

[46] C. MacKenzie and W. Rogers, 'Autonomy, Vulnerability and Capacity', (2013) 9 *International Journal of Law in Context* 37, 43.

[47] Ibid.

ourselves and what we value in life are conceptions of the values that are influenced, caused, or constituted by our social relationships and social conditions. Social–relational factors are essential in the development of our capacity for autonomous decision making.[48] We are probably over-confident, if anyone, of being actually capable of shaking off the shackles of their relational and social context to form values genuinely 'of their own'.

3. Issue specific or person specific

One of the issues which has troubled the courts, as mentioned above, is whether the test for capacity should be act or person specific. In other words, do we ask 'does P have capacity to do this kind of act?' or 'does P have capacity to do this act in relation to this person at this time?'. As noted above, in many circumstances the court has preferred the act specific test. So in relation to marriage the question is whether the person understood the nature of marriage, not whether they understood the nature of marriage in relation to this person.[49]

At first sight the debate seems an odd one. Surely in respect of a particular decision we need to ask whether P understood the information necessary for this particular decision, not a general matter. I suggest the courts in a number of contexts have preferred the 'act specific' approach for two reasons. First, it means the courts can avoid what might be seen as inappropriate decision making. Take the example of marriage. An assessment of whether P understands what marriage is about is far less controversial than whether P understands what marriage to X will be like. The issue is even more pertinent to sex.

Second, an assessment which is 'act specific' is far easier for social workers or other carers to deal with. If it is decided that P understands the nature of sex, then they can conclude that P is able to decide with whom to have sex. However, if the test is seen as person specific then the social workers or carers must determine on each occasion whether P understands what sex with X will be like. As it was put in *A Local Authority v TZ*:[50] 'To require the issue of capacity to be considered in respect of every person with whom TZ contemplated sexual relations would not only be impracticable but would also constitute a great intrusion into his private life.' Hence in relation to sex, the courts have taken the approach that capacity to have sex is act specific.[51] Mostyn J in *D Borough Council v AB*[52] stated:

---

[48] J. Herring, *Relational Autonomy and Family Law* (Berlin, Springer 2014).
[49] *D Borough Council v B* [2012] Fam 36.　　[50] [2013] EWHC 2322 (COP).
[51] *A Local Authority v TZ* [2013] EWHC 2322 (COP).
[52] [2011] EWHC 101 (COP).

I therefore conclude that the capacity to consent to sex remains act-specific and requires an understanding and awareness of: the mechanics of the act; that there are health risks involved, particularly the acquisition of sexually transmitted and sexually transmissible infections; that sex between a man and a woman may result in the woman becoming pregnant.[53]

Leveson P held the focus is on a general capacity to consent to sex, 'which is not tied down to a particular partner, time and place'.[54]

Despite these reasons for the courts preferring an act specific approach, it is hard to justify in terms of the principle of autonomy. Using an act specific approach in relation to sex or marriage or indeed any intimate activity is artificial. As Baroness Hale put it in *R v C*:[55]

My Lords, it is difficult to think of an activity which is more person- and situation-specific than sexual relations. One does not consent to sex in general. One consents to this act of sex with this person at this time and in this place. Autonomy entails the freedom and the capacity to make a choice of whether or not to do so. This is entirely consistent with the respect for autonomy in matters of private life which is guaranteed by article 8 of the European Convention for the Protection of Human Rights and Fundamental Freedoms. The object of the 2003 Act was to get away from the previous 'status'-based approach which assumed that all 'defectives' lacked capacity, and thus denied them the possibility of making autonomous choices, while failing to protect those whose mental disorder deprived them of autonomy in other ways.

Indeed I would question whether anyone of us can answer the abstract question 'do you have capacity to consent to sex'? Inevitably the answer will be 'it all depends'. It depends on whether you are intoxicated, terrified, asleep, and so forth. Inevitably it all depends upon the individual, the circumstances, and the situation. The idea you can consent to sex ignores the huge variation in understandings, even for a particular person, about the meaning of sex acts in different contexts.[56] Sex may be: a moment of fun; an expression of commitment; a physical release; and/or an act of spiritual union, at different times for different people (or for the same person at different times, or for different people at the same time). Asking whether a person can consent to sex assumes we have a monolithic understanding of it. At most an assessment might consider 'can we imagine a scenario in which this person is able to consent to sex', but such a test is not providing any helpful guidance to social workers and carers.

---

[53] *A Local Authority v TZ* [2013] EWHC 2322 (COP) explained that if P was gay or lesbian then the last factor did not need to be understood. This means that it is easier to have capacity to have gay sex than straight sex.
[54] *IM v Liverpool* [2014] EWCA Civ 37.   [55] [2009] UKHL 42.
[56] J. Herring, 'Mistaken Sex', [2005] *Criminal Law Review* 511.

Further, it is far from straightforward when to apply which test. In *York v PC*[57] the conclusion that the test for marriage was act specific but the decision to cohabit was person specific could have led to the conclusion that a person had capacity to marry but not cohabit. McFarlane LJ reasoned that although some decisions (such as the decision to marry or divorce) involve 'understanding matters of status, obligation and rights'[58] and are thus status or act specific, other decisions (such as decisions as to contact and residence) may be person specific and 'may well be grounded in the specific factual context'.[59] However, this seems a very lawyerly distinction and the person on the street would assume the capacity to marry to include the capacity to live together.[60]

Both McFarlane J in *PC v York* and Leveson P in *IM v Liverpool* proposed that the distinction between person and act specific decisions was based on the statutory distinction between the kinds of decisions the court can make orders about if a person lacks capacity (MCA, s. 17) and those which they cannot (MCA, s. 27). So as s. 27 refers to marriage, that indicates it is an act specific test and not situation specific. Yet what activities the court has jurisdiction over with regards to an incapacious person is a fundamentally distinct question to how the court ought to assess whether a person has capacity. There are good reasons why an authority should not be able to determine, for example, that it would be in the best interests of a person lacking capacity to have sex (and consent to sex on their behalf). However, those reasons do not help us determine how we assess capacity.

In truth the decision about whether a person is acting autonomously can only be made with reference to the substance of the decision and the context in which the decision takes place. In making a decision about whether to have sex on a particular occasion with a particular person, people might always take into account some general factors (e.g. the risk of pregnancy) but most of the other factors will depend on the particular individual concerned and the broader context. In part this is because (as will be elaborated shortly) capacity is not just a matter of intellectual comprehension of facts, but an evaluative judgement. That judgement is exercised in relation to a particular person and particular time. The current law in its use of the act specific test is deeming a person to have capacity in cases when, at least on some occasions, they may not autonomously be deciding to act in that way.

---

[57] [2013] EWCA Civ 478.   [58] Ibid., para. 38.   [59] Ibid., para. 37.
[60] J. Herring and J. Wall 'Understanding Capacity: "The Heart May Easily Overrule the Head"', (2014) 4 *Elder Law Journal* 190.

4. The determination of relevant information

To have capacity and be autonomous one must understand the relevant information to make the decision. However, much depends here on what constitutes 'relevant information'. That in turn will often depend on how one interprets the question to be decided.

Consider, for example, the question in *A Local Authority v Mr and Mrs A*[61] of whether Mrs A had capacity to make a decision about contraception. While she understood the fact contraception stopped her becoming pregnant, she did not understand that if she did become pregnant, given her history, it was nearly inevitable that any child born to her would be removed at birth. She wanted to have and care for a child and so chose to stop taking the contraception. The finding that she had sufficient understanding to make the decision must be questioned. It should be remembered that the outcome of the decision is that she is going to undergo the pain and discomfort of pregnancy and birth; followed by the agony of having her children removed. We are justifying this in the name that this respects her autonomy. But her choice in this case was very different from the outcome that arose. Again we see here the law opting for a narrow interpretation of capacity, meaning that a person's decision is respected, without it being an autonomous decision in a rich sense. While that may be appropriate in relation to decisions over minor issues, to rely on it when the decision involves a major aspect of a person's well-being is unjustified.

5. The diagnostic test

As already mentioned, the fact a person does not understand the relevant information does not lead to a finding that they lack capacity if the reason for that failure does not result from a mental disorder.[62] So, in *PC v York*,[63] although the Court of Appeal considered PC's failure to understand the violent nature of her husband and therefore to fail to understand some key facts about what cohabitation with him would be like, that had not been shown to be a result of the mental disorder. Hedley J held it was related to PC's impairment, but the Court of Appeal held that such terminology did not capture the 'causal nexus' that was required by the wording of the statute.

McFarlane LJ explained that despite the 'understandable professional concern',[64] 'the structure and provisions of the MCA 2005 are to be applied

---

[61] [2010] EWHC 1549 (Fam). [62] *Redbridge v G* [2014] EWCOP 485.
[63] [2013] EWCA Civ 478. [64] Ibid., para. 41.

with clarity and care in order to ensure that the autonomy of the individual is not eroded by the court in a case which, in reality, does not come within the statutory provisions'. However, that view, with respect, is misguided. The Court had concluded that PC failed to understand the information about cohabitation needed to make the decision: in effect the cohabitation she imagined she was choosing was completely different to the cohabitation that would take place. In what sense then is it respecting her autonomy, her choice, to let her cohabit? We are not, thereby, respecting a choice, or at least not a choice she has made. Lewison LJ concluded his judgment noting: 'We must leave PC free to make her own decision, and hope that everything turns out well in the end.'[65] But the point was she was not making her own decision. What she was choosing was not what was going to happen to her.

Further, the diagnostic requirement can be difficult. The exact reason why a person does not understand a piece of information may be complex.[66] In *PC v York,* we knew that despite NC's convictions, PC did not believe that NC had committed the serious sexual offences. As it could not be proved this was because of her mental impairment she was found to have capacity under the MCA. McFarlane LJ did not speculate as to what, if not her mental impairment, caused this disbelief; it may be *because of* PC's love and affection for NC, or trust of NC. As the court could not say with confidence that it was her learning disability per se which clouded her understanding of the truth, incapacity had not been shown. However, I suggest this is too strict a requirement.

Whether the inability (s. 3) is *caused by* a mental impairment (s. 2) will depend on how widely or narrowly we understand 'impairments of the mind'. If a learning disability can be associated with emotional immaturity and lack of insight, then isolating the particular aspect of PC's personhood that led her not to understand NC is incredibly complex. This is especially so in decisions about intimate lives. Could someone *with* capacity explain why they love someone? The root of such feelings or perceptions about another is hard to discover in those with full capacity, let alone someone of questionable capacity.

Another way of challenging the diagnostic requirement is that it breaches the United Nations Convention on the Rights of Persons with Disabilities. Article 12(2) provides that people with disabilities may enjoy legal capacity 'on an equal basis with others in all aspects of life'. Yet here if we have two people

---

[65] Ibid., para. 62.
[66] J. Wall and J. Herring, 'Capacity to Cohabit: Hoping "Everything Turns out Well in the End" *PC v City of York*', [2013] *Child and Family Law Quarterly* 471.

with delusions, the one whose delusion is as a result of a mental disorder is treated differently from one which is not.[67] It is, I suggest, hard to explain why that should be so.

6. Different kinds of impairment

Making a decision requires, as the MCA indicates, both an understanding of the information and an ability to use that information.[68] This requires both a set of preferences or goals and the ability to use the information to achieve goals. It is the ability to select preferences and to work towards them which shows that capacity is not an entirely cerebral activity. It requires a person to value an outcome. As Charland[69] argues: '[W]ithout the emotion system to generate values and fix preferences to guide and direct reason, the prefrontal subject remains hopelessly paralysed in the fact of innumerable theoretical possible alternatives and hypothetical consequences.' This means that a person's ability to make a decision can be impaired by an emotional interference as much as an intellectual failure to understand. A good example can be seen with some people with anorexia nervosa who can 'understand the evidence that they are unhealthily underweight and at physical danger, and they can see the ways in which anorexia nervosa impoverishes their life. At the same time, the profound emotions tell them that eating to put on weight is dangerous and that they will be safer if they lose still more weight'. [70] Similarly major depression 'can interfere with decision-making capacity, although not because of any lack of understanding of relevant information, but rather due to stifling negativity or impassive indifference towards future possibilities'.[71] Another example is that 'women with intellectual disabilities', Doyle[72] argues, 'are predisposed to being both subservient to the wishes of others ... and are more likely to be unable to refuse consent to sexual activity when initiated by another'.

---

[67] Although it is arguable that the person with the disability is treated more favourably in that they can be protected by the Mental Capacity Act 2005.

[68] J. Wall and J. Herring, 'Capacity to Cohabit', (n. 66).

[69] L. Charland, 'Is Mr. Spock Mentally Competent? Competence to Consent and Emotion', (1998) 5 *Philosophy, Psychiatry & Psychology* 67, at 73.

[70] T. Hope, J. Tan, A. Stewart, and J. McMillian, 'Agency, Ambivalence and Authenticity: The Many Ways in Which Anorexia Nervosa Can Affect Autonomy', (2013) 9 *International Journal of Law in Context* 20, at 30.

[71] F. Freyenhagen and T. O'Shea, 'Hidden Substance: Mental Disorder as a Challenge to Normatively Neutral Accounts of Autonomy', (2013) 9 *International Journal of Law in Context* 53, at 56.

[72] S. Doyle, 'The Notion of Consent to Sexual Activity for Persons with Mental Disabilities', (2010) 31 *Liverpool Law Review* 111, at 112.

There is some indication that the courts have failed to take sufficiently seriously the impact of emotional disturbance on P's capacity. For example the Court of Appeal in *IM v Liverpool* ultimately held that in the context of consent to sex 'ability to use and to weigh information is of limited relevance'.[73] They explained that as a person with full capacity does not typically engage in a refined analysis and weighting of the relevant information that pertains to the decision to consent to a sexual relationship, the use and weight of the relevant information is of limited relevance in assessing whether someone has the capacity to consent to sexual relations.

The assumption here seems to be that once a person has intellectual understanding of sex, there are visceral, even animalistic, instincts that fulfil the capacity and exclude the importance of valuing or weighing towards the goals. Yet, as just argued, the ability to set, value, and work towards goals is an essential part to capacity. Fully capacitous persons make decisions using unimpaired affective attitudes, their sexual *preferences* and *desires*, their *concern of* or *hope* for pregnancy, their *fear* of or *indifference* towards transmittable diseases. So, to make a decision it is not enough to just understand the 'relevant information', be that the mechanics of sexual intercourse, the medical consequences of under-nutrition, or the addictive content of narcotics. Making a decision also requires us to attribute value to these facts, such as the relational consequences of sexual intimacy, the desire to gain or loose weight, the goal of longevity of life, or a hedonistic lifestyle.

Hence, there are a number of instances where a person is able to understand the information that is relevant to their decision, but their decision is driven by overriding affective attitudes (fears, anxieties, desires). Despite being able to use and weigh the relevant information, their ability for autonomous decision-making is impaired. Such people may well be found to have capacity within the MCA, but would not be autonomous.

Solving the problem

This chapter has highlighted six situations which illustrate that there are gaps between being assessed as having capacity under the MCA and being genuinely autonomous. This raises the concerning possibility that a court would determine that, because a person has been found to have capacity, the court cannot intervene to protect them (despite genuine concern as to their autonomy). For example, in *PC v York*, although the Court of Appeal claimed

---

[73] [2014] EWCA Civ 17, para. 64.

to be respecting PC's autonomy by not interfering in her decision, as they themselves admitted, her decision was based on a fundamental misunderstanding of the facts. Respecting a decision based on a major mistake is not respecting autonomy. It is also a failure of the legal system to comply with its obligations under the Human Rights Act 1998 and the European Convention on Human Rights, to take reasonable steps to protect vulnerable adults from violence and harm, as set out in Chapter 5. So what can be done?

Redefining capacity

One response to the gaps we have identified between capacity and autonomy is to redefine capacity to bring it in line with the notion of autonomy. This clearly has attractions, but brings with it difficulties. For instance, to develop a definition of capacity that covered all the issues raised above would prove complex and likely unusable in a clinical setting. The practical requirements for finding capacity in patients necessitates that doctors be able to use it in a clinical setting. Straightforwardness is particularly important if a doctor is to be held to account if they have failed to meet the legal standards. More significantly it would not deal with the issue of the sharp divide between having and not having capacity, which was criticized above.

A rather different response might be to suggest we should seek to promote the decision-making of everyone. Ginerva Richardson uses the UN Convention on the Rights of Persons with Disabilities (CRPD) to make this point:

Under the CRPD, the approach is very different. The emphasis has moved from substitute to supported decision-making. Decisions are no longer to be made, however benignly, on behalf of the person with disability; instead she is to be supported and encouraged to make her own decisions. In its purest form there is no point beyond which legal capacity is lost. There is no binary divide. Article 12 of the Convention provides:

(1) 'States Parties reaffirm that persons with disabilities have the right to recognition everywhere as persons before the law.'
(2) 'States Parties shall recognize that persons with disabilities enjoy legal capacity on an equal basis with others in all aspects of life.'

These two paragraphs can be read as requiring the law to give the same status and respect to decisions made by people with mental disabilities, however great the impact of those disabilities on their decision-making, as it gives to the decisions made by others. *Legal* capacity should not be dependent on *mental* capacity."[74]

This decision is excellent in so far as the decision is P's decision. Supported decision making carries with it dangers that the supporter makes the decision

---

[74] G. Richardson, 'Mental Capacity in the Shadow of Suicide: What Can the Law Do?', (2013) *International Journal of Law in Context* 87.

and labels it as P's. Further there is a danger that a decision that is not truly autonomous is treated as P's autonomous decision when it is not.

Blurring the capacity/non-capacity line

Elsewhere Stephen Gilmore and I have advocated an approach which requires us to balance the strength of autonomy with the degree of harm.[75] As argued earlier in this chapter, some decisions are richly autonomous: they reflect a genuine part of the person's life vision, and are made with a full understanding of the consequences; while other decisions are only weakly autonomous: they represent no more than a whim or casual preference and may not involve a careful consideration of the consequences. So on the autonomy side of the scale, the weight attached to the decision will vary depending on how richly autonomous it is. A very richly autonomous decision may be sufficient to outweigh even a serious harm to an individual. However, a weakly autonomous decision may not. That is not to say weakly autonomous decisions count for nothing. The weakly autonomous decision may be sufficient to outweigh a decision with only a very minor amount of harm.

While I find that a highly appealing approach I accept it would require a complete reworking of the MCA.[76] Any resulting statutory formulation would become remarkably complex. A more pragmatic way forward, at least in the short term, has already been found by the courts, and that is their use of the inherent jurisdiction to protect vulnerable adults. This has enabled the court to deal with those of marginal capacity and protect them from serious harms, while still acknowledging their decisions deserve some respect. I will explore that in Chapter 4.

Relational autonomy

Further thinking about the points made in this chapter highlights the fiction presented by the model of autonomy commonly presented.[77] The traditional notion of autonomy promotes the concept of an isolated patient deciding for himself what is in his best interests (the image of 'the male in the prime of his life'),[78] whereas in fact we live lives based on interdependent

---

[75] S. Gilmore and J. Herring, ' "No" is the Hardest Word', (n. 42).

[76] It is possible that the courts could start again with a new way of interpreting the Mental Capacity Act, but it is hard to imagine the courts taking a complete volte face at this stage.

[77] J. Herring, *Relational Autonomy*, (n. 48).

[78] A. Donchin, 'Understanding Autonomy Relationally', (2001) 26 *Journal of Medicine and Philosophy* 365.

relationships.[79] It assumes that we can say straightforwardly 'this is my life' and I can do what I want with it, ignoring the deep interconnections explored in Chapter 2. We need therefore to recognize that for most patients the question is not simply 'what is best for me?', but rather, 'given the responsibilities I owe to those in relationships with me and the responsibilities owed to me by others, what is the most appropriate course of action?'[80] We need a vision of autonomy that promotes the values of love, loyalty, friendship, and care.[81] We need to examine people's choices in light of the relationships within which they live and the feelings of worry, concern for others, and obligations that they may have.[82] Such an approach can be found in some writings on relational autonomy.

In a helpful discussion on relational autonomy, Natalie Stoljar[83] considers a woman deciding whether to take hormone replacement therapy for menopausal symptoms. Such a woman is likely to be given all the relevant medical facts:

However, the decision-making process will likely be influenced by factors in addition to a weighing up of the medical evidence that is presented to the woman, including her education, race, and class; her conception of herself and her unique experience of menopause; cultural norms such as that looking young is attractive and valued whereas looking old is unattractive and devalued; the attitude of family members to the symptoms of menopause; the support of family members for the woman's decision; and so on. The complexity of all these factors and the uncertainty experienced by the woman in weighing them up may lead to diminished self-trust. Informed consent, as an opportunity concept, is inadequate to ensure that agents *exercise* their preference formation with the required subject-referring attitudes. The process of preference formation that we call informed consent is therefore not sufficient for autonomy.

With these concerns in mind she advocates the following:

Taking relational autonomy seriously suggests that in addition to securing informed consent, health care providers have an important role to play in promoting patient autonomy. Providers must be alert to the social conditions that affect patients' capacities for autonomous reasoning. For example, internalized norms may undermine an

---

[79] J. Herring, 'The Caesarean Section Cases and the Supremacy of Autonomy' in M. Freeman and A. Lewis (eds), *Law and Medicine* (Oxford, Oxford University Press 2000), at 278.

[80] R. West, *Caring for Justice* (New York, New York University Press 1997).

[81] C. Mackenzie and N. Stoljar (eds), *Relational Autonomy* (New York, Oxford University Press 2000).

[82] S. Dodds, 'Choice and Control in Feminist Bioethics' in C. Mackenzie and N. Stoljar (eds), *Relational Autonomy* (New York, Oxford University Press 2000).

[83] N. Stoljar, 'Informed Consent and Relational Conceptions of Autonomy', (2011) 36 *Journal of Medicine and Philosophy* 375.

agent's sensitivity to the options that are available to her; and cultural or family expectations may erode a patient's 'self-referring attitudes' and lead to diminished self-confidence and self-esteem. The provider must therefore take positive steps to counteract these effects, for instance, encourage imaginative reflection on different options and create the conditions in which patients truly feel authorized to speak for themselves.

We are all inevitably influenced by our family and broader society. How we view ourselves and what we value in life are conceptions of the values that are influenced, caused, or constituted by our social relationships and social conditions. Social–relational factors are essential in the development of our capacity for autonomous decision making.[84] We are probably overconfident, if anything, of being actually capable of shaking off the shackles of their relational and social context to form values genuinely 'of their own'. This is why we are somewhat sympathetic to great thinkers of the past who express views which, while orthodox in their day, now seem misguided or even offensive. We recognize that even the greatest thinkers to some extent adopt the values of their day.

However, a relational autonomy approach must recognize that relationships can undermine as well as enhance autonomy. Social relationships or social conditions can undermine our capacity for autonomous decision-making by influencing the content and impairing the authenticity of our affective attitudes.[85] A relationship of domestic abuse, for example, can rob a person of self-worth, self-respect, and self-esteem and thereby the ability to assign weight to their preferences and desires, which is essential to practical reasoning.[86] Where this sense of self-worth is impaired, a person is vulnerable to deferring excessively to the preferences and desires of others.

There is a tension here. Relationships are key to our identity. As Catriona Mackenzie argues: 'as *agents*, our practical identities and value commitments are constituted in and by our interpersonal relationships and social environment.' At the same time those relationships can undermine our sense of self. This need not unduly worry a relational theorist, indeed it can highlight the significance of relationships to the nature of the self, and reveal what is particularly wrong about the misuse of a relationship to manipulate another.[87] How, though, can we distinguish between a

---

[84] J. Herring, *Relational Autonomy*, (n. 48).

[85] The points in this paragraph are particularly relevant for issues around supported decision making. Given the emphasis placed on supported decision making in the UN Convention on the Rights of Persons with Disabilities that may be particularly significant.

[86] T. Grovier, 'Self-trust, Autonomy and Self-esteem', (1993) 8 *Hypatia* 99.

[87] See J. Herring, 'The Serious Wrong of Domestic Abuse and the Loss of Control Defence' in A. Reed and M. Bohlander (eds), *Loss of Control and Diminished Responsibility* (Aldershot, Ashgate 2011).

relationship which establishes identity and one which controls? Mackenzie helpfully suggests that 'self-trust' and 'self worth' are key. Relationships that build these up are compatible, even essential, to full autonomy. She explains:

[T]o claim normative authority over her life an agent must have a conception of herself as the legitimate source of that authority; as able, and authorized, to speak for herself. What underwrites this self-conception ... are certain affective attitudes toward oneself—attitudes of self-respect, selftrust, and self-esteem.[88]

This discussion has revealed that the common assumption underpinning traditional autonomy—I make my decision for my life—is far too simplistic. We need an understanding of autonomy that recognizes that our lives and decisions are intertwined with others. Respect for autonomy must recognize this and acknowledge the responsibilities that go with relationships. This means autonomy becomes less about me having my way; and more a negotiation between different people over how their interconnected lives can flourish.

Conclusion

Jonathan Glover writes:

For many of us would not be prepared to surrender our autonomy with respect to the major decisions of our life, even if by doing so our other satisfactions were greatly increased. There are some aspects of life where a person may be delighted to hand over decisions to someone else more likely to bring about the best results. When buying a secondhand car, I would happily delegate the decision to someone more knowledgeable. But there are many other decisions which people would be reluctant to delegate even if there were the same prospect of greater long-term satisfaction. Some of these decisions are relatively minor but concern ways of expressing individuality [...] Even in small things, people can mind more about expressing themselves than about the standard of the result. And, in the main decisions of life, this is even more so.[89]

This quote captures a strong intuition that many people feel about the importance of autonomy. The law seeks to protect autonomy through the notion of mental capacity, as defined in the Mental Capacity Act 2005. This chapter has argued that the current law is flawed in two important ways.

---

[88] C. Mckenzie, 'Relational Autonomy, Normative Authority and Perfectionism', (2008) 39 *Journal of Social Philosophy* 512, 513.

[89] J. Glover, *Causing Death and Saving Lives* (London, Penguin 1990), 80–1.

First, it has set out six situations in which a person will be deemed to have capacity under the Mental Capacity Act 2005, but should not be regarded as being able to make an autonomous decision. Where a person has made a mistake over an important issue; where they have competing views; where there is a clash between the first and second order desires; where they lack the emotional requirements to make a decision; it does not follow that following their decision is in fact respecting their autonomy. It may be respecting a choice which is not truly theirs; or is respecting a decision made for a different set of facts to the ones they are facing in the real world. I have advocated an approach that recognizes that decisions can be more or less autonomous. We should balance how richly the autonomous decision is with the amount of harm it will cause if the decision is respected. The greater the harm that will be suffered if the decision is followed, the more richly autonomous the decision needs to be. By contrast, the more beneficial the results that will follow from the decision, the less richly autonomous it needs to be. As a pragmatic proposal I have suggested that we retain the current Mental Capacity Act approach, but have supported the development of the vulnerable adult jurisdiction to deal with cases where following the decisions of the marginally capacitous will cause them serious harm. We shall discuss this further in the next chapter.

This chapter has also argued that the norms said to underpin autonomy, the image of the fully informed, rational, emotionally restrained man making a decision, is a fiction we should reject. Our decisions are, in fact, commonly the result of forces outside our control and our values are rarely freely chosen. More significantly our decisions are rarely 'ours', but are the result of consultation and discussion. They are made in the context of our relationships, reflecting the obligations we owe to those around us. This does not require us to abandon autonomy, but to rethink it in a deeply relational way.[90]

---

[90] C. Mackenzie, 'The Importance of Relational Autonomy and Capabilities for an Ethics of Vulnerability' in C. Mackenzie, W. Rogers, and S. Dodds (eds), *Vulnerability* (Oxford, Oxford University Press 2014), 3.

4

The Use of the Inherent Jurisdiction
and Vulnerable People

Introduction

The courts in recent years have developed the use of the inherent jurisdiction to protect 'vulnerable adults'. In this chapter I will explore the use of the jurisdiction. Its use has recently become extensive and it is a settled part of the law's response to the protection of vulnerable people. Sir James Munby P describes it, extrajudicially, as 'a lusty infant which is by now well advanced into adolescence and gives every indication that it will survive to achieve its majority'. This chapter will pick up on the discussion in Chapter 3. The use of the inherent jurisdiction challenges the binary divide between those who have capacity and those who do not, set up in the Mental Capacity Act 2005. It does this by offering the potential for legal intervention when a person has capacity, but only just.

There is no doubt that the jurisdiction is highly controversial. It is a departure from the general proposition that a person with capacity has autonomy to make decisions for themselves. The controversy is all the greater because, as acknowledged by Sir James Munby P, who has played a significant role in developing the jurisdiction in a series of key decisions, it is an 'example of judicial law making'.[1]

Despite this criticism that has been made of the jurisdiction this chapter will support its use and encourage its development. The chapter will start with an exploration of the historical background to the jurisdiction before exploring its renaissance in more recent years.

---

[1] J. Munby, 'Protecting the Rights of Vulnerable and Incapacitous Adults—The Role of the Courts: An Example of Judicial Law Making', [2014] *Child and Family Law Quarterly* 64, on which I draw throughout this chapter.

The historical background

The inherent jurisdiction of the court has a well-established pedigree. However, in the twentieth century it was primarily used for children. Its use for cases involving adults was virtually unknown until the decisions of *Re F (Mental Patient: Sterilisation)*[2] and *Airedale NHS Trust v Bland*.[3] Following those decisions, the use of jurisdiction blossomed, especially in the twenty-first century. By 2005 Munby J (as he then was) was able to state:

> It is now clear … that the court exercises what is, in substance and reality, a juris-diction in relation to incompetent adults which is for all practical purposes indis-tinguishable from its well-established *parens patriae* or wardship jurisdictions in relation to children. The court exercises a 'protective' jurisdiction in relation to vul-nerable adults just as it does in relation to wards of court.[4]

To understand the controversy surrounding the use of the jurisdiction it is helpful to appreciate why it had been assumed that the inherent jurisdiction only existed in relation to children. The *parens patriae* inherent jurisdiction was justified as necessary for a court to authorize medical treatment for chil-dren. The jurisdiction was based on the fact that parents are normally able to consent to medical treatment but that if the child did not have a parent, or the parent was not undertaking their role, the court needed a jurisdiction to act in *loco parentis*. Given the law accepted the child could not make the decision and give the clear legal acknowledgement of the idea that others could make a decision on behalf of the child, it was no great stretch to ensure that someone was available to make decisions where a parent could not do so. However, the same reasoning did not apply to adults. The common law has not had a concept of a next of kin or close family member being able to consent on behalf of an adult.

However, Sir James Munby suggests that this argument overlooks the his-torical basis for the jurisdiction. He argues that medieval kings and queens were *parens patriae* as part of their responsibilities for any of their subjects who were not able to look after themselves.[5] That would include children and adults who lacked capacity to make decisions for themselves. That was put onto a statutory footing and explicitly acknowledged when in 1540 the Court of Wards and Liveries was created specifically to deal with children, 'idiots',

---

[2] [1990] 2 AC 1.   [3] [1993] AC 789.
[4] *Re SA (Vulnerable Adult with Capacity: Marriage)* [2005] EWHC 2942 (Fam), para. 37.
[5] See G. R. Elton, *The Tudor Revolution in Government* (Cambridge, Cambridge University Press 1953), at 219–23.

and 'lunatics'.[6] That court was abolished in 1646 and the jurisdiction, at least in relation to children, came to the Chancery courts, where it remained until transferred to the Family Division in 1971. However, it was less clear what happened to the jurisdiction over the 'idiots and lunatics'. That, it seems, was not adopted within the Chancery courts. Sir James Munby explains that the jurisdiction following the Restoration was assigned by letters patent under the Great Seal to the Lord Chancellor and subsequently the Master of the Rolls and Lords Justices of Appeal. In 1956 it was assigned to the Lord Chancellor and the judges of the Chancery division. However, in 1960 when the Mental Health Act 1959 was passed, the warrant was revoked. While the jurisdiction governing financial affairs of incapacitated adults was transferred to the Court of Protection, it was commonly thought that in relation to non-financial matters no one was given the jurisdiction. Sir James Munby suggests the jurisdiction was 'inadvertently abolished', although whether it was that or that the jurisdiction was placed on hold, with no one given entitlement to exercise it, is a moot point. The lacuna of the jurisdiction over those lacking capacity was acknowledged and indeed the Mental Capacity Act 2005 was a response to the concerns over it.

In 1987 in *T v T*[7] Wood J, dealing with an adult who lacked capacity, acknowledged that the *parens patriae* jurisdiction was the most suitable to be used in the case, but held it was no longer available for adults. However, he held the declaratory jurisdiction was available and that he was able to make a declaration that the operation would be lawful, even though the patient could not consent. This, he explained, was not the court giving consent to the procedure, but rather based on the principle that 'where the patient is suffering from such mental abnormality as never to be able to give such consent, a medical adviser is justified in taking such steps as good medical practice "demands" '.[8] This use of the declaratory jurisdiction was supported by the House of Lords in *Re F (Mental Patient: Sterilisation)*.[9] Lord Goff relied on the principle of necessity to explain the declaratory jurisdiction:

[N]ot only (1) must there be a necessity to act when it is not practicable to communicate with the assisted person, but also (2) the action taken must be such as a reasonable person would in all the circumstances take, acting in the best interests of the assisted person.

Note that the significance of the reference to necessity is that it is not the declaration of the court which renders the act lawful (as it might be if the

---

[6] H. E. Bell, *An Introduction to the History and Records of the Court of Wards & Liveries* (Cambridge, Cambridge University Press 1953), ch VI.
[7] [1988] Fam 52.   [8] *T v T* [1988] Fam 52, 68.   [9] [1990] 2 AC 1, 59.

court made an order under the *parens patriae* jurisdiction); rather the court is declaring what the current law is or how the current law would apply. It is stating, not changing, the legal position.

A further point emphasized by Sir James Munby is that the doctrine of necessity relied upon in these cases is separate from the doctrine of necessity as understood in the criminal law, which applies only in highly unusual cases where the act is seen as promoting the lesser of two evils.[10] Rather, it relies on the doctrine of agency of necessity as developed in mercantile law.

That may seem a rather technical point, but it has potentially significant ramifications. In its early days when the declaration was authorizing a proposed behaviour, the doctrine seemed to rely on the *Bolam* test.[11] It would determine whether the proposed course of behaviour would be accepted by a respected body of medical opinion. At one level it is understandable that the court interpreted it this way. The court under the declaratory jurisdiction was determining whether a doctor was acting unlawfully and therefore committing a criminal offence. It would be surprising if a doctor acting in line with a respected body of medical opinion was acting unlawfully. As the court was confirming the legality of the decision made by the doctor, rather than making the decision itself, it is unsurprising the *Bolam* test was used.

Yet it was the use of the *Bolam* test that made the declaratory jurisdiction problematic by the mid-1990s. For example, it meant that if a patient lacked capacity then how they would be treated would depend on which doctor happened to seek a declaration first. The problem was well illustrated by *Re NK*[12] where a dispute arose as to whether a mentally disabled woman should be sterilized. There was a division of medical opinion and the matter was brought to the court. With both views being *Bolam* reasonable, the court was put in an impossible position and the judge was left with little option but to declare it was both lawful for her to be sterilized and not to be.

There was also a difficulty in cases where there was a dispute concerning a person who lacked capacity, but there was no question of illegality involved. Imagine, for example, a case where there was a dispute over whether an adult lacking capacity should live with his mother or father, who had separated. There would be no potentially unlawful acts which could be declared lawful. The court could do no more than declare it would be lawful for the adult to live with either the mother or father. The declaratory jurisdiction did not

---

[10] See for example *Re A (Children)* [2000] EWCA Civ 254, [2000] 4 All ER 961 (the 'conjoined twins case').

[11] *Bolam v Friern Hospital Management Committee* [1957] 1 WLR 58.

[12] (1990) 4 April (unreported), discussed in J. Munby, 'Protecting the Rights of Vulnerable and Incapacitous Adults', (n. 1).

provide a route for choosing between two lawful activities. In *Re C*[13] and *Cambridgeshire County Council v R (An Adult)*[14] it was determined that there was no jurisdiction to deal with disputes of this kind. In effect, in cases where there were disputes over residence of adults lacking capacity there appeared to be no way for the courts of resolving them.

From 1994 the courts started a shift in their approach. In *Frenchay Healthcare NHS Trust v S*[15] Bingham MR signalled a move away from the *Bolam* approach in medical issues and emphasized that the court needed to determine what was in the best interests of the patient. The courts also started to move away from the language of a declaration of legality. In *Re S (Hospital Patient: Court's Jurisdiction)*,[16] there was a dispute between a wife and lover of a man who lacked capacity, over his residence and care. Significantly, Sir Thomas Bingham MR in the Court of Appeal stated that 'in cases of controversy ... the courts have treated as justiciable any genuine question as to what the best interests of a patient require or justify'. This indicated that the jurisdiction was not limited to medical issues. The Court of Appeal also indicated that injunctions could be granted, and this freed it from the inhibitions imposed by limiting the courts to a declaration.

The decisive moves in recognizing the jurisdiction came in in the late 1990s in *Re F (Adult: Court's Jurisdiction)*[17] and *Re S (Adult Patient: Sterilisation)*.[18] These cases seem simply to accept that it was necessary to put the old shackles on the jurisdiction to one side. The focus for the courts was promoting the best interests of the individual and protecting their rights and so was not limited to declarations. Emphasis was placed on human rights and particularly Article 8 of the European Convention on Human Rights, protected by the Human Rights Act 1998. This required the court to make orders protecting the human rights of the patient, rather than simply authorizing a proposed course of conduct. Sir James Munby P also suggests that the widening and rethinking of the jurisdiction reflected the fact that the Family Division was experiencing an increase in the volume of cases involving incapacitated adults. The declaratory necessity doctrine was clearly not adequate to deal with the kinds of cases coming before the courts. Quite simply, something had to be done.

Following those decisions the case-law has developed rapidly. In *City of Sunderland v PS*[19] and *Re SA*[20] Munby J confirmed the existence of the inherent jurisdiction to protect adults lacking capacity:

It is now clear ... that the court exercises what is, in substance and reality, a jurisdiction in relation to incompetent adults which is for all practical purposes

---

[13] [1993] 1 FLR 940.   [14] [1995] 1 FLR 50.   [15] [1994] 1 WLR 601.
[16] [1996] Fam 1.   [17] [2001] Fam 38.   [18] [2001] Fam 15.
[19] [2007] EWHC 623 (Fam).   [20] [2005] EWHC 2942 (Fam).

indistinguishable from its well-established parens patriae or wardship jurisdictions in relation to children. The court exercises a 'protective jurisdiction' in relation to vulnerable adults just as it does in relation to wards of court.[21]

And:

the court can regulate everything that conduces to the incompetent adult's welfare and happiness.[22]

One notable feature about these comments is that the jurisdiction is put in very broad terms. It was certainly not limited to medical matters. In *City of Sunderland v PS*[23] Munby J states that:

[T]he court has jurisdiction to grant whatever relief in declaratory form is necessary to safeguard and promote the vulnerable adult's welfare and interests, just as there is also no doubt that the court has a wide and largely unfettered jurisdiction to grant appropriate injunctive relief.

The courts are sensitive to the fact that the jurisdiction in this area has no clear statutory or jurisdictional basis. Lord Donaldson of Lymington MR[24] used this justification:

[T]he common law is the great safety net which lies behind all statute law and is capable of filling gaps left by that law, if and in so far as those gaps have to be filled in the interests of society as a whole. This process of using the common law to fill gaps is one of the most important duties of the judges.

Munby J echoed this in his extrajudicial statement:

[T]he law must always be astute to protect the weak and helpless, not least in circumstances where, as so often happens in these cases, the very people they need to be protected from are those who ought to be their natural protectors—their parents, partners, other close relatives or friends.[25]

The jurisdictional difficulties could also be overcome by reference to the obligations under the Human Rights Act. The state is required to protect vulnerable people, as indeed are the courts, as explored in Chapter 5. Munby J states: 'The inherent jurisdiction has evolved, continues to evolve and must indeed continue to evolve if the court is properly to comply with its obligations under the Convention.'

Not long after the inherent jurisdiction became fully recognized, it was thrown into doubt by the passing of the Mental Capacity Act 2005. The next section will explore the relationship between them.

---

[21] Ibid. para. 37.　　[22] Ibid. para. 45.　　[23] [2007] EWHC 623 (Fam), para. 13.
[24] [1990] 2 AC 1, 13.
[25] J. Munby, 'Protecting the Rights of Vulnerable and Incapacitous Adults', (n. 1), 73.

The relationship between the inherent jurisdiction and the Mental Capacity Act 2005

The primary challenge to the burgeoning jurisdiction was the passing of the Mental Capacity Act 2005 (MCA). It was argued in a series of cases after the 2005 Act came into force that the legislation governed the law on mental capacity issues and so there was no room left for the jurisdiction to protect vulnerable adults. The argument was based on the alleged principle[26] summarized in *Bennion on Statutory Interpretation*[27] that 'where an enactment codifies a rule of common law … it is presumed to displace that rule altogether'.

The argument has been firmly rejected by the courts.[28] In *Westminster City Council v C*[29] Wall LJ was clear:

I am in no doubt that the inherent jurisdiction to protect the welfare of vulnerable adults, confirmed in this court in *Re F (Adult: Court's Jurisdiction)* [2001] Fam 38, survives, albeit that it is now reinforced by the provisions of the Mental Capacity Act 2005.

A series of cases has now taken the same line.[30] In *BL v BYJ*[31] Macur J confirmed that that the inherent jurisdiction 'supplemented' the Mental Capacity Act 2005 but was not abolished by it.

The Court of Appeal provided authoritative support for the existence of the jurisdiction in *DL v A Local Authority.*[32] Theis J, whose judgment at first instance was approved by the Court of Appeal, provided seven reasons[33] why the inherent jurisdiction survived the passing MCA:

1. The jurisdiction prior to the MCA applied to cases and issues beyond those involving loss of mental capacity. The Act could not, therefore, be said to completely cover the cases that fell within the jurisdiction.

2. The 'essence of this jurisdiction is to be flexible and to be able to respond to social needs'. Its flexible nature meant it could not be extinguished by legislation intended to deal with a particular set of cases.

---

[26] *Black v Forsey* [1988] SC (HL) 28.
[27] F. Bennion, *Bennion on Statutory Interpretation* (5th edn, London, Butterworths 2007), 1250.
[28] See also *XCC v AA* [2012] EWHC 2183 (COP).
[29] [2008] EWCA Civ 198, para. 54.
[30] For example *A Local Authority v A* [2010] EWHC 978 (Fam).
[31] [2010] EWHC 2665 (Fam).   [32] [2012] EWCA Civ 253.
[33] He states eight reasons, but the last is that the jurisdiction existed in the past but that does not really seem a plausible argument.

3. The MCA did not contain provisions which explicitly excluded the use of the jurisdiction and in the Parliamentary debates it had not been suggested that the legislation was designed to abolish the jurisdiction.

4. An adult may be found to be incapacitated, but not fall under the MCA. It was necessary for the courts to be able to make orders to protect such people.

5. Several decisions had used the inherent jurisdiction since the MCA had come into force.

6. The obligations the state has under the European Convention on Human Rights and the Human Rights Act 1998 to protect vulnerable adults and that required the court to retain the inherent jurisdiction.

7. The jurisdiction exists to enable a person to make decisions for themselves and so does not undermine the principles underpinning the MCA, which is about making decisions for those lacking capacity.

The Court of Appeal approved of this reasoning and emphasized the fourth point in particular:

Where, on a strict mental health appraisal, such an individual does not lack capacity in the terms of the MCA 2005 and therefore falls outside the statutory scheme, but other factors, for example coercion and undue influence, may combine with his borderline capacity to remove his autonomy to make an important decision, why, one may ask, should that individual not be able to access the protection now afforded to adults whose mental capacity puts them on the other side of that borderline?[34]

Although the MCA has not abolished the use of the inherent jurisdiction it seems generally agreed that the inherent jurisdiction should not apply to cases where the MCA could apply. So, where a person lacks capacity under the MCA, that legislation should be used where it can be. In *DL*, having determined that the jurisdiction exists post the MCA, the Court of Appeal went on to emphasize that the jurisdiction is 'targeted solely at those adults whose ability to make decisions for themselves has been compromised by matters other than those covered by the MCA'.[35] Davis LJ explained:

Where cases fall precisely within the ambit of the MCA 2005 and are capable of being dealt with under its provisions there is no room for—as well as no need for invocation of the inherent jurisdiction. However, even in the case of an adult who lacks capacity within the meaning of the MCA 2005, it appears that the inherent

---

[34] Ibid. para. 65.   [35] Ibid. para. 66.

jurisdiction remains available to cover situations not precisely within the reach of the statute.[36]

What is rather surprising is that the inherent jurisdiction has been used not only in cases where a person has capacity under the terms of the MCA or other legislation, but where the details of the legislation deny jurisdiction to make the order.

A NHS Trust v Dr A[37] involved Dr A, who was seeking asylum in the United Kingdom. His passport was taken by the UK Border Agency and he went on a hunger strike to protest about this. He was detained under the Mental Health Act 1983 (MHA) after he became suicidal and had obsessive thoughts. An application was made to authorize artificial nutrition and hydration under the MCA. The case fell into a legislative loophole. The Court of Protection was satisfied that he lacked capacity to refuse nutrition and hydration. However since he was detained under the MHA he could not fall within the Deprivation of Liberty Safeguards and so the MCA could not be used. The treatment could not be authorized under the MHA because the nutrition and hydration were not treatments for his mental illness. Nevertheless Baker J held that in these circumstances the inherent jurisdiction could be used to authorize the treatment.

The case does look like one which fell into the legislative scheme of both the MCA and MHA, and yet both Acts contained provisions which did not permit the use of the proposed treatment. It might seem surprising, therefore, that the inherent jurisdiction could be used. One response may be simply to suggest that the gap highlighted by the case is an error and an oversight by Parliament. But that does not seem an entirely satisfactory response to the issue. Perhaps the best justification relies on the Human Rights Act claim that the courts are not permitted to leave a person without protection of their rights if there is a jurisdiction that is theoretically applicable.

Another case where the issue arose was *Re D*.[38] D, who had severe learning difficulties, was subject to an arranged marriage to her cousin. The cousin was rough and abusive with D and an assessment was then undertaken. It was found that D lacked capacity to consent to sexual relations. Concerns were raised that if the marriage was found invalid this would put D in a difficult position within her community as being seen to have engaged in sex outside marriage or as being shamed because her marriage had been invalidated. Parker J nevertheless held the marriage invalid. She accepted that the MCA did give the Court of Protection (CoP) jurisdiction to invalidate a

---

[36] Ibid. para. 70.   [37] [2013] EWHC 2442 (COP).
[38] *Re D* [2012] EWHC 2183 (COP).

marriage. Even though she had capacity and even though the CoP did not have jurisdiction under the MCA to make the order, the inherent jurisdiction could apply. The point being made here was that the order sought could not be made under the MCA, but that did not mean the order could not be made under the inherent jurisdiction.

It seems then that the current position is that where there is jurisdiction under the MCA or the MHA, that legislation should be used, but if an order cannot be made under that legislation and the court is persuaded an order should be made, the inherent jurisdiction is available.

We are now in a position to summarize in more detail the current scope of the inherent jurisdiction.

Who is subject to the inherent jurisdiction?

As just outlined, where a person lacks capacity as defined under the MCA and an appropriate order can be made under that legislation, the inherent jurisdiction should not be used. However, it can be used in cases where a person lacks capacity as defined by that legislation. But what is the precise scope of the jurisdiction? That is what I will consider next.

A General Definition

Munby J in *SA*,[39] in a judgment approved by the Court of Appeal in *DL*,[40] was reluctant to define those who fell within the jurisdiction:

It would be unwise, and indeed inappropriate, for me even to attempt to define who might fall into this group in relation to whom the court can properly exercise its inherent jurisdiction. I disavow any such intention.[41]

Nevertheless he did go on to give some indication of the kind of people who might fall within the jurisdiction, in a key quote (I will refer to this as the 'key statement' subsequently):

A vulnerable adult who, even if not incapacitated by mental disorder or mental illness, is, or is reasonably believed to be, either (i) under constraint or (ii) subject to coercion or undue influence or (iii) for some other reason deprived of the capacity to make the relevant decision, or disabled from making a free choice, or incapacitated or disabled from giving or expressing a real and genuine consent.

---

[39] [2005] EWHC 2942 (Fam).   [40] [2012] EWCA Civ 253.
[41] [2005] EWHC 2942 (Fam), para. 77.

Munby J went on to clarify that the three categories he has identified are not exclusive:

I am not suggesting that these are separate categories of case. They are not. Nor am I suggesting that the jurisdiction can only be invoked if the facts can be forced into one or other of these headings. Quite the contrary. Often, indeed, the facts of a particular case will exhibit a number of these features. There is, however, in my judgment, a common thread to all this. The inherent jurisdiction can be invoked wherever a vulnerable adult is, or is reasonably believed to be, for some reason deprived of the capacity to make the relevant decision, or disabled from making a free choice, or incapacitated or disabled from giving or expressing a real and genuine consent. The cause may be, but is not for this purpose limited to, mental disorder or mental illness. A vulnerable adult who does not suffer from any kind of mental incapacity may nonetheless be entitled to the protection of the inherent jurisdiction if he is, or is reasonably believed to be, incapacitated from making the relevant decision by reason of such things as constraint, coercion, undue influence or other vitiating factors.[42]

It should be noted that although the term 'vulnerable adult' was used by Munby J in that dicta, he went on to make it clear it should not be seen as limiting the scope of the jurisdiction:

The inherent jurisdiction is not confined to those who are vulnerable adults, however that expression is understood, nor is a vulnerable adult amenable as such to the jurisdiction. The significance in this context of the concept of a vulnerable adult is pragmatic and evidential: it is simply that an adult who is vulnerable is more likely to fall into the category of the incapacitated in relation to whom the inherent jurisdiction is exercisable than an adult who is not vulnerable. So it is likely to be easier to persuade the court that there is a case calling for investigation where the adult is apparently vulnerable than where the adult is not on the face of it vulnerable.[43]

So it is clear that those labelled 'vulnerable adults' can be subject to the jurisdiction, being vulnerable is neither a necessary nor a sufficient condition to fall within the jurisdiction.

The judiciary have been keen to maintain the flexibility of the jurisdiction. In *City of Sunderland v PS*[44] Munby J held that the doctrine 'continues to evolve'. Singer J made precisely a similar point when he said in *Re SK (Proposed Plaintiff) (an Adult by way of her Litigation Friend)*[45] that the jurisdiction is 'sufficiently flexible ... to evolve in accordance with social needs and social values'. In light of these comments it is more appropriate to describe

---

[42] Ibid. para. 79.   [43] Ibid. para. 80.   [44] [2007] EWHC 623 (Fam).
[45] [2004] EWHC 3202 (Fam), para. 8.

the kind of people who might fall within the jurisdiction, rather than draw a clear boundary.

Munby P, in the dicta quoted above, makes it clear that the jurisdiction applies to those who have capacity, as defined by the MCA, but whose ability to make an effective decision has been severely impaired. In *BL v BYJ*[46] Macur J held that the jurisdiction applied to those who had capacity for MCA purposes, but were 'incapacitated' by external faces 'whatever they may be'.[47] This is a good starting point. As we have seen in Chapter 3, not all cases of incapacity are covered by the MCA. In particular a person only lacks capacity under the MCA if their incapacity is as a result of 'an impairment of, or a disturbance in the functioning of, the mind or brain'. A person may suffer an impairment in their ability to make a decision due to external forces that do not impact directly on a functioning of the brain. They would not fall within the MCA, but still lack the ability to make an autonomous decision.[48]

A key question is whether the jurisdiction extends beyond people who cannot make decisions and covers those people whose decision-making ability is impaired. It seems clear Munby P did intend the jurisdiction to extend beyond those who cannot make decisions. First, as already emphasized he made clear the importance of keeping the jurisdiction flexible. Second, the key statement above (see p. 80) opens with the words 'even if not incapacitated' and then goes on to refer to those who are 'deprived of the capacity ... or disabled'. That indicates that a person may be disabled in their exercise of capacity without being incapacitated as such. Third, the category of those who are 'disabled from giving or expressing real or genuine consent' seems to clearly include those who are able to give what might be legally consent, but it is not a 'real or genuine consent'. Mostyn J states the jurisdiction applies to those who cannot give 'true' consent.[49] I suggest, therefore, that the jurisdiction extends beyond those who lack capacity due to forces other than impairment or disturbance in the functioning of the mind or brain, to any whose decision making capacity is impaired.[50]

It is clear that Munby J in his rulings was seeking to avoid strait-jacketing the jurisdiction. Given the range of cases which the jurisdiction has been used for, it is understandable that he does not want to limit it. This approach was also taken by MacFarlane LJ in the Court of Appeal in *DL*:

[I]t is not easy to define and delineate this group of vulnerable adults, as, in contrast, it is when the yardstick of vulnerability relates to an impairment or disturbance in

---

[46] [2010] EWHC 2665 (Fam).
[47] *LBL v RYJ* [2010] EWHC 2665 (COP), para. 62.   [48] Ibid. para. 79.
[49] *Nottinghamshire Healthcare NHS Trust v RC* [2014] EWCOP 1317.
[50] *A Local Authority v A* [2010] EWHC 978 (Fam), para. 68.

the functioning of the mind or brain. Nor is it wise or helpful to place a finite limit on those who may, or may not, attract the court's protection in this regard. The establishment of a statutory scheme to bring the cases in this hinterland before the Court of Protection would (as Professor Williams described) represent an almost impossible task, whereas the ability of the common law to develop and adapt its jurisdiction, on a case by case basis, as may be required, may meet this need more readily.[51]

It is worth exploring some of the categories mentioned in Munby P's key statement further, while remembering that they are not to be seen as a conclusive list.

Constraint

One category of vulnerable people is those under constraint. Munby J explains:

It does not matter for this purpose whether the constraint amounts to actual incarceration. The jurisdiction is exercisable whenever a vulnerable adult is confined, controlled or under restraint, even if the restraint is only of the kind referred to by Eastham J in *Re C* (*Mental Patient: Contact*) [1993] 1 FLR 940. It is enough that there is some significant curtailment of the freedom to do those things which in this country free men and women are entitled to do.[52]

This seems surprisingly broad. Much depends on what is regarded as a 'significant curtailment' of the freedom to do the things people are entitled to do. Poverty, ill health, or emotional disorders could all be a significant curtailment in what people are entitled to do. Indeed such curtailment is common among those that might be regarded as vulnerable adults. Clearly Munby J has in mind those who are detained in a hospital or other place. But he states the concept is wider than that. The category is separate from the next (coercion or undue influence) and so it may be focused on cases where there are physical restrictions on what the person may do.

Coercion or undue influence

On this Munby J stated:

What I have in mind here are the kind of vitiating circumstances referred to by the Court of Appeal in *In Re T* (*Adult: Refusal of Treatment*) [1993] Fam 95, where a vulnerable adult's capacity or will to decide has been sapped and

---

[51] [2012] EWCA Civ 253, para. 63.
[52] *Re SA* [2005] EWHC 2942 (Fam), para. 66.

overborne by the improper influence of another. In this connection I would only add, with reference to the observations of Sir James Hannen P in *Wingrove v Wingrove* (1885) 11 PD 81, of the Court of Appeal in *In re T* (*Adult: Refusal of Treatment*) [1993] Fam 95, and of Hedley J in *In re Z* (*Local Authority: Duty*) [2004] EWHC 2817 (Fam), [2005] 1 WLR 959, that where the influence is that of a parent or other close and dominating relative, and where the arguments and persuasion are based upon personal affection or duty, religious beliefs, powerful social or cultural conventions, or asserted social, familial or domestic obligations, the influence may, as Butler-Sloss LJ put it, be subtle, insidious, pervasive and powerful. In such cases, moreover, very little pressure may suffice to bring about the desired result.[53]

It is worth bringing out several points here. The first is that the individual's decision making must have been 'sapped or overborne'. It is not sufficient simply to demonstrate that they have been put under pressure. Indeed, it is obvious that could not be so. In a whole range of circumstances medical professionals, social workers, friends, and relatives might encourage a person to make a decision and indeed in doing so create pressure, but that can hardly be sufficient to render them unable to make the decision.

Second, it must be shown that the pressure is 'improper'. Again there may be circumstances in which it is proper to put pressure on someone, especially if the decision they might otherwise make will cause them or others serious harm. A social worker may encourage a person with dementia to move into a care home. That encouragement is not necessarily improper.[54]

Third, the quote acknowledges that the emphasis should be on the impact of the pressure not the amount of the pressure or the nature of it. As Munby J notes, 'very little pressure' may be required in some cases to overbear the will of the individual. So the focus should be on the impact of the pressure, not its nature. Further, as the court notes, there are a range of ways pressures might be used, from families to friends, from domestic to religious. Interestingly included within the list are 'social and cultural conventions'. This suggests there may be cases where the pressure is not overt, but part of the background expectations an individual is facing. It is also notable that the courts will be sensitive to the fact that in a relationship one party may come to dominate another, and then there may be little, if any pressure, needed to overcome a vulnerable person's will.[55] In *A Local Authority v A*[56] Bodey J, in assessing a wife's capacity to refuse to take contraception, concluded: 'In view of what I find to be the completely unequal dynamic in

---

[53] *Re SA* [2005] EWHC 2942 (Fam), para. 67.
[54] Although one can imagine cases where it would be improper.
[55] *D v R* [2010] EWHC 2405 (COP).   [56] [2010] EWHC 1549 (Fam).

the relationship between Mr and Mrs A, I am satisfied that her decision not to continue taking contraception is not the product of her own free will.'

As will be readily apparent, none of these factors indicate there is a bright line to be drawn. Indeed both the impact of pressure and the extent to which it is improper are both matters of degree.

Other disabling circumstances

Munby J on these stated:

Other disabling circumstances: What I have in mind here are the many other circumstances that may so reduce a vulnerable adult's understanding and reasoning powers as to prevent him forming or expressing a real and genuine consent, for example, the effects of deception, misinformation, physical disability, illness, weakness (physical, mental or moral), tiredness, shock, fatigue, depression, pain or drugs. No doubt there are others.[57]

Munby J makes it clear that this category is open-ended. Although a wide set of things which might impair capacity are listed, it is made clear that more can be added.[58] Again it is worth emphasizing that it is insufficient simply to show that a vulnerable adult's understanding or reasoning powers were affected by the circumstances; it must be sufficient to do so in a way which means the person was unable to give a real and genuine consent.

Summarizing the overall approach

The courts have wisely avoided anything that is like a precise statutory definition of who is a vulnerable adult to whom the jurisdiction applies. Instead they have spoken in more abstract terms of dealing with cases where a person's capacity is impaired or lost due to outside events. In *XCC v AA*[59] the approach was put in terms of individuals whose 'autonomy had been compromised by a reason other than mental incapacity'.[60] This is where the discussion in Chapter 3 is so significant. There it was argued that the definition of incapacity under the MCA failed to capture all the cases where a person was not truly autonomous. While not put precisely in those terms, it is suggested that what the courts are seeking to identify are cases where there is not autonomy in this full sense, even if there may be some form of capacity.

---

[57] *Re SA* [2005] EWHC 2942 (Fam).
[58] *Key v Key* [2010] EWHC 408 (Ch) an eighty-nine year old man whose wife of sixty-five had died the week before was found to lack capacity to make a will. His severe grief and depression meant he did not have capacity. Such a case might fall outside the MCA.
[59] [2012] EWHC 2183 (COP).   [60] Ibid., para. 43.

Abusive relationships

One clear example of this would be where a person is in a relationship where their partner dominates them so that they are unable to make decisions for themselves. In deciding whether to invoke the jurisdiction the court will need persuading that the pressure is sufficient to mean the person's decision is not truly their own.

The leading case is *DL v A Local Authority*.[61] The appeal proceeded on a set of 'assumed facts', although the details were disputed. Mrs L was ninety-five and she was married to Mr L who was eighty-five. They lived with their son DL, who was in his fifties. The house was owned by Mr L. Mrs L suffered physical disabilities and received regular visits from health and social care professionals. Grave concerns arose over the treatment of Mr and Mrs L by their son. The local authority was concerned about the couple's well-being, after reports of assaults, threats, and controlling behaviour from DL. This was said to be aggressive and to have on occasions resulted in violence. The chronicle of his behaviour included:

physical assaults, verbal threats, controlling where and when his parents may move in the house, preventing them from leaving the house, and controlling who may visit them, and the terms upon which they may visit them, including health and social care professionals providing care and support for Mrs L. There have also been consistent reports that DL is seeking to coerce Mr L into transferring the ownership of the house into DL's name and that he has also placed considerable pressure on both his parents to have Mrs L moved into a care home against her wishes.[62]

At the time the proceedings started neither Mr nor Mrs L lacked capacity under the MCA and had sufficient understanding to make decisions about their relationship with their son.[63] They wished to remain with him.

The local authority sought injunctions to control DL's behaviour; however, the MCA could not be used because the couple had capacity to make decisions about their relationship with the son (at least at that time of the initial application).[64] It therefore sought to invoke the inherent jurisdiction. Initially proceedings were heard before Ward LJ *ex parte* and he restrained DL from,

---

[61] [2012] EWCA Civ 253.   [62] Ibid. para. 52.

[63] Under invitation from the court the Official Solicitor investigated the case to determine wither Mr and Mrs L were under the influence of DL. The independent social work expert appointed by the Official Solicitor visited Mr and Mrs L and reported that Mr L was unduly influenced by DL so that his ability to make a decision was compromised. However, the influence was not so strong that Mrs L was unable to make to make her own decision.

[64] It also rejected an application for an ASBO (an anti-social behaviour order) under the Crime and Disorder Act 1998 and an application under s. 153A of the Housing Act 1996.

inter alia, assaulting, threatening to assault, or preventing the couple from having contact with friends. His order also included an order prohibiting him from 'seeking to persuade or coerce ML into moving into a care home or nursing home' or acting in a degrading or coercive way. By the time the case came to an *inter partes* hearing Mr L had lost capacity to make the decision.

Theis J made an order under the MCA in relation to Mrs L and under the inherent jurisdiction in relation to Mr L restraining DL's behaviour towards his parents and other professionals. DL appealed. Before the Court of Appeal the key issue was whether there was jurisdiction to protect Mr and Mrs L. The local authority recognized that Mrs L wanted to preserve her relationship with her son and opposed taking proceedings. Mr L was more critical of DL, but did not seem willing to take action against his wife's wishes. As already mentioned the Court of Appeal rejected an argument that the inherent jurisdiction had not survived the passing of the MCA. MacFarlane LJ went on to justify the jurisdiction in these terms:

My conclusion that the inherent jurisdiction remains available for use in cases to which it may apply that fall outside the MCA 2005 is not merely arrived at on the negative basis that the words of the statute are self-limiting and there is no reference within it to the inherent jurisdiction. There is, in my view, a sound and strong public policy justification for this to be so. The existence of 'elder abuse', as described by Professor Williams, is sadly all too easy to contemplate. Indeed the use of the term 'elder' in that label may inadvertently limit it to a particular age group whereas, as the cases demonstrate, the will of a vulnerable adult of any age may, in certain circumstances, be overborne. Where the facts justify it, such individuals require and deserve the protection of the authorities and the law so that they may regain the very autonomy that the appellant rightly prizes.[65]

Davies LJ acknowledged there were concerns about personal autonomy. He referred to the arguments of Miss Lieven, counsel for DL:

Miss Lieven stressed the importance of personal autonomy. She expressed concern to the effect that the retention of the inherent jurisdiction might for the future be resorted to by public authorities, pursuing a 'Big Brother' agenda, with a view to ensuring that adults make decisions which conform to an acceptable, state decided, norm (I put it in my words, not hers). I acknowledge the point but do not share the concern. It is, of course, of the essence of humanity that adults are entitled to be eccentric, entitled to be unorthodox, entitled to be obstinate, entitled to be irrational. Many are. But the decided authorities show that there can be no power of public intervention simply because an adult proposes to make a decision, or to tolerate a state if affairs, which most would consider neither wise nor sensible. There has to be much more than simply that for any intervention to be justified: and any

---

[65] [2012] EWCA Civ 253, para. 63.

such intervention will indeed need to be justified as necessary and proportionate. I am sure local authorities, as much as the courts, appreciate that. It is at all events neither possible nor appropriate exhaustively to define 'vulnerability' for this purpose. Cases which are close to the line can safely be left to be dealt with under the inherent jurisdiction by the judges of the Family Division on the particular facts and circumstances arising in each instance.

This case demonstrates an astute awareness of the impact of abuse within the context of an intimate relationship. It is aware that respecting the views of an abused person may not be respecting their autonomous wishes, if their self-worth and self-understanding has been undermined by the abuse.

A further example, already mentioned, is *A Local Authority v A*[66] where Bodey J, in finding a wife to lack capacity to refuse contraception, referred to the 'completely unequal dynamic' in the relationship.

It should not be assumed that every individual in an unequal relationship will be found to be subject to the vulnerable adult jurisdiction. That claim failed in *BL v BYJ*,[67] a case involving an eighteen-year-old with severe learning difficulties and a dispute over where she wished to live. Macur J concluded:

I am not satisfied that it has been established before me that she is unable to recognise and withstand external pressure to appropriate degree nor that she is or is likely to be subject to physical constraint or behaviour that will impact upon her free will and ability and capacity to reach decisions concerning residence, care and contact. All the evidence in the papers before me suggests that even during her minority she was able to withstand the external desires of others by her physical resistance to the same; that she has been able to withstand decisions enforced upon her and that she has been able to verbalise her wishes. The difficulty, as I apprehend it to be, arising from the approach of others to the expression of those wishes.[68]

Autonomy

At the heart of the attack on the inherent jurisdiction in *DL* was the view that people should enjoy the rights of autonomy if they have capacity. Lord Reid in *S v McC: W v W*[69] stated:

English law goes to great lengths to protect a person of full age and capacity from interference with his personal liberty. We have too often seen freedom disappear in other countries not only by coups d'état but by gradual erosion: and often it is the first step that counts. So it would be unwise to make even minor concessions.[70]

---

[66] [2010] EWHC 1549 (Fam).   [67] [2010] EWHC 2665 (Fam).
[68] Ibid., para. 63.   [69] [1972] AC 25.   [70] Ibid., 34.

This was rejected by the Court of Appeal and a number of reasons underpin their decision. First, that there are cases where a person may lack capacity, even if they do not fall within the definition of lack of capacity in the MCA. For those who lack the ability to make a free choice it is not interfering in their autonomy to override their 'wishes', because their 'wishes' may not reflect a genuine choice of theirs.

Second, there may be those who have the capacity to protect themselves at a theoretical level, but are actually unable to use that capacity to ensure they avoid harm. Kay LJ in *DL* explained:

Where a person lacks capacity in the sense of s2(1) of the MCA 2005, he has the protection provided by that statute. A person at the other end of the scale, who has that capacity and is not otherwise vulnerable, is able to protect himself against unscrupulous manipulation, if necessary by obtaining an injunction against his oppressor. This case is concerned with a category of people who, in reality, have neither of those remedies available for their protection. It would be most unfortunate if, by reference to their personal autonomy, they were to be beyond the reach of judicial protection. For the reasons given by my Lords, they are not.[71]

Third, some cases have emphasized that there is not a tension between the vulnerable adult jurisdiction and autonomy, because the jurisdiction is designed to facilitate and enable a person to make decisions for themselves, free from pressures or restraints that are impairing them. So, rather than undermining the principle of autonomy, it is enabling it. Bodey J in *A Local Authority v A*[72] explained the purpose of the jurisdiction very succinctly:

The purpose, in respect of a capacitated but vulnerable adult, is to create a situation where he or she can receive outside help free of coercion, to enable him or her to weigh things up and decide freely what he or she wishes to do. In respect of an incapacitated adult, I consider the same should apply, except that the aim of providing him or her with relief from the coercion is first to gain capacity and, if achieved, then to enable him or her to reach a free decision.

It is unclear whether this dicta and similar are setting down a strict rule that the jurisdiction can only be used with the end of enabling a person to regain capacity. We will be returning to this question later (see p. 91) and it will be argued it is not. However, if that interpretation is incorrect, that Bodey J's view is taken as imposing a limit on the jurisdiction, this will in effect impose a restriction on who can be covered by it. A strict interpretation would mean it is not available in cases where the person cannot be enabled to have capacity. Then there seems little difficulty for the courts intervening in a

---

[71] [2012] EWCA Civ 253, para. 79.   [72] [2010] EWHC 1549 (Fam).

case where the individual's capacity is impaired or lost through an oppressive relationship. We might hope that removing them from that oppressive situations will enable them with support, to regain the ability to make decisions for themselves. In other cases we might not be able to remove the impairment to enable the capacity. Then on that view the jurisdiction would not be available. However, for reasons which I will discuss later, I reject the view that the jurisdiction's intervention should be limited to cases where autonomy can be restored.

Best interests

If the inherent jurisdiction applies to a vulnerable adult, the court must make the order which is in the best interests of that person. Inevitably there is considerable overlap with the best interests test as it applies to those who fall under the MCA, although the provisions of the MCA concerning best interests do not technically apply to the assessment of best interests under the inherent jurisdiction. That said, it is likely that an inherent jurisdiction assessment of best interests will take into account the factors mentioned in the MCA. The court will take into account a wide range of interests and weigh them up. Munby J's comments in *Re MM (An Adult)*[73] summarize the approach well:

MM's welfare is the paramount consideration. The focus must be on MM's best interests, and this involves a welfare appraisal in the widest sense, taking into account, where appropriate, a wide range of ethical, social, moral, emotional and welfare considerations. Where, as will often be the case, the various factors engaged pull in opposite directions, the task of ascertaining where the individual's best interests truly lie will be assisted by preparation of a 'balance sheet' of the kind suggested by Thorpe LJ in *Re A (Male Sterilisation)* [2000] 1 FLR 549 at page 560. This will enable the judge, at the end of the day, to strike what Thorpe LJ referred to as 'a balance between the sum of the certain and possible gains against the sum of the certain and possible losses'.

I will not here repeat the literature on what counts as best interests and how the courts determine best interests under the MCA.[74] That is extensive.[75] Instead, I will focus on asking whether there is any reason to think that the best interest operates differently in respect of vulnerable adults as it does

[73] [2007] EWHC 2003 (Fam).
[74] C. Foster and J. Herring, *Altruism, Welfare and the Law* (Amsterdam, Springer 2015).
[75] For a summary see J. Herring, *Medical Law and Ethics* (Oxford, Oxford University Press 2014), ch 3.

under the MCA. Here are some issues which might be thought to suggest there is a difference.

Autonomy enhancing

There are *dicta* which support a view that the primary role for intervention in cases of a vulnerable adult should be to enable a person to make decisions for themselves. In *LBL v RYJ*[76] the argument 'that the inherent jurisdiction of the court may be used in the case of a capacitous adult to impose a decision upon him/her whether as to welfare or finance' was fiercely rejected. Instead the role of the court is 'to facilitate the process of unencumbered decision-making by those who they have determined have capacity free of external pressure or physical restraint in making those decisions'.[77] Bodey J in *A Local Authority v A*[78] stated:

The purpose, in respect of a capacitated but vulnerable adult, is to create a situation where he or she can receive outside help free of coercion, to enable him or her to weigh things up and decide freely what he or she wishes to do. In respect of an incapacitated adult, I consider the same should apply, except that the aim of providing him or her with relief from the coercion is first to gain capacity and, if achieved, then to enable him or her to reach a free decision.[21]

There is some indication of support for this approach in *DL*: 'Where the facts justify it, such individuals require and deserve the protection of the authorities and the law so that they may regain the very autonomy that the appellant rightly prizes.'[79]

While some[80] have suggested that these *dicta* indicate that a court cannot impose a solution on a vulnerable adult, and can only take steps to enable them to make a decision, I would reject that reading. I suggest all they are saying is that there are cases where the appropriate response is to take steps to enable the person to make the decision for themselves. It is reading too much into this to say the inherent jurisdiction cannot be used to 'impose a decision' on a vulnerable adult. That is clear from Munby J's judgment in *City of Sunderland v PS*[81] where he accepted that under the inherent jurisdiction an adult can be 'placed at and remain in a specified institution such as, for example, a hospital, residential unit, care home or secure unit. It is equally clear that the court's

---

[76] [2010] EWHC 2665 (COP).   [77] Ibid., para. 62.
[78] [2010] EWHC 1549 (Fam).
[79] *DL v A Local Authority* [2012] EWCA Civ 253, para. 63.
[80] A. Brammer, 'Safeguarding the Elusive, Inclusive Vulnerable Adult' in J. Wallbank and J. Herring (eds), *Vulnerabilities, Care and Family Law* (Abingdon, Routledge 2014).
[81] [2007] EWHC 623 (Fam).

powers extend to authorizing that person's detention in such a place and the use of reasonable force (if necessary) to detain him and ensure that he remains there'.[82] That can also be seen from the repeated references to the importance of the fact the jurisdiction meets the positive duties to protect vulnerable adults under Articles 3 and 8 were emphasized.[83] Those obligations may require the use of force and detention to ensure a vulnerable adult is protected. Indeed McFarlane LJ expressly acknowledged in *DL*[84] that the jurisdiction could extend beyond the creation of a 'safe space' to enable a vulnerable adult to make the decision themselves, and could involve making long-term injunctive relief.

What can fairly be stated is that, to use the phrase adopted by the Court of Appeal in *DL*, the role of the courts is to be 'facilitative, rather than dictatorial'.[85] Where possible a person should be enabled to make their choice. It is helpful in this context to distinguish cases where the source of the vulnerability is 'internal' and where it is 'external' (or what might alternatively be termed 'inherent' and 'situational' vulnerability).[86] Where the source of a person's vulnerability may be external to the person—for example, when that person is in an abusive relationship, or where they are subject to the over-bearing influence of another person such that they are unable to exercise a free choice—we might believe there is hope their autonomy can be restored if we can remove them from that vulnerability. They may just need 'breathing space'.[87] However, where the source of a person's vulnerability is internal to the person: for example when the person has a cognitive impairment, it may not be readily remedied by a court order.

It is clear from *DL* itself that a 'facilitative' approach may not always be feasible. A person under the strong influence of another may not be able to make a free decision or be protected without a degree of dictatorial intervention. That may be necessary to protect their human rights.[88] This conclusion is supported in the judgment of Parker J in *NCC v PB*[89] where she expressly rejected a claim that the inherent jurisdiction could not involve the use of force or deprivation of liberty. She accepted that while the 'inherent jurisdiction exists to protect, liberate and enhance personal autonomy' it may be necessary to impose a regime of care 'if that is the only way in which [P's] interests can be safeguarded. To be maintained in optimum health, safe,

---

[82] Ibid. para. 16.

[83] See also *Re S (Adult Patient) (Inherent Jurisdiction: Family Life)* [2002] EWHC 2278 (Fam); and *Re MM* [2007] EWHC 2003 (Fam).

[84] *DL v A Local Authority* [2012] EWCA Civ 253.   [85] Ibid. para. 67.

[86] M. Dunn, I. Clare, and A. Holland, 'To Empower or to Protect? Constructing the "Vulnerable Adult" in English Law and Public Policy', (2008) 28 *Legal Studies* 234.

[87] *YLA v PM* [2013] EWHC 4020 (COP), para. 231.

[88] *Re D* [2012] EWHC 2813 (COP).   [89] *NCC v PB* [2014] EWCOP 14.

warm, free from physical indignity, and cared for is in itself an enhancement of autonomy.'[90]

Family members and vulnerable adults

What about cases where a vulnerable person is to be removed from the care of their family. In *Local Authority X v MM*[91] Munby J rejected an argument that a vulnerable adult could only be removed from their family in the case of significant harm. The basis of that argument was that children cannot be removed from their parents in the absence of a finding that they have suffered or are likely to suffer significant harm.[92] Munby J rejected that analysis, but nevertheless confirmed that the starting point was that incapacitated adults would be better living with a family than in state care. As Munby J stated: 'We have to be conscious of the limited ability of public authorities to improve on nature. We need to be careful not to embark upon "social engineering". And we should not lightly interfere with family life.' He went on to say that any intervention in the family life of a vulnerable adult would require proof that there was a real possibility of abuse and a demonstrated need to protect a vulnerable adult. Further:

[T]he court must be careful to ensure that in rescuing a vulnerable adult from one type of abuse it does not expose her to the risk of treatment at the hands of the State which, however well intentioned, can itself end up being abusive of her dignity, her happiness and indeed of her human rights.

The court must also take into account the Article 8 rights to respect for family life which may exist between a vulnerable adult and their family living with them.[93] While that right can be interfered with if necessary to protect the vulnerable adult, it has to be shown that intervention was necessary and proportionate.[94]

Deprivation of liberty and Article 5

Similarly the courts in applying the inherent jurisdiction will take into account the right under Article 5 not to be deprived of liberty without the legal safeguards. Lord Kerr in *Cheshire West*[95] explained the notion of liberty:

[T]he state or condition of being free from external constraint. It is predominantly an objective state. It does not depend on one's disposition to exploit one's freedom. Nor is it diminished by one's lack of capacity.

---

[90] Ibid., para. 120.   [91] [2007] EWHC 2003 (Fam).
[92] Children Act 1989, s. 31.   [93] *City of Sunderland v PS* [2007] EWHC 623 (Fam).
[94] *A Local Authority v A* [2010] EWHC 978 (Fam).
[95] *P v Cheshire West and Chester Council* [2014] UKSC 19, para. 76.

A deprivation of liberty was said to be whether the person is 'under continuous supervision and control and [is] not free to leave'.[96] Lady Hale in *Cheshire* explained the test applied regardless of a person's capacity:

If it would be a deprivation of my liberty to be obliged to live in a particular place, subject to constant monitoring and control, only allowed out with close supervision, and unable to move away without permission even if such an opportunity became available, then it must also be a deprivation of the liberty of a disabled person. The fact that my living arrangements are comfortable, and indeed make my life as enjoyable as it could possibly be, should make no difference. A gilded cage is still a cage.[97]

This means that where a person is being detained, the court must ensure the detention can be justified in terms of Article 5.

Cases where the inherent jurisdiction was not used

It is worth mentioning two cases where the vulnerable adult jurisdiction appears to have been overlooked. In *York CC v PC*[98] (discussed pp. 49 and 65) it was found that a woman with intellectual impairments who was planning to cohabit with her husband lacked capacity to understand the information and weigh it up to make that decision. However, the difficulties in decision making were not shown to be as a result of her mental impairment and hence she did not lack capacity for the purposes of the MCA. This seems like a perfect case for using the vulnerable adult jurisdiction. It had been determined she lacked an understanding of the relevant information and so lacked capacity, although as it was not due to a mental disorder it fell outside the MCA. Yet, surprisingly, the Court of Appeal failed to even consider the use of the jurisdiction. McFarlane LJ states:

There may be many women who are seen to be in relationships with men regarded by professionals as predatory sexual offenders. The Court of Protection does not have jurisdiction to act to 'protect' these women if they do not lack the mental capacity to decide whether or not to be, or continue to be, in such a relationship ... The statute respects their autonomy so to decide and the Court of Protection has no jurisdiction to intervene.[99]

That dicta is hard to understand given that the inherent jurisdiction to protect vulnerable adults gives precisely the jurisdiction he denied.

---

[96] *HL v United Kingdom* (Application No 45508/99) (2004) 40 EHRR 761.
[97] [2014] UKSC 19, para. 46.   [98] [2013] EWCA Civ 478.
[99] *DL v A Local Authority* [2012] EWCA Civ 253.

Unsurprisingly, the decision has been subject to fierce criticism.[100] Leaving aside the jurisdictional issue, it also fails to take account of the obligations on the court by virtue of the Human Rights Act 1998. Even in terms of principle it is hard to justify. Lewison LJ states 'adult autonomy is such that people are free to make unwise decisions, provided that they have the capacity to decide', but the court had concluded that she misunderstood a key fact relating to her decision. So in what sense did she have capacity?

A less controversial case of where the jurisdiction was not used was *Wandsworth Clinical Commissioning Group v IA*.[101] IA was fifty-nine years old with diabetes and partially blind. He was assaulted and as a result suffered cognitive impairment, leaving him with difficulties with organization, judgment, and controlling his decision making. Issues arose as to whether he had capacity to make decisions about his medical treatment, his residence and care, and management of property and affairs. The assessment of capacity was problematic and generally accepted to be finely balanced. The difficulties were exacerbated by his reluctance to co-operate fully with the capacity tests and he was described as 'difficult, mischievous and capricious, while also humorous and amiable'. The court in determining capacity emphasized that the threshold of capacity should not be set 'unduly high' and concluded that, despite his impairments, he did have capacity. Surprisingly Cobb J then concluded his decision about where he had to live had to be respected, despite the dangers imposed. Again, it would have been open to the court to explore the use of the inherent jurisdiction, given the marginal finding of capacity. It may well have been that given the risks faced by returning home were not great, the court would still have decided to respect his view.

Conclusion

I fully accept that the academic reaction to the use of the inherent jurisdiction for vulnerable adults has not been positive.[102] John Coggon describes it as 'troubling',[103] although he goes on to see it as 'a testament to the weakness of a general received wisdom concerning autonomy'. Barbara Hewson describes

---

[100] J. Wall and J. Herring, '*Capacity to Cohabit:* Hoping "Everything Turns Out Well in the End" *PC v City of York*', [2013] *Child and Family Law Quarterly* 471.

[101] [2014] EWHC 990 (COP).

[102] E. Cave, 'Determining Capacity to Make Medical Treatment Decisions: Problems Implementing the Mental Capacity Act 2005', (2015) 36 *Statute Law Review* 86.

[103] J. Coggon, 'Would Responsible Medical Lawyers Lose their Patients', (2012) 20 *Medical Law Review* 130.

the use of the jurisdiction as 'remarkable'[104] and questions whether the jurisdiction has any legitimate basis. She believes the case law raises important constitutional principles. Jo Miles has argued that if such a jurisdiction is needed to protect vulnerable adults it should be created by Parliament and not the courts.[105]

Yet one final advantage to the use of the vulnerable adult jurisdiction is that the law is brought close in line to the ideals in the United Nations Convention on the Rights of Persons with Disabilities. The ability to intervene and make decisions will discriminate less on the grounds of whether a person has a mental disorder and enable the law to provide a set of protective mechanisms for those who lack autonomy.

This chapter, read in the light of the previous chapter, provides, I suggest, a sound justification for the jurisdiction. It is a helpful acknowledgement that a person may have legal capacity for the purposes of the MCA, yet not be able to make a properly autonomous decision. In such a case it can hardly be said to be respectful of autonomy to grant legal weight to their decision. The jurisdiction is also a recognition that autonomy is not an all-or-nothing concept, but should be understood as scalar. A richly autonomous decision deserves more respect than a weakly autonomous one. The inherent jurisdiction enables a more subtle approach to be taken to autonomy. Finally, and importantly, the jurisdiction ensures the state and the courts are able to meet their obligations to protect the human rights of vulnerable adults. And that is the topic of the next chapter.

---

[104] B. Hewson, ' "Neither Midwives nor Rainmakers"—why *DL* is wrong', [2013] *Public Law* 415.
[105] J. Miles, 'Family Abuse, Privacy and State Intervention', [2011] 70 *Cambridge Law Journal* 31.

5

Vulnerable Adults and Human Rights

Introduction

This chapter will explore human rights and vulnerability. Although every person is entitled to the same basic human rights,[1] the European Court of Human Rights and the English courts have established that there are special rights for vulnerable adults and subsequently special obligations on the state to protect vulnerable adults from abuse.[2] These rights in the English context can be found in the European Convention on Human Rights (ECHR), given effect in English law currently through the Human Rights Act 1998.[3] Reference will also be made to the Council of Europe Convention on Preventing and Combating Violence against Women and Domestic Violence (the Istanbul Convention). The United Kingdom has signed this Convention, but is yet to put it into effect.[4]

There are two particular difficulties in developing a human right to protection, which will be recurrent themes in this chapter. The first is how we can balance protection rights and 'autonomy rights' of the vulnerable adult in a case where they do not want protection. The second is how to put a reasonable limit on what the state is required to do to protect vulnerable adults.

The right to protection

The ECHR recognizes that there is a right to be protected from violence. A brief summary will be offered of this right, before it is explored in

---

[1] In preparing this chapter I have drawn from work I have completed with Shazia Choudhry, especially S. Choudhry and J. Herring, *European Human Rights and Family Law* (Oxford, Hart 2010) and S. Choudhry and J. Herring, 'Righting Domestic Violence', (2006) 20 *International Journal of Law, Policy and the Family* 95.

[2] A. Timmer, 'A Quiet Revolution: Vulnerability in the European Court of Human Rights' in M. Fineman and A. Grear (eds), *Vulnerability* (Aldershot, Ashgate 2013).

[3] At the time of writing there is debate over whether the Human Rights Act 1998 will be repealed. It is assumed that if it is repealed something essentially similar will replace it.

[4] Although other legal instruments could be used, as could arguments from principle. See for example, *Guyez and Sanchez v Spain (X and Y Intervening)* (C-483/09 and C-1/10) (Court of Justice of the European Union; 15 September 2011).

detail. The Convention recognizes that the state has a duty to take reasonable steps to protect one person from abuse at the hands of another,
where that abuse threatens an individual's rights under ECHR Articles
2, 3, or 8. For example, Article 2 prohibits a state from intentionally and
unlawfully taking a life. But it does much more than that. It requires
the state to protect citizens from a risk of death at the hands of others.[5]
The same is true of the right to protection from torture or inhuman or
degrading treatment under Article 3 and the right to respect for private
life under Article 8. That is because the state has an obligation to protect
the rights of the citizen, regardless of the source of interference in their
rights.[6] A state will infringe an individual's right under Articles 2, 3, or
8 if it is aware that they are suffering the necessary degree of abuse at the
hands of another and fails to take reasonable,[7] adequate,[8] or effective[9]
steps to protect that individual from interference in their rights.[10] The
obligation on the state is enhanced in cases where the individual is vulnerable. The obligations imposed on the state include to ensure that there
is an effective legal deterrent to protect victims from abuse; to ensure that
there is a proper legal investigation and prosecution of any infringement
of the individual rights; and where necessary to intervene and remove a
victim from a position where they are suffering conduct which is prohibited by one of the articles.[11] Hence states have been found to infringe
Article 3 when they have been aware that children are being abused but
have not taken steps to protect them;[12] where the law on sexual assault
required proof that the victim had physically resisted the sexual assault;[13]
and where the police failed to properly investigate or take steps to prosecute men alleged to have committed sexual assaults.[14] Article 14 which
prohibits discrimination in the protection of rights may also be relevant
in some cases.

The basic right to protection from violence and abuse is also found in the
Istanbul Convention. Article 4, para. 1 states: 'Parties shall take the necessary legislative and other measures to promote and protect the right for
everyone, particularly women, to live free from violence in both the public
and the private sphere.' This right is not restricted to the state refraining

---

[5] *Opuz v Turkey* (2010) 50 EHRR 28.

[6] *Valiuliené v Lithuania* (Application no. 33234/07), para. 72.

[7] *Z v UK* [2001] 2 FCR 246.   [8] *A v UK* [1998] 3 FCR 597, para. 24.

[9] *Z v UK* [2001] 2 FCR 246, para. 73.   [10] *E v UK* [2002] 3 FCR 700.

[11] See S. Choudhry and J. Herring, *European Human Rights and Family Law*, (n. 1), ch. 8 and ch. 9.

[12] *E v UK* [2002] 3 FCR 700.   [13] *MC v Bulgaria* (2005) 40 EHRR 20.

[14] Ibid.

from committing violence itself. It imposes positive obligations on the state to enact and give effect to laws that protect women from domestic violence. As Article 5, para. 2 of the Istanbul Convention states: 'Parties shall take the necessary legislative and other measures to exercise due diligence to prevent, investigate, punish and provide reparation for acts of violence covered by the scope of this Convention that are perpetrated by non-State actors.' Further, Article 18(1) states: 'Parties shall take the necessary legislative or other measures to protect all victims from any further acts of violence.'[15] Having generally introduced the issues, these will be explored in more detail. Under the ECHR analysis the right to protection depends on three key issues:

1. Proof of an interference in the rights of the victim.
2. Proof the state agency had the necessary knowledge of the interference.
3. Proof that the state failed to act as it should.

Those three requirements will be explored separately.

Proof of an interference of a right

Article 2

Article 2 of the ECHR states:

1. Everyone's right to life shall be protected by law. No one shall be deprived of his life intentionally save in the execution of a sentence of a court following his conviction of a crime for which this penalty is provided by law.
2. Deprivation of life shall not be regarded as inflicted in contravention of this article when it results from the use of force which is no more than absolutely necessary:
   a. in defence of any person from unlawful violence;
   b. in order to effect a lawful arrest or to prevent the escape of a person lawfully detained;
   c. in action lawfully taken for the purpose of quelling a riot or insurrection.

Article 2 prohibits the state from intentionally and unlawfully taking life. It is normally relatively straightforward whether or not this right has been breached. A few points are worth making here.

The first is that the right is restricted to the intentional taking of life. An accidental killing will not be covered by Article 2, but may be covered by

---

[15] Article 18(1).

other Articles. Second, the European Court in *Vo v France*[16] took the view that whether a foetus was protected by Article 2 was within the margin of appreciation. So it was up to individual states to determine whether or not a foetus was a person protected by Article 2. In English law it is reasonably well established that a foetus does not become a person for legal purposes until birth, although prior to birth it has interests which are protected.[17] Third, the right is not an absolute one. There are circumstances in which the right can be justifiably breached, for example in cases of self-defence. I will not go into the details of these.

Article 2 has been applied in cases which go beyond the more obvious cases of a person being murdered. In *Watts v United Kingdom* [18]the applicant complained that her transfer from her existing care home to another care home would reduce her life expectancy. The court held[19] that a badly managed transfer of elderly residents of a care home could well have a negative impact on their life expectancy as a result of the general frailty and resistance to change of older people. It followed that Article 2 was 'applicable'. The operational duty was, therefore, capable of being owed in such circumstances, but for various reasons, the claim failed on the facts.

Article 3

Article 3 of the ECHR states: 'No one shall be subjected to torture or to inhuman or degrading treatment or punishment.' How are these terms to be understood? The first point to make is that Article 3 requires proof of some kind of treatment. This indicates that an illness or mental condition itself will not fall within Article 3. However, as stressed in *Pretty v UK*, the impact of the illness may be exacerbated by conduct and so bring the case within Article 3.[20] So, it might, for example, fall within Article 3 if a wheelchair user is pulled out of their chair and they are unable to get back in, but not if an able-bodied person is pulled from a chair and is able to return easily to their seat.

That point having been made we can turn to the definition of the three terms used in Article 3, although it is worth pointing out that they are not really three separate categories, but rather three overlapping terms that capture certain kinds of conduct.

---

[16] (2005) 40 EHRR 12.
[17] For detail on the law see J. Herring, 'The Loneliness of Status: The Legal and Moral Significance of Birth' in F. Ebtehaj, J. Herring, M. Johnson, and M. Richards (eds), *Birth Rites and Rights* (Oxford, Hart 2011).
[18] (2010) 51 EHRR 66.   [19] Ibid., para. 88.   [20] [2002] ECHR 423, para. 52.

Torture

The European Court has rarely addressed the definition of torture.[21] This is because of the three kinds of conduct prohibited in Article 3, torture is seen as worse than inhuman or degrading treatment.[22] If therefore the court is satisfied that the conduct infringes Article 3 because it is inhuman or degrading treatment, then there is no need to consider whether it also amounts to torture.[23] In *Salman v Turkey*[24] the definition provided in the United Nations Convention Against Torture was approved:

[A]ny act by which severe pain or suffering, whether physical or mental, is intentionally inflicted on a person for such purposes as obtaining from him or a third person information or a confession, punishing him for an act he or a third person has committed or is suspected of having committed, or intimidating or coercing him or a third person, or for any reason based on discrimination of any kind, when such pain or suffering is inflicted by or at the instigation of or with the consent or acquiescence of a public official or other person acting in an official capacity. It does not include pain or suffering arising only from, inherent in or incidental to lawful sanctions.[25]

Aisling Reidy[26] in her analysis suggests that there are three elements in torture

1. The infliction of severe mental or physical pain or suffering.
2. The intentional or deliberate infliction of the pain.
3. The pursuit of a specific purpose, such as gaining information, punishment or intimidation.

In *Aksoy v Turkey*[27] a man was detained and:

... on the second day of his detention he was stripped naked, his hands were tied behind his back and he was strung up by his arms in the form of torture known as 'Palestinian hanging'. While he was hanging, the police connected electrodes to his genitals and threw water over him while they electrocuted him. He was kept blindfolded during this torture, which continued for approximately thirty-five minutes.

The Court found this amounted to torture. They explained:

In the view of the Court this treatment could only have been deliberately inflicted; indeed, a certain amount of preparation and exertion would have been required

---

[21] L. McGregor, 'Applying the Definition of Torture to the Acts of Non-State Actors: The Case of Trafficking in Human Beings', (2014) *Human Rights Quarterly* 210.

[22] *Ilascu v Moldova and Russia* [GC] (Application no. 48787/99), 8 July 2004, para. 440.

[23] See for example *Opuz v Turkey* (2010) 50 EHRR 28.   [24] (2002) 34 EHRR 17.

[25] UN Convention on the Prohibition of Torture and Other Cruel, Inhuman, or Degrading Ill-Treatment or Punishment (Convention Against Torture).

[26] A. Reidy, *The Prohibition of Torture: A Guide to the Implementation of Article 3 of the European Convention on Human Rights* (Council of Europe 2003).

[27] Application no. 21987/93.

to carry it out. It would appear to have been administered with the aim of obtaining admissions or information from the applicant. In addition to the severe pain which it must have caused at the time, the medical evidence shows that it led to a paralysis of both arms which lasted for some time ... The Court considers that this treatment was of such a serious and cruel nature that it can only be described as torture.[28]

Aydin v Turkey[29] accepted that rape could be torture. It concluded:

[T]he accumulation of acts of physical and mental violence inflicted on the applicant and the especially cruel act of rape to which she was subjected amount to torture in breach of Article 3 of the Convention. Indeed the Court would have reached this conclusion on either of these grounds taken separately.

The case lists a number of factors that contributed to that finding:

Rape of a detainee by an official of the State must be considered to be an especially grave and abhorrent form of ill-treatment given the ease with which the offender can exploit the vulnerability and weakened resistance of his victim. Furthermore, rape leaves deep psychological scars on the victim which do not respond to the passage of time as quickly as other forms of physical and mental violence. The applicant also experienced the acute physical pain of forced penetration, which must have left her feeling debased and violated both physically and emotionally.

Aydin v Turkey,[30] therefore, does not unquestionably conclude that all rape is per se torture (her youth and the fact that the rape was performed by officials were emphasized), although it is clear that in many cases it will be.[31] In *MC v Bulgaria*[32] Article 3 was used in relation to failure to prosecute a 'date rape', but this time it was not made clear whether rape fell under the label 'torture' or 'inhuman or degrading treatment'. So, although it seems a rape will always fall within Article 3,[33] whether it is always 'torture' or not is unclear, although it is as clear as it can be.

Inhuman or degrading treatment

The phrase 'inhuman treatment' in Article 3 includes actual bodily harm or intense physical or mental suffering.[34] In *Mudric v Moldova*[35] it was not the beatings themselves so much as the anxiety and emotional impact of

---

[28] Ibid., para. 64.   [29] [2005] ECHR 325.   [30] [2005] ECHR 325.
[31] A. Edwards, 'The Feminizing of Torture Under International Human Rights Law', (2006) 19 *Leiden Journal of International Law* 349.
[32] *MC v Bulgaria* (2005) 40 EHRR 20.
[33] *DSD v Commissioner of Police of the Metropolis* [2014] EWHC 436 (QB).
[34] *Ireland v the United Kingdom* (1978) 2 EHRR 25.   [35] Application no. 74839/10.

them which was said to bring the case within Article 3. To be inhuman the court will consider whether the conduct was premeditated and whether it was 'applied for hours at a stretch'.[36]

'Degrading treatment' includes conduct which humiliates or debases an individual; or shows a lack of respect for, or diminishes, human dignity. It also includes conduct which arouses feelings of fear, anguish, or inferiority capable of breaking an individual's moral and physical resistance.[37] In considering whether treatment is 'degrading' the Court will have regard to whether its object was to humiliate and debase the victim and the effect on the victim. Hence corporal punishment can fall within this category, even if the physical injuries caused are relatively minor.[38] Clearly serious physical assaults will fall into this category. But less serious incidents, especially when occurring over a prolonged period of time can too. In *Pretty v UK*[39] it was held that 'fear, anguish *or* inferiority' could be involved in degrading treatment. So, psychological mistreatment can fall within the category of degrading treatment.[40]

The court has also made it clear that the assessment of treatment is relative and will depend upon all the circumstances of the case. Factors that have been taken into account by the court have included the nature and context of the treatment, its duration, its physical and mental effects, and in some cases the sex, age, and state of health of the victim.[41] Thus, just because a form of conduct is not degrading treatment for one person does not mean that it cannot be so for another.

Vulnerable adults and Article 3

There are several issues which are worth exploring further in relation to Article 3 in so far as those who may be classified as vulnerable adults are concerned.

First, conduct which would not breach Article 3 for some people might in relation to a vulnerable adult. In *Mudric v Moldova*[42] it was emphasized that whether the conduct is sufficiently severe to fall into Article 3 will depend on the circumstances of the case and that includes the physical and mental effects of the behaviour and the 'sex, age and state of health of the victim'.[43] This is

---

[36] *Dordevic v Croatia* (2012) EHRR 1640, para. 95.
[37] *Wieser v Austria* (Application no. 2293/03), para. 36; *Dordevic v Croatia* (2012) EHRR 1640, para. 95.
[38] *Campbell and Cosans v UK* (1982) 4 EHRR 293; *Tyrer v UK* (1978) 2 EHRR 1.
[39] *Pretty v UK* [2002] ECHR 423, para. 52.
[40] *Valiuliené v Lithuania* (Application no. 33234/07), para. 69.
[41] S. Choudhry and J. Herring, *European Human Rights and Family Law*, (n. 1), ch 2.
[42] Application no. 74839/10.   [43] Ibid., para. 93.

significant because a low level abuse might be readily shrugged off by some, but to a vulnerable adult it may be taken as particularly severe. Or indeed, it might be added, what might be serious emotional abuse to an average person might have little impact on others. In *Đorđević v Croatia*[44] a vulnerable man was harassed and abused by a group of children. The court found the course of conduct amounted to a breach of Article 3 and his inability to protect himself was emphasized. The continued harassment had caused physical injuries and feelings of fear and helplessness, and these were all sufficient to fall within the remit of Article 3. In *TM and CM v Moldova*[45] the experiences of a child seeing her mother being abused by her father were an infringement of her Article 3 rights.

Second, in a series of cases the courts have been willing to find the impact of abusive relationships as falling within Article 3. Depression, learned helplessness and alienation, post-traumatic stress disorder, guilt, and denial have been cited as resulting from abusive relationships.[46] This suggests that an on-going relationship in which the vulnerable adult is subject to a series of incidents, which seen individually might appear minor but which create an atmosphere of coercive control, could amount to a breach of Article 3. A lack of respect of a person's humanity can be included.[47] In serious cases persistent infantilization and emotional abuse could, therefore, fall within Article 3, even if physical violence has not taken place. As the Parliamentary Assembly, Council of Europe, Committee on Equal Opportunities for Women and Men[48] put it: 'It has been demonstrated that violence in the home is like a form of torture. The victims are injured physically and psychologically and humiliated in body and soul. Like torture, conjugal violence is something that goes on and on.' This was accepted in the concurring opinion of Judge Pinto de Albuquerque in *Valieneuli* where it was held:

[I]t is self-evident that the very act of domestic violence has an inherent humiliating and debasing character for the victim, which is exactly what the offender aims at. Physical pain is but one of the intended effects. A kick, a slap or a spit is also aimed at belittling the dignity of the partner, conveying a message of humiliation and degradation. It is precisely this intrinsic element of humiliation that attracts the applicability of Article 3 of the Convention.[49]

---

[44] *Dordevic v Croatia* (2012) EHRR 1640, para. 96.   [45] Application no. 26608/11.

[46] R. Wolf, 'Elder Abuse and Neglect: Causes and Consequences' (1997) 31 *Journal of Geriatric Psychiatry* 153.

[47] *Albert and Le Compte v Belgium*, 10 February 1983, Series A, no. 58, para. 22.

[48] Parliamentary Assembly, Council of Europe, Committee on Equal Opportunities for Women and Men, *Domestic Violence* (2002), para. 12.

[49] *Valiulienė v Lithuania* (Application no. 33234/07), concurring opinion of Judge Pinto De Albuquerque.

Third, where the abuse is targeted at a vulnerability it may be more likely to be found to breach Article 3. The courts may be more willing to find a relationship where one party is exploiting a vulnerable adult is one of coercive control and so degrading of them. This may be a relationship which would be a classic example of domestic abuse, but might include other relationships where one party has sought to control the life of a vulnerable adult. It might be argued that where the abuser is particularly exploiting the vulnerability of the other party this is likely to make the activities particularly degrading. This kind of argument could be used in relation to a series of disturbing cases (to be discussed in Chapter 7) where people have befriended vulnerable adults in order to exploit or humiliate them.

A fourth, important point is that the consent of a victim to the conduct in question does not negate the fact there is a breach of Article 3.[50] Of course, the fact that the victim is 'happy' with the abuse might mean it falls short of amounting to inhuman or degrading treatment in borderline cases. Article 3 is drafted in absolute terms and so once the conduct is classified as torture or inhuman or degrading treatment there is no scope for a consent defence. Apparent consent might impact on the extent of the obligation of the state to respond as the public authorities are only to take *reasonable* measures to protect an individual's Article 3 rights.[51] We will explore that further later.

Article 8

Article 8 of the ECHR states that:

1. Everyone has the right to respect for his private and family life, his home and his correspondence.
2. There shall be no interference by a public authority with the exercise of this right except such as in accordance with the law and is necessary in a democratic society in the interests of national security, public safety or the economic well-being of the country, for the prevention of disorder or crime, for the protection of health or morals, or for the protection of the rights and freedoms of others.

Private life

Included within the right to respect for private life is the right to bodily integrity. Assaults would therefore amount to a breach of Article 8 rights. The right also covers 'psychological integrity' and 'a right to personal develop-ment, and the right to establish and develop relationships with other human

---

[50] M. Addo and N. Grief, 'Does Article 3 of the European Convention on Human Rights Enshrine Absolute Rights?', (1998) 9 *European Journal of International Law* 510.

[51] *E v UK* [2002] 3 FCR 700.

beings and the outside world'.[52] Article 8 'can sometimes embrace aspects of an individual's physical and social identity'.[53] Therefore, personal names,[54] gender identification, sexual orientation,[55] and sexual life[56] all fall within Article 8. In *Dordević v Croatia*[57] it was held that witnessing domestic violence against a parent could fall within Article 8.[58]

Family life and the home

A consideration of 'family life' for the purposes of Article 8 necessitates, at first, a definition of what actually constitutes a 'family'. This is broadly defined and can include unmarried couples, but would require some kind of blood relationship or common life.[59] Of most relevance to vulnerable adults is that a vulnerable adult who is living with family carers will be able to claim a right to family life.[60]

The definition given to a 'home' by Strasbourg has been a wide one, though it should be noted that this aspect of Article 8 is not dependent upon, or directed to the protection of, property interests or contractual rights. The test used to establish a 'home' was further expanded by the Commission in *Buckley v UK*[61] when the court described the 'home' as 'an autonomous concept which does not depend on classification under domestic law. Whether or not a particular habitation constitutes a "home" which attracts the protection of Article 8(1) will depend on the factual circumstances, namely, the existence of sufficient and continuous links.'

Qualification of right

Unlike Article 3, Article 8 is a qualified right. It is permissible for the state to fail to respect an individual's right to respect for private life under Article 8(1) if para. 2 is satisfied. So, if the level of abuse is not sufficient to engage Article 3 but falls within Article 8, then it is necessary to balance the Article 8 rights and interests of other parties. It would therefore be possible to make an argument that the rights of the abuser, or perhaps even the victim, justify the state in not intervening in an Article 8 case, while those factors would not need to be considered in an Article 3 case. That said,

---

[52] *A v Croatia* [2010] ECHR 1506; *Pretty v UK* (2002) 12 BHRC 149, para. 61.
[53] *Haas v Switzerland* (2013) EHRR 429, para. 50.
[54] *Burghartz v Switzerland* (Application no. 10328/83).
[55] *Dudgeon v the United Kingdom*, 22 October 1981, § 41, Series A no. 45.
[56] *Laskey, Jaggard, and Brown v the United Kingdom*, 19 February 1997, § 36, *Reports of Judgments and Decisions* 1997-I.
[57] Application no. 41526/10, para. 97.
[58] See also *Eremia v Moldova* (Application no. 3564/11).
[59] S. Choudhry and J. Herring, *European Human Rights and Family Law*, (n. 1).
[60] J. Herring, *Caring and the Law* (Oxford, Hart 2013).   [61] (1996) 23 EHRR 101.

those issues are most likely to arise in the context of positive obligations on the state, in the third of my overarching questions (what is required of the state?) rather than ascertaining whether there has been a breach of Article 8 rights. So I will not discuss the issue further at this point.

Vulnerability and Article 8

As with Article 3, an appreciation of the relational context is important. An abusive relationship that imposes physical, psychological, or emotional harm could therefore infringe Article 8. So too could a relationship which inhibited the victim's interaction with others. If the abuse interfered in the way that a vulnerable adult interacted with their family this could amount to an interference with her right to respect for her family life.

A court may accept that a 'vulnerable person' may be more open to having their psychological wellbeing negatively impacted than other people. Emotional abuse may be more likely to have an impact on their private life than would be the case with others.

Article 14: The right to protection from discrimination

Article 14 of the ECHR states: 'The enjoyment of the rights and freedoms set forth in this Convention shall be secured without discrimination on any ground such as sex, race, colour, language, religion, political or other opinion, national or social origin, association with a national minority, property, birth or other status.' It should be noted that Article 14 is not a standalone right, but can only be used in conjunction with another right. So, the claimant might want to show that their Article 8 rights have been infringed in a way which is discriminatory contrary to Article 14. Even if the claim does not fall precisely within the terms of a right, it has been held that Article 14 can be relied upon if it is within the 'ambit' of another right.[62]

It might legitimately then be questioned whether bringing in Article 14 adds significantly to a claim. The reason it does is that it becomes much harder to justify an interference with a right if Article 14 is involved too. So while, for example, a national interest might justify an interference with an individual's Article 8 rights, if the interference was discrimination on the grounds of sex, then the national interest would have to be very substantial indeed to justify the interference.

Just because a person is a vulnerable adult does not, of itself, bring a person within Article 14, but a vulnerable person may well fall within one of the established categories. Race and sex are explicitly included. The words 'such

[62] *Dordevic v Croatia* (2012) EHRR 1640, para. 157

as' in Article 14 indicates that this is not a closed list. Indeed the European Court of Human Rights has shown itself willing to add to the list. It seems that both disability[63] and age are included by implication.[64] Arguably, in the future the law may develop to add vulnerability generally to the list.

In *Opuz v Turkey*[65] the failure to adequately respond to domestic violence amounted to sex discrimination.[66] Reference was made to various international documents to support the view of the CEDAW Committee that 'violence against women, including domestic violence, is a form of discrimination'. In *Opuz* it was emphasized that women were far more likely to be subject to domestic violence and so a systematic failure to respond to the issue disproportionately impacted on women. In *Mikulic v Croatia*[67] it was emphasized:

> In the Court's opinion, the combination of the above factors clearly demonstrates that the authorities' actions were not a simple failure or delay in dealing with violence against the applicant, but amounted to repeatedly condoning such violence and reflected a discriminatory attitude towards her as a woman. The findings of the United Nations Special rapporteur on violence against women, its causes, and consequences only support the impression that the authorities do not fully appreciate the seriousness and extent of the problem of domestic violence and its discriminatory effect on women.

The failure to respond to domestic violence was held to be a breach of both Article 3 and Article 14.[68] This approach is entirely justifiable. A worldwide study by the World Health Organization found rates of women suffering physical or sexual violence at the hands of an intimate partner at some point in her life varying across countries between 15 per cent and 71 per cent, with most countries falling between 29 per cent and 62 per cent.[69] The European Parliamentary Assembly 'found for women between 16 and 44 years of age, domestic violence is thought to be the major cause of death and invalidity, ahead of cancer, road accidents and even war'.[70]

---

[63] *Kiyutin v Russia* (2011) 53 EHRR 364.

[64] *Rutherford (No 2) v Secretary of State for Trade and Industry* [2006] UKHL 19.

[65] *Opuz v Turkey* (2010) 50 EHRR 28.

[66] M. Burton, 'The Human Rights of Victims of Domestic Violence: *Opuz v. Turkey*', [2010] *Child and Family Law Quarterly* 131; P. Londono, 'Developing Human Rights Principles in Cases of Gender-based Violence: *Opuz v Turkey* in the European Court of Human Rights', (2009) 9 *Human Rights Law Review* 662.

[67] Application no. 53176/99, para. 93.

[68] See also *TM and CM v Moldova* (Application no. 26608/11).

[69] World Health Organization, *Multi-country Study on Women's Health and Domestic Violence Against Women* (WHO, 2005).

[70] European Parliamentary Assembly Recommendation 1582, *Domestic Violence Against Women* (2002), para. 2.

Domestic violence not only relies on existing inequalities within society, it reinforces them. For example, the attempts by the male perpetrators of abuse to prevent their female partners entering the workplace or public arena work with wider social forces which restrict women's access to the workplace. Michelle Madden Dempsey[71] explains:

[T]he patriarchal character of individual relationships cannot subsist without those relationships being situated within a broader patriarchal social structure. Patriarchy is, by its nature, a social structure—and thus any particular instance of patriarchy takes its substance and meaning from that social context. If patriarchy were entirely eliminated from society, then patriarchy would not exist in domestic arrangements and thus domestic violence in its strong sense would not exist ... Moreover, if patriarchy were lessened in society generally then *ceteris paribus* patriarchy would be lessened in domestic relationship as well, thereby directly contributing to the project of ending domestic violence in its strong sense.

The gendered aspect of domestic abuse is therefore crucial to its understanding.

The vast majority of domestic violence takes place against women, although many men are subject to violence from their partners.[72] Most violence by women against men is quite different from violence by men against women because women's violence is often in self-defence rather than being an aspect of an ongoing oppressive relationship.[73] Also, where men are the victims the injuries involved tend to be less serious.

Level of knowledge required

As we shall see when we move onto the third question on what is required of the state, this can be broken down into two kinds of intervention: general protection and specific intervention. General protection obligations require the state to ensure that there are in place legal provisions to protect individuals and which are effectively enforced. Questions of knowledge generally are not relevant to those duties because it is obvious that, generally speaking, people can have their human rights abused. Here we will focus on cases of specific obligation where there is a claim that the state has an obligation to protect a particular individual.

---

[71] M. Madden Dempsey, 'Towards a Feminist State: What Does "Effective" Prosecution of Domestic Violence Mean?' (2007) 70 *Modern Law Review* 908, 938.

[72] C. Mirless-Black, *Home Office Research Study 191: Domestic Violence* (Home Office, 1999). E. Buzawa and C. Buzawa, *Domestic Violence: The Criminal Justice Response* (London, Sage 2003), 13.

[73] R. Dobash and R. Dobash, 'Women's Violence to Men in Intimate Relationships', (2004) 44 *British Journal of Criminology* 324, 343.

The duty on the state to take reasonable steps only applies if the state knew or ought to have known the victim's rights were at risk of being breached. [74] In *Opuz v Turkey* (discussing the right to life) it was explained:

For a positive obligation to arise, it must be established that the authorities knew or ought to have known at the time of the existence of a real and immediate risk to the life of an identified individual from the criminal acts of a third party and that they failed to take measures within the scope of their powers which, judged reasonably, might have been expected to avoid that risk.[75]

As is clear from the quote the particular duty to protect from abuse of human rights is not restricted to cases where the state knew of the abuse, but also applies in cases where it ought to have known of the abuse.[76] However, if the state could not reasonably have known of the risk then the state cannot be blamed for not intervening. This, combined with the third overarching question (what is reasonably expected of the state?), is needed so that the burden on the state is not disproportionate or impossible to perform.[77]

The leading case on the awareness of risk is *Osman v UK*.[78] A school teacher named Paget Lewis had developed an infatuation with a teenage pupil (Ahmet Osman). He engaged in a set of odd behaviours. This included spreading rumours that Osman was in a sexual relationship with another boy (LG) and stalking LG, changing his name to Osman, bursting the tyres of Osman's father's car, pouring paraffin into the Osman family home and smearing dog excrement on the doorstep, driving a car into a van which carried LG, and telling LG he would 'get him'. The police were told of all that had happened and assured the Osmans they would protect the family. However, the police took no effective action and Paget Lewis killed Osman's father, and injured Osman and the school's deputy headmaster. The family sued the police, unsuccessfully, in the UK Courts. The European Court in *Osman v UK* accepted that in principle a state authority could be found to breach human rights for failing to protect one citizen from a threat to their life from another. The court held:

[I]t must be established to [the court's] satisfaction that the authorities knew or ought to have known at the time of the existence of a real and immediate risk to the life of an identified individual or individuals from the criminal acts of a third party and that they failed to take measures within the scope of their powers which, judged reasonably, might have been expected to avoid that risk.[79]

[74] *Osman v UK* (1998) 29 EHRR 245.   [75] (2010) 50 EHRR 28, para. 129.
[76] *Z v UK* [2001] 2 FCR 246.   [77] *Opuz v Turkey* (2010) 50 EHRR 28.
[78] (1998) 29 EHRR 245.   [79] Ibid., para. 116.

However, perhaps surprisingly, the court held that Article 2 was not violated on the facts of the case:

In the view of the Court the applicants have failed to point to any decisive stage in the sequence of the events leading up to the tragic shooting when it could be said that the police knew or ought to have known that the lives of the Osman family were at real and immediate risk from Paget-Lewis. While the applicants have pointed to a series of missed opportunities which would have enabled the police to neutralise the threat posed by Paget-Lewis, for example by searching his home for evidence to link him with the graffiti incident or by having him detained under the Mental Health Act 1983 or by taking more active investigative steps following his disappearance, it cannot be said that these measures, judged reasonably, would in fact have produced that result or that a domestic court would have convicted him or ordered his detention in a psychiatric hospital on the basis of the evidence adduced before it. As noted earlier, the police must discharge their duties in a manner which is compatible with the rights and freedoms of individuals. In the circumstances of the present case, they cannot be criticised for attaching weight to the presumption of innocence or failing to use powers of arrest, search and seizure having regard to their reasonably held view that they lacked at relevant times the required standard of suspicion to use those powers or that any action taken would in fact have produced concrete results.[80]

While it might seem a slightly surprising conclusion it is worth remembering that hindsight can make circumstances appear more threatening that might reasonably appear at the time. In particular, in that case it had not yet been established whether Paget-Lewis was responsible for the activities, many of which he had denied. Further, it might be thought that the earlier acts appeared bizarre, rather than directly threatening. There had not been an explicit threat to kill any member of the Osman family.

According to *Perevedentsevy v Russia*,[81] looking at Article 2, there needs to be a 'real and imminent' risk of death to generate the duty to intervene. These appear to be two separate requirements. First, the risk must not be fanciful. It is, of course, easy to say that in retrospect there was a real risk of a breach of a right, but the court will make the assessment based on the knowledge of the authorities at the time. The likelihood of risk seems to be relevant both to whether the duty arises and to what might be reasonably expected of the state. The higher the risk, the more might be expected of the state, and the lower, the less may be required. If that approach is taken then 'real risk' can be interpreted as a relatively low hurdle. If the risk is a low one then less will be required of the state; whereas more can be expected in cases of a higher risk. The second requirement is that it is an imminent risk. Again

---

[80] Ibid., para. 121.   [81] Application no. 39583/05, para. 92.

it may well be that this is largely subsumed into the question of what is reasonably expected of a public authority. The further the risk is into the future, the harder it will be to state the state should be required to intervene immediately. That said, it is possible to imagine cases where although the risk is in the future, the state's only effective opportunity to intervene is now, in which case an intervention might reasonably be expected. It would, therefore, be preferable to delegate the 'imminence' requirement to the reasonableness factor rather than retain it as a separate requirement.

The uncertainty over the facts can be a significant factor in these cases. In *Danini v Italy*[82] a couple separated and both contacted the police to complain of the other's violence. The police failed to intervene and the man killed the woman. The Commission, in not finding a breach of Article 2, emphasized that there were competing versions of the facts and so the situation was not sufficiently clear to produce an Article 2 duty to intervene. Although it might be noted in that case that the killer had a history of a psychiatric disorder, that itself was not taken as sufficient to justify intervention.

A fairly restrictive approach to the positive duty to protect has been taken in the domestic case law. In *Van Colle v Chief Constable of Hertfordshire Police* and *Smith v Chief Constable of Sussex Police*[83] a man accused of theft approached witnesses and persuaded them not to give evidence. Giles Van Colle refused to be intimidated. He had reported the threats to the police but they did little to protect him and he was later shot dead. Claims brought by his family that the police had infringed his Article 2 rights succeeded before the Court of Appeal. However, they were rejected by the House of Lords. The Court of Appeal was influenced by the argument that the 'Osman duty' (i.e. the duty to protect people) required a lower threshold of risk if the state had exposed an individual to the risk to his or her life. In this case that had occurred because he had been asked to be a witness at a trial. However, this was rejected by the House of Lords, who held that the Osman test was consistent and did not vary, depending on whether the state was involved in the creation of the risk. On the facts of the case the standard Osman threshold was not met. It had not been shown from the facts passed to the police that the threat to Van Colle was real and imminent. Lord Bingham said:

The test of real and immediate risk is one not easily satisfied, the threshold being high, and I would for my part accept that a court should not likely find that a

---

[82] Application no. 22998/93.   [83] [2008] UKHL 50.

public authority has violated one of an individual's fundamental rights or freedoms, thereby ruling, as such a finding necessarily does, that the United Kingdom has violated an important international convention.[84]

The approach was confirmed by the European Court of Human Rights in *Van Colle v United Kingdom*.[85]

A little more can be said about two particular categories of cases. First, domestic violence.

When deciding whether the risk is 'real and imminent' the courts have shown an awareness that domestic violence is common and where it has occurred it is particularly likely to reoccur. In *Kontrová v Slovakia*[86] a woman on several occasions alleged to police that her husband had been repeatedly violent to her. She later complained he had a gun and was threatening to kill her and the children. This was sufficient to alert them to a 'real risk' of threat to life, meaning they breached her human rights when they failed to respond to the threats and he later killed his children and himself.

Second, cases of would-be suicide have troubled the courts. The duty applies to those whose risk to infringing their rights comes from themselves, by way of self-harm or suicide. In *Savage v South Essex Partnership NHS Foundation Trust*[87] Carol Savage had been detained at a hospital under the Mental Health Act 1983. Due to alleged inadequate supervision she was able to leave the hospital and committed suicide. Her daughter claimed under s. 7 Human Rights Act 1998 that the public authority had breached her mother's Article 2 rights by failing to protect her life. The House of Lords held that she was at 'real and immediate' risk of committing suicide; indeed that was why she had been detained under the 1983 Act. Reasonable steps could have been taken to prevent Ms Savage killing herself and these were not taken. Similarly in *Rabone v Pennine Care NHS Trust*,[88] Melanie Rabone, who was aged twenty-four and had suffered from bouts of severe depression, was a voluntary patient at the hospital. She was assessed as at high risk of deliberate self-harm and suicide, but the hospital allowed her home leave, which she took and committed suicide. Again the Supreme Court found that the authorities were aware of the risk of suicide. Lord Dyson in *Rabone* emphasized that the risk was 'immediate', meaning 'present and continuing'.[89] That, he found, was clearly established on the facts of the case.

---

[84] Ibid., para. 30.   [85] (2013) 56 EHRR 23, para. 88.
[86] Application no. 7510/04.   [87] [2009] 1 AC 681; [2010] EWHC 865 (QB).
[88] [2012] UKSC 2.   [89] *Opuz v Turkey* (2010) 50 EHRR 28, para. 134,

What is required of the state?

A state will infringe an individual's right under Article 3 if it is aware that she or he is suffering the necessary degree of abuse at the hands of another and fails to take reasonable,[90] or adequate,[91] or effective[92] steps to protect that individual.[93] There is a particular obligation on the state to protect the human rights of vulnerable people.[94] The obligations can extend to intervening and removing a victim from a position where she or he is suffering conduct which is prohibited by Articles 3 or 8.[95] Hence states have been found to infringe Article 3 when they have been aware that children are being abused but have not taken steps to protect them.[96] To complete a successful claim it needs to be shown that had the public authority acted properly then there was a substantial chance of the breach not occurring.[97] It does not need to be shown that the breach would not have occurred but for the intervention, just that there was a real chance it would not have.

We will explore these issues further.

General duties

There is a duty on the state to put in place laws which generally speaking ensure that citizens' rights are protected. This means there must be effective criminal law to deter violent crimes[98] and an effective mechanism for law enforcement.[99] As Article 5.2 of the Istanbul Convention puts it: 'Parties shall take the necessary legislative and other measures to exercise due diligence to prevent, investigate, punish and provide reparation for acts of violence covered by the scope of this Convention that are perpetrated by non-State actors.' In *Menson v United Kingdom*[100] Article 2 was said to impose 'a duty on that State to secure the right to life by putting in place effective criminal law provisions to deter the commission of offences against a person backed up by law enforcement machinery for the prevention of suppression and punishment of breaches of such provisions'. This requires an effective legislative and administrative

---

[90] *Z v UK* [2001] 2 FCR 246.
[91] *A v UK* [1998] 3 FCR 597, para. 24.   [92] *Z v UK* [2001] 2 FCR 246, para. 73.
[93] *E v UK* [2002] 3 FCR 700.   [94] *A v UK* [1998] 3 FCR 597, para. 20.
[95] See S. Choudhry and J. Herring, *European Human Rights and Family Law*, (n. 1), ch. 8 and 9.
[96] *E v UK* [2002] 3 FCR 700.   [97] *Rabone v Pennine Care NHS Trust* [2012] UKSC 2.
[98] *Valiulienė v Lithuania* (Application no. 33234/07), para. 75.
[99] *Vosylius v United Kingdom* (2013) 57 EHRR SE20.
[100] [2003] EHRR CD220.

framework.[101] That said, the European Court acknowledges that the positive obligations imposed on the national authorities by the Convention may be met in a range of possible ways and the Court should not usurp the States' role in selection the appropriate way.[102] Tort law, criminal law, and regulation law may all have their part to play. Of course, although the state is required to take reasonable steps to prevent, suppress, and punish breaches of Convention rights, that does not mean that it is liable simply because a crime is committed.[103]

Included within the administrative framework is a duty to conduct 'a proper and open investigation into deaths for which the state might be responsible'.[104] If there are criminal proceedings they should be brought reasonably promptly.[105] The obligation also applies in cases of breaches of Article 3[106] and Article 8 too,[107] although presumably the depth of the investigation might depend on the severity of the abuse.[108]

In *DSD v Commissioner of Police of the Metropolis*[109] the claimants brought an action against the police under the Human Rights Act claiming that the police's failure to investigate the behaviour of a serial rapist led to their rapes and this was an infringement of their rights under Articles 3 and 8. Green J concluded that they could bring the claim. He explained the significance behind the duty to investigate and prosecute crimes:

The purpose behind this duty is to secure confidence in the rule of law in a democratic society, to demonstrate that the State is not colluding with or consenting to criminality, and, to provide learning to the police with a view to increasing future detection levels and preventing future crime ... The investigation must be independent, impartial and subject to independent scrutiny.

He also helpfully listed some factors which might be relevant in determining whether the investigation was compatible with human rights obligations: '[T]he resources available to the police; the nature of the offence; whether the victim fell into an especially vulnerable category; whether the operational failures were caused by (up-stream) systemic failings in the law or in the practices of the police.'

---

[101] *Oneryildiz v Turkey* (2005) 41 EHRR 20, para. 89.
[102] *Eremia v Moldova* (Application no. 3564/11).
[103] *Valiulienė v. Lithuania* (Application no. 33234/07), para. 75.
[104] *Rabone v Pennine Care NHS Trust* [2012] UKSC 2.
[105] *Opuz v Turkey* (2010) 50 EHRR 28, para. 150.
[106] *M v Italy* (2013) 57 EHRR 29.
[107] *Eremia v Moldova* (Application no. 3564/11); *CAS & CS v Romania* [2012] ECHR 512.
[108] *DSD v Commissioner of Police of the Metropolis* [2014] EWHC 436 (QB).
[109] Ibid.

Specific duties: operational

Baroness Hale in *Savage*[110] explained that 'the positive protection obligation under Article 2 is generally an obligation to have proper systems in place. But in some circumstances an operational duty to protect a particular individual is triggered. The latter duty is not engaged by ordinary medical negligence alone.' This duty is to take measures 'which, judged reasonably, might have been expected to avoid that risk'.[111] The same is said in relation to Article 3, if the state is aware an individual is at risk of suffering torture or inhuman or degrading treatment. The state is under an obligation to take reasonable steps to intervene.

However, reasonableness is key here. The Courts are all too aware that interpreted too broadly this could be an enormous burden on public authorities. In *Dordevic v Croatia*[112] it was emphasized:

Bearing in mind the difficulties in policing modern societies, the unpredictability of human conduct and the operational choices which must be made in terms of priorities and resources, the scope of this positive obligation must, however, be interpreted in a way which does not impose an impossible or disproportionate burden on the authorities. Not every claimed risk of ill-treatment, therefore, can entail for the authorities a Convention requirement to take operational measures to prevent that risk from materialising.

Inevitably the police hear of all kinds of allegations and concerns and it is not possible to respond to every one by putting in place an effective protection mechanism. The courts have limited the duty in several ways. It only applies when the state is aware that a particular individual is at risk of their rights being infringed.[113] It does not, for example, apply in cases where there is simply a dangerous person 'on the loose'. Another limiting factor is whether the risk is 'an "ordinary" risk of the kind that individuals in the relevant category should reasonably be expected to take or is it an exceptional risk?'[114] So a distinction was drawn in *Stoyanovi v Bulgaria*[115] between the kind of risks that a solider must expect in the course of their job and a member of the public. So the duty arises only in the cases of unusual risks against an identified person.

It is helpful to look at some of the categories of cases where questions about the specific operational duty has arisen.

Suicide

The leading case in the domestic law is *Rabone*.[116] The Supreme Court confirmed that there was a positive duty on the state to take reasonable steps to avoid a real

---

[110] *Savage v South Essex Partnership NHS Foundation Trust* [2009] 1 AC 691.
[111] *Van Colle v UK* (2013) 56 EHRR 23, para. 88.
[112] (2012) EHRR 1640, para. 139.   [113] *Van Colle v UK* (2013) 56 EHRR 23.
[114] Lord Dyson in *Rabone v Pennine Care NHS Trust* [2012] UKSC 2.
[115] [2010] ECHR 1782.   [116] *Rabone v Pennine Care NHS Trust* [2012] UKSC 2.

and immediate risk of suicide but only where the person was in care of the state. So, there is a duty on the public authorities to take reasonable steps to prevent known suicide risks from committing suicide in the case of prisoners,[117] immigrants kept in administrative detention,[118] and conscript soldiers. The duty does not seem to apply simply to a member of the public known to be a suicide risk. The duty applies to patients detained under the Mental Health Act 1983[119] and in *Rabone* itself was applied to a psychiatric patient voluntarily in public health care.[120] The Supreme Court held that drawing a distinction between formally and informally detained patients was one of 'form not substance' and so did not matter. It was the vulnerability of the victim, the nature of the risk, and the assumption of responsibility which were key, rather than their official legal status. Applying these to the case at hand, Ms Rabone was extremely vulnerable, was a genuine suicide risk, and the trust had assumed responsibility for her welfare and safety by accepting her at the hospital as a voluntary patient. Given the risk of suicide it was found that the hospital could and should have detained her and not permitted her to leave. There was a real and significant risk of suicide of which the Trust knew or ought to have known and they had not taken all reasonable steps to prevent the risk eventuating. So, there was a breach of their duty.

Lord Dyson in *Rabone* summarized the thinking of the court:

[I]f there was a real and immediate risk of suicide at that time, of which the trust was aware or ought to have been aware, then in my view the trust was under a duty to take reasonable steps to protect Melanie from it. She had been admitted to hospital because she was a real suicide risk. By reason of her mental state, she was extremely vulnerable. The trust assumed responsibility for her. She was under its control. Although she was not a detained patient, it is clear that, if she had insisted on leaving the hospital, the authorities could and should have exercised their powers under the MHA to prevent her from doing so.

Care of the state

More generally when a person is in the care of the state there is a duty to protect that person's human rights. So there is a duty on the state to take reasonable steps to ensure one prisoner's human rights are not infringed by another prisoner.[121] As Lord Rodger in *Mitchell v Glasgow City Council*[122] held:

The obligation of the United Kingdom under article 2 goes wider, however. In particular, where a state has assumed responsibility for an individual, whether by taking

---

[117] *Keenan v United Kingdom* (2001) 33 EHRR 913.
[118] *Slimani v France* (2006) 43 EHRR 49.
[119] *Savage v South Essex Partnership NHS Foundation Trust* [2008] UKHL 74.
[120] *Reynolds v UK* (Application no. 2694/08).
[121] *Edwards v United Kingdom* (2002) 35 EHRR 487.   [122] [2009] AC 874, para. 66.

him into custody, by imprisoning him, detaining him under mental health legislation, or conscripting him into the armed forces, the state assumes responsibility for that individual's safety. So in these circumstances police authorities, prison authorities, health authorities and the armed forces are all subject to positive obligations to protect the lives of those in their care.

In that case this duty was not held to apply to a vulnerable family being housed by a local authority. Although the authority was aware they were at risk of abuse the authority had not undertaken especial responsibility of them and were not aware of a specific allegation of abuse.

Even where a person is in the care of the state it does not follow that every breach of human rights is the responsibility of the state. In *Powell v United Kingdom*[123] a boy died after negligent treatment in a hospital. The *Osman* duty was held not to apply. The court held:

> The court accepts that it cannot be excluded that the acts and omissions of the authorities in the field of health care policy may in certain circumstances engage their responsibility under the positive limb of article 2. However, where a contracting state had made adequate provision for securing high professional standards among health professionals and the protection of the lives of patients, it cannot accept that matters such as error of judgment on the part of a health professional or negligent coordination among health professionals in the treatment of a particular patient are sufficient of themselves to call a contracting state to account from the standpoint of its positive obligations under article 2 of the Convention to protect life.[124]

What is important to note about this passage is that it is not saying that Article 2 does not apply in a straightforward case of a patient receiving inadequate care at a hospital. Rather it is saying that the duty under Article 2 is met more readily where the state has in place procedures to ensure generally there are high medical standards among professionals and ensure provision for the protection of the lives of patients. In such cases where a medical professional has been negligent it does not follow that the state has failed to comply with its duties.

Responsibility for the danger

The duty is particularly likely to arise in cases where the state is responsible for the danger. In *Oneryildiz v Turkey*[125] the applicant lived on a slum on the edge of a refuse tip. The applicant's house was engulfed in a slide. The Grand Chamber of the ECHR held that the authorities ought to have known that

---

[123] (2000) 30 EHRR CD 362.   [124] Ibid., 364.
[125] (2005) 41 EHRR 20.

the tip constituted a real and immediate risk to the lives of those who lived close by. Therefore the authorities 'had a positive obligation under article 2 of the Convention to take such preventive operational measures as were necessary and sufficient to protect those individuals, especially as they themselves had set up the site and authorised its operation, which gave rise to the risk in question'. That case may be distinguished from *Mitchell v Glasgow City Council*,[126] where a local authority housed a family in an estate where other residents abused the family. The authority could not be found responsible for the actions of other residents.

A case closer to the borderline was *Mammadov v Azerbaijan*,[127] where police officers were attempting to evict the applicant and his family from their house. During the attempt the applicant's wife set fire to herself. It was held that the state had triggered the specific situation and that the state agents had become or ought to become aware of the risk of suicide. The court stated:

[I]n a situation where an individual threatens to take his or her own life in plain view of state agents and, moreover where this threat is an emotional reaction directly induced by the state agents' actions or demands, the latter should treat this threat with the utmost seriousness as constituting an imminent risk to that individual's life, regardless of how unexpected that threat might have been.

Domestic violence

One line of cases where the courts have found a breach is domestic violence cases.[128] The court has heard a sad litany of claims where victims of domestic violence have reported their concerns about abuse and threats to the authority, but these have not been taken seriously and later death or serious injury occurred. In such cases, if the authorities have not taken reasonable steps to protect victims they will be found to have breached the victims' human rights.

In *Kontrová v Slovakia*,[129] where a report of domestic violence was ignored by the authorities, the court listed what was expected:

inter alia, accepting and duly registering the applicant's criminal complaint; launching a criminal investigation and commencing criminal proceedings against the applicant's husband immediately; keeping a proper record of the emergency calls and advising the next shift of the situation; and taking action in respect of the allegation that the applicant's husband had a shotgun and had made violent threats with it.

---

[126] [2009] AC 874, para. 66.   [127] [2009] ECHR 2079.
[128] *Eremia v Moldova* Application no. 3564/11.   [129] Application no. 7510/04.

The failure to comply with these led to a finding of a breach of the applicant's Article 2 rights when the husband killed the children.

In *Opuz v Turkey*[130] the court concluded that the state could have foreseen a lethal attack given the series of violent incidents reported to them and could have done more to protect the mother, even though she had withdrawn her complaints. The Court explained:

In the Court's opinion, it does not appear that the local authorities sufficiently considered the above factors when repeatedly deciding to discontinue the criminal proceedings against H.O. [the man]. Instead, they seem to have given exclusive weight to the need to refrain from interfering in what they perceived to be a 'family matter' ... Moreover, there is no indication that the authorities considered the motives behind the withdrawal of the complaints.[131]

In *Bevacqua and S v Bulgaria* the applicant was the victim of domestic violence. She successfully argued that her and her child's rights under Article 8 had been violated as the authorities had failed to protect them from the former husband's violence. The European Court of Human Rights held:

At the relevant time Bulgarian law did not provide for specific administrative and policing measures (in relation to domestic violence) and the measures taken by the police and prosecuting authorities on the basis of their general powers did not prove effective [...] In the Court's view, the authorities' failure to impose sanctions or otherwise enforce Mr N.'s obligation to refrain from unlawful acts was critical in the circumstances of this case, as it amounted to a refusal to provide the immediate assistance the applicants needed. The authorities' view that no such assistance was due as the dispute concerned a 'private matter' was incompatible with their positive obligations to secure the enjoyment of the applicants' Article 8 rights.[132]

A similar approach can be found in *A v Croatia*,[133] which emphasized that it was not simply a matter of obtaining court orders; the state must ensure that they are effectively enforced if it is to meet its obligations under Article 8.[134] In *Wilson v United Kingdom*[135] it was held that victims of domestic violence are particularly vulnerable and this leads to an enhanced obligation to protect victims of domestic violence. This was confirmed in *Söderman v Sweden*.[136]

---

[130] [2009] ECHR 33401/02.
[131] Ibid., para. 143.   [132] European Court of Human Rights; 12 June 2008.
[133] *A v Croatia* [2010] ECHR 1506.
[134] See also *Hajduova v Slovakia* (Application no. 2660/03).
[135] Application no. 10601/09.   [136] (2013) 57 EHRR 29.

Vulnerable

There is a particularly heavy obligation on the state to protect the Article 3 rights of vulnerable people, such as children,[137] and victims of domestic violence,[138] and ethnic minorities.[139] It should be added that the vulnerability here can either be a group identity (e.g. by being a child or member of an oppressed group) or by one's particular situation (e.g. by being a victim of domestic abuse). In relation to children it has been said that 'measures must be aimed at ensuring respect for human dignity and protecting the best interests of the child'.[140] It seems being a woman per se is not accepted as vulnerability.[141]

In *Söderman v Sweden*[142] the obligation to protect children was said to stem not only from the ECHR but also 'from other international instruments, such as, *inter alia*, Articles 19 and 34 of the United Nations Convention on the Rights of the Child and Chapter VI, "Substantive criminal law", of the Council of Europe Convention on the Protection of Children against Sexual Exploitation and Sexual Abuse'.[143]

Significantly, in cases of vulnerable people the duty is owed even where there is no particular assumption of care by the state. Lord Dyson in *Rabone* explained:

When finding that the article 2 operational duty has been breached, the ECtHR has repeatedly emphasised the vulnerability of the victim as a relevant consideration. In circumstances of sufficient vulnerability, the ECtHR has been prepared to find a breach of the operational duty even where there has been no assumption of control by the state, such as where a local authority fails to exercise its powers to protect a child who to its knowledge is at risk of abuse as in *Z v United Kingdom*.[144]

Autonomy

In determining what is a reasonable response of the state a balance must be struck between respecting the right to protection we are discussing and the right to make decisions about one's own life, also protected by Article 8. For example in relation to the suicide cases, Lady Hale in *Rabone*[145] accepted: 'There is a difficult balance to be struck between the right of the individual patient to freedom and self-determination and her right to be prevented from taking her own life.' This issue is particularly likely to be

---

[137] *A v UK* [1998] 3 FCR 597, para 20.
[138] *Wilson v United Kingdom* (Application no. 10601/09).
[139] *Secic v Croatia* (2009) 49 EHRR 408.   [140] (2013) 57 EHRR 29, para. 81.
[141] *Valiulienė v Lithuania* (Application no. 33234/07).   [142] (2013) 57 EHRR 29.
[143] Ibid., para. 82.   [144] [2001] ECHR 333.
[145] *Rabone v Pennine Care NHS Trust* [2012] UKSC 2.

pertinent for a court when an order is sought to protect an individual, when that person is opposing the order.

So, how can these competing rights and interests be balanced? The right under Article 3 is an absolute one. Unlike many of the other rights mentioned in the European Convention there are no circumstances in which it is permissible for the state to infringe this right. This makes it clear that the rights of another party cannot justify an infringement of someone's Article 3 rights. So, for example, it cannot be successfully argued that a family's right of privacy justifies non-intervention by the state if that non-intervention is an infringement of one family member's Article 3 rights. Indeed, and perhaps this is more controversial, it is suggested that other rights of the victim cannot justify an infringement of Article 3. In other words, in a domestic violence case the state cannot justify its failure to protect a victim's Article 3 rights by referring to that person's right to respect for private life. Where Article 3 is engaged the state must take reasonable steps to protect the victim, regardless of her wishes.

However, unlike Article 3, Article 8 is a qualified right. It is permissible for the state to fail to respect an individual's right to respect for private life under Article 8(1) if para. 2 is satisfied. So, if the level of abuse is not sufficient to engage Article 3 but falls within Article 8, then it is necessary to balance the Article 8 rights and interests of other parties. It would therefore be possible to make an argument that the rights of autonomy of the victim justify the state in not intervening in an Article 8 case. I will argue that in most cases this balancing of rights will still fall down in favour of intervention.

First, a strong pro-prosecution approach would not necessarily reflect the autonomous wish of the victim. It may be that she has been pressurized into withdrawing her co-operation in proceedings. It should not be forgotten what the impact of domestic violence can be: low self-esteem, dependence upon the perpetrator, feelings of hopelessness about ending the violence, and a tendency to minimize or deny the violence. If we do attach weight to the views of the victim in deciding whether or not to prosecute all we will do is open up victims to further abuse as the defendant seeks to pressurize the victim into withdrawing her complaint. The *Opuz v Turkey*[146] case is a good example of where although the victim made complaints to the police, the victim withdrew them in the face of threats from the defendant.

In considering whether the behaviour infringes Articles 3 or 8 it is important to look at the conduct in the context of the whole relationship. The experiences of victims of domestic abuse show that it is best understood not

---

[146] [2009] ECHR 33401/02.

as simply a series of violent or abusive acts, but rather as a programme of 'coercive control' (to use Evan Stark's[147] phrase) or 'patriarchal terrorism' or 'intimate terrorism' (to use Michael Johnson's phrase).[148] Michael Johnson distinguishes intimate terrorism from what he calls 'situational couple violence' or 'mutual violence'. Patriarchal terrorism is 'violence enacted in the service of taking general control over one's partner'.[149] By contrast, in situational couple violence or mutual violence, there is violence but there is no attempt to control the relationship. Rather, an incident of violence arises in a moment of conflict during an intimate relationship which is not generally marked with inequality. It involves a lashing out in self-defence, anger, or frustration, rather than an attempt to exercise control.

Understanding the impact of domestic abuse requires an appreciation of its controlling intent and impact. This can only be understood by looking at the relationship between the parties as a whole. Psychologist Mary Ann Dutton[150] explains:

Abusive behaviour does not occur as a series of discrete events. Although a set of discrete abusive incidents can typically be identified within an abusive relationship, an understanding of the dynamic of power and control within an intimate relationship goes beyond these discrete incidents. To negate the impact of the time period between discrete episodes of serious violence—a time period during which the woman may never know when the next incident will occur, and may continue to live with on-going psychological abuse—is to fail to recognize what some battered woman experience as a continuing 'state of siege'.

The whole aim of the behaviour of the abuser is to dominate the victim and diminish her sense of self-worth. This is done by restricting the victim's access to work; isolating her from friends; manipulating the victims emotionally; and physical attacks. Physical violence, then, is but one tool used in the relationship to keep one party inferior.[151] When considering whether or not the conduct amounts to domestic violence and thereby to generate the right to protection, it is important to look at the relationship as a whole and not simply individual acts.

Second, even if there is a genuine request for non-intervention, there is a balance between protecting the current autonomous wish of the victim with

---

[147] E. Stark, *Coercive Control* (New York, Oxford University Press 2007).

[148] M. Johnson, 'Apples and Oranges in Child Custody Disputes: Intimate Terrorism vs. Situational Couple Violence', (2005) 2 *Journal of Child Custody* 43.

[149] Ibid.

[150] M. Dutton, 'Understanding Women's Response to Domestic Violence', (2003) 21 *Hofstra Law Review* 1191, 1204.

[151] O. Rachmilovitz, 'Bringing Down the Bedroom Walls: Emphasizing Substance Over Form in Personalized Abuse', (2007) 14 *William and Mary Journal of Women & Law* 495.

the increase in autonomy they may experience if they were removed from the abuse. Many victims in these cases have conflicting wishes. They want to remain in the relationship, but they want the abuse to stop. In such a case it is not easy to determine what is promoting their autonomy. It is not possible to respect these two conflicting desires. I suggest that where the abuse is low level, the infringement on autonomy in remaining in the relationship will be limited. However, in more serious cases the autonomy arguments will be in favour of removal. It must be remembered that being in an abusive relationship is itself undermining of autonomy. Leaving a person to suffer abuse, but who does not want to be protected, is not necessarily justified in the name of autonomy.

It may be argued that my approach is giving insufficient respect for the notion of a private life. Katherine O'Donovan,[152] before criticizing the argument, suggests: 'Home is thought to be a private place, a refuge from society, where relationships can flourish uninterrupted by public interference.' Some therefore consider it essential that the law should 'stay out of the home'. This argument must be resisted. Catharine Mackinnon characterized the ideology of privacy as 'a right of men "to be let alone" to oppress women one at a time'.[153] Even if there is value in the notion of the privacy of the family life, I argue there are good reasons in favour of state intervention in cases of domestic violence.

A good starting point for rethinking the nature of privacy is to ask: Why should the state respect the private life of its citizens? One popular answer lies in the concept of autonomy. Each person should be entitled to develop her/his own understanding of the 'good life'. We could have a state that attempted to enforce a beneficial lifestyle on each citizen, telling her/him what to read, eat, and do, but most people would find such a society repellent, not least because living in a society of 'clones' would be boring indeed. So, the notion of privacy plays a role in allowing us to develop our lives and intimate relations in the ways we wish. This produces a wide range of different personalities and lifestyles which provide part of the enjoyment of life. But, so understood, privacy is not necessarily a negative concept about state non-intervention, but rather about an enabling of each individual to flourish as a person. As Elisabeth Schneider argues,[154] the state needs to promote 'a more affirmative concept of privacy, one that encompasses liberty, equality, freedom of bodily integrity, autonomy and self-determination, which is important to women

---

[152] K. O'Donovan, *Family Law Matters* (Pluto 1993), at 107.

[153] C. Mackinnon, *Feminism Unmodified* (Cambridge MA, Harvard University Press 1987), 32.

[154] E. Schneider, 'The Violence of Privacy', in M. Fineman and R. Myktiuk (eds), *The Public Nature of Private Violence* (Abingdon, Routledge 1994).

who have been battered'. For those with power that may be possible with little intervention from the state. However, for the less powerful, state intervention may be necessary to enable a person (or groups of people) to live their lives fully. Adopting such an approach means that privacy is not a concept which prevents state intervention in incidents of domestic violence but one which in fact requires it. Without state intervention a victim of domestic violence will be prevented from pursuing her vision of the good life. As we have seen, domestic abuse is typically about the control of a woman's life. So, then, if the state wishes to promote privacy in this sense—the ability to thrive in one's attempt to do what they wish with their lives—then protection from violence is required. To leave a person in an abusive relationship which is restricting her ability to develop her life as she wishes is not respecting her privacy: quite the opposite. Properly understood, therefore, privacy is a reason in favour of intervention, not against it.[155]

Third, there are strong state reasons which can justify prosecuting a case of domestic violence, even where the victim does not want intervention. There are the interests of the community in expressing a clear message that domestic violence is unacceptable and will be taken very seriously by the state.[156] It is important to remember that prosecutions are brought by the state and not the victim. Battering can be seen as causing public harm: it can cause increased costs to the state, extensive loss to the economy of police time, victims having to take time off work, etc. In the United Kingdom, it has been estimated that domestic violence alone costs the economy £5.8 billion per year.[157] More than this, domestic violence is caused by and reinforced by patriarchy. As the state upholds and maintains patriarchy, it has responsibility for it and so is under a duty to mitigate its effects. To rely on Schneider's words:

[H]eterosexual intimate violence is part of a larger system of coercive control and subordination; this system is based on structural gender inequality and has political roots … In the context of intimate violence, the impulse behind feminist legal arguments [is] to redefine the relationship between the personal and the political, to definitively link violence and gender.[158]

---

[155] J. Herring and R. Taylor, 'Relocating Relocation', (2006) 18 *Child and Family Law Quarterly* 517. See also S. Choudhry and H. Fenwick, 'Taking the Rights of Parents and Children Seriously: Confronting the Welfare Principle and the Human Rights Act', (2005) 25 *Oxford Journal of Legal Studies* 453.

[156] M. Madden Dempsey, *Prosecuting Domestic Violence* (Oxford, Oxford University Press 2009) describes how effective prosecution of domestic violence can exhibit the characteristics of a feminist state.

[157] S. Walby, *The Cost of Domestic Violence* (Home Office, 2004).

[158] E. Schneider, 'The Violence of Privacy' in M. Fineman and R. Myktiuk (eds), *The Public Nature of Private Violence* (Abingdon, Routledge 1994) 5–6.

Fourth, even if these arguments are not accepted, the issue cannot be cat-egorized as private where children are involved.[159] A UNICEF report sug-gests that up to one million children in the United Kingdom are living with domestic violence.[160] There is widespread acceptance that children raised in a household where there is domestic violence suffer in many ways, as compared to households where there is not.[161] This includes psychological disturbance and often a feeling that they are to blame for the violence.[162] The impact of the domestic violence on the mother may itself harm the child.[163] Indeed, one study of children who had suffered abuse showed that 39 per cent of them had come from families in which there was domestic violence.[164] Marianne Hester found that children were present in 55 per cent of cases of domestic violence.[165] Ten per cent of children who witnessed domestic violence wit-nessed their mother being sexually assaulted.[166]

There has been considerable debate over how the law should respond to cases of domestic abuse where the victim does not want a criminal prosecu-tion to be brought.

Even if these arguments are accepted, it may be argued that there are insurmountable problems in putting a strong pro-prosecution policy into practice. One of the difficulties of domestic violence is that often the only witnesses to the violence are the two parties themselves. In many cases it is one person's word against another's. This requires the courts to make orders that may infringe important rights of either party on the basis of meagre evidence. If the court makes the wrong decision, an innocent person may be removed from his or her home, or a victim may be denied protection from further violence. An obvious objection to a pro-prosecution approach is that without the evidence of the victim it is going to be extremely difficult to obtain a conviction. The incident is often only witnessed by the victim: so, in a practical sense, is it possible to prosecute where the victim opposes the

---

[159] M. Hester, C. Pearson, and N. Harwin, *Making an Impact—Children and Domestic Violence: A Reader* (York, Jessica Kingsley 2007).

[160] UNICEF *Behind Closed Doors: The Impact of Domestic Violence on Children* (UNICEF, 2006).

[161] K. Kitzmann, N. Gaylord, A. Holt, and E. Kenny, 'Child Witnesses to Domestic Violence: A Meta-analytic Review', (2003) 71 *Journal of Consultative Clinical Psychology* 339.

[162] Barnardo's, *Bitter Legacy* (Barnardo's 2004).

[163] L. Radford and M. Hester, *Mothering Through Domestic Violence* (York, Jessica Kingsley 2006).

[164] E. Farmer and S. Pollock, *Substitute Care for Sexually Abused and Abusing Children* (London, John Wiley & Sons 1998).

[165] M. Hester, *Who Does What to Whom? Gender and Domestic Violence Perpetrators* (London, Northern Rock 2009).

[166] A. Mullender, *Tackling Domestic Violence: Providing Support For Children Who Have Witnessed Domestic Violence* (Home Office, 2005).

prosecution? Those who wish to see more extensive prosecution in this area might suggest two solutions.

One would be to compel victims of domestic violence to testify under pain of imprisonment for contempt of court. This has few supporters. As the primary justification offered for intervention is the protection of the rights of the victim and any children, to imprison the victim would undermine that aim. The second alternative has more support. This involves a prosecution without the involvement of the victim. At present it is very rare for this to happen.[167] Louise Ellison[168] has argued that 'victimless prosecution' is the way forward.[169] She argues that, although it is often assumed that without victim involvement a prosecution is not possible, more imaginative policing and prosecution techniques would make it feasible. She discusses, for example, the use of cameras as soon as the police arrive on the scene, to capture objective evidence of injuries. She recommends that police procedure in domestic violence cases should be premised on the assumption that there will be a 'victimless prosecution'.[170] There may also need to be changes to the law of evidence—and in particular the hearsay rule and the admissibility of previous convictions—to assist in victimless prosecution. The advantages of victimless prosecution are clear: it involves less invasion of the victim's autonomy if the victim is opposed to it; the victim can avoid the pressures associated with giving evidence in these kinds of cases; and it can prevent threats or other pressures being used to dissuade victims from participating in litigation. Of course none of this should be seen as seeking not to prosecute with the victim's consent; much more should be done to enable and encourage the victim to support the litigation. The use of specialist domestic violence police, advisors,[171] prosecutors, and courts might assist in these procedures.[172] The pilot studies to date indicate that in specialist domestic violence courts, victimless prosecutions have been successfully brought.[173]

To summarize, I am not arguing in favour of a mandatory prosecution policy. However, wherever there is a reasonable chance of success a prosecution should be brought in all cases, save in cases of the least serious domestic

---

[167] S. Edwards, *Briefing Note: Reducing Domestic Violence* (Home Office, 2000).

[168] L. Ellison, 'Responding to Victim Withdrawal in Domestic Violence Prosecutions', (2002) *Criminal Law Review* 760; L. Ellison, 'Prosecuting Domestic Violence Without Victim Participation', (2002) 65 *Modern Law Review* 834.

[169] See also S. Edwards, *Briefing Note: Reducing Domestic Violence* (Home Office, 2000) arguing for a greater willingness to use victims' written statements in cases where victims are unwilling to give evidence in court.

[170] Crown Prosecution Service, *Policy for Prosecuting Cases of Domestic Violence* (CPS, 2009).

[171] E. Howarth, L. Stimpson, D. Baran, and A. Robinson, *Safety in Numbers* (Hestia Fund 2009).

[172] Crown Prosecution Service, *Policy for Prosecuting Cases of Domestic Violence* (CPS 2009).

[173] M. Burton, *Domestic Violence: Literature Review* (LSC 2009).

abuse, where the victim strongly opposes the prosecution. This approach is in fact required under the European Convention on Human Rights to ensure protection of the rights of victims.

Criminal law remedies alone will not be enough to ensure there is protection from abuse. There may be insufficient evidence for a criminal prosecution, or for some other reason a prosecution is not feasible. Then providing civil remedies to ensure protection is essential for a legal system seeking to protect the rights of victims from domestic abuse.

Remedies for breach of human rights

In domestic law the primary remedy for an applicant who has not been protected by a public authority is via the Human Rights Act 1998 and a claim under section 7. The alternative possibility of using tort law has proved less fruitful.

The leading case is *Michael v Chief Constable of South Wales Police*.[174] Joanna Mitchell called 999 and she said that her former partner had attacked her and said he would return to hit her. Later, she said he was returning to kill her, although that may have been indistinct. The operator passed on the call but did not mention the threat to kill. The call was downgraded as not immediate but then a further call upgraded it, but by the time the police arrived she had been stabbed to death by Williams. Her estate sought damages for negligence and breach of duty under Article 2 through a Human Rights Act claim. The chief constable sought to strike out the claim. Before the Court of Appeal the negligence claim was struck out, but the Article 2 claim was permitted to proceed. The case went to the Supreme Court only in terms of the negligence claim.

In relation to the law on tort the Supreme Court followed the approach taken in *Hill v Chief Constable of West Yorkshire*.[175] There, while Lord Keith's leading speech recognized the general law of tort applied to the police as much as anyone else, it was held that 'the general duty of the police to enforce the law did not carry with it a private law duty towards individual members of the public'.[176] Lord Toulson in *Michael* summarized Lord Keith's reasoning:

He concluded that it would be contrary to the public interest to impose liability on the police for mistakes made in relation to their operations in the investigation and

---

[174] [2015] UKSC 2.
[175] [1989] AC 53.
[176] *Michael v Chief Constable of South Wales Police* [2015] UKSC 2.

suppression of crime. He said that the manner and conduct of such an investigation must necessarily involve a variety of decisions to be made on matters of policy and discretion, such as which particular line of inquiry is most advantageously to be pursued and what is the most advantageous way to deploy available resources. Many such decisions would not be appropriate to be called in question, but elaborate investigation of the facts might be necessary to ascertain whether or not this was so. A great deal of police time and expense might have to be put into the preparation of a defence to the action. The result would be a significant diversion of police manpower and attention from their most important function. He also said that the imposition of liability might lead to the exercise of the investigative function being carried out in a defensive frame of mind. He concluded that the Court of Appeal had been right to take the view that the police were 'immune from an action of this kind on grounds similar to those which in *Rondel v Worsley* [1969] 1 AC 191 were held to render a barrister immune from actions for negligence in his conduct of proceedings in court'.[177]

As Lord Toulson noted, the use of 'immunity' was 'unfortunate'[178] and led to the Strasbourg Court in *Osman v United Kingdom*[179] finding that an exclusion of liability for the police was a restriction on access to the court in violation of Article 6. The European Court later backtracked on that in *Z v United Kingdom*[180] when it accepted that the Supreme Court in *Osman* was saying that a duty of care might not normally be found, rather than an exemption based on status. *Brooks v Commissioner of Police of the Metropolis*[181] made it clear that what was being talked about in *Hill* was not a 'blanket immunity' but rather an absence of a duty of care.

The case law has made it clear that it is not impossible for a duty of care to arise where there has been an assumption of responsibility by the police towards a citizen and reliance on that by the citizen. In *An Informer v A Chief Constable*[182] the claimant contacted the police about a business associate whom he suspected was engaged with criminal activities and was persuaded to act as an informant. The police explained what they wanted him to do and promised to treat his safety and that of his family as a priority. Later as part of the prosecution he was investigated for economic crimes and orders were made limiting his ability to transfer property. The Court of Appeal accepted the police owed him a duty of care to protect his physical well-being, but rejected an argument that that included a duty of care towards his economic interests.

Similar approaches have been taken with regard to emergency services. In *Capital & Counties Plc v Hampshire County Council*[183] the Court of Appeal heard three cases concerning alleged negligence of the fire brigade

---

[177] Ibid., para. 41.   [178] Ibid., para. 42.   [179] (1998) 29 EHRR 245.
[180] (2001) 34 EHRR 97.   [181] [2005] UKHL 24, [2005] 1 WLR 1495.
[182] [2013] QB 579.   [183] [1997] QB 1004.

in response to an emergency call. Liability was found in one case where the fire brigade had ordered a sprinkler system to be turned off, leading to more extensive damage occurring than would otherwise have happened, but none was found in the two other cases where the fire brigade had failed to take steps they could have taken to limit the damage. The general approach taken was that where the emergency services had exacerbated the harm then they could be liable, but not where they had simply failed to take steps they could have taken to protect the citizen.[184] A rather different approach is taken to an ambulance service[185] because it is seen as part of the health service.

Lord Toulson accepted that generally tort law does not impose liability for omissions, save in two exceptions:

The first is where D was in a position of control over T and should have foreseen the likelihood of T causing damage to somebody in close proximity if D failed to take reasonable care in the exercise of that control. ... [186]

The second general exception applies where D assumes a positive responsibility to safeguard C under the *Hedley Byrne* principle, as explained by Lord Goff in *Spring v Guardian Assurance Plc*. It is not a new principle. It embraces the relationships in which a duty to take positive action typically arises: contract, fiduciary relationships, employer and employee, school and pupil, health professional and patient. The list is not exhaustive.[187]

As a result Lord Toulson suggested that generally failures by the police in a case like *Michael* would not be covered by tort law. The police had not undertaken a special duty towards the victim. No special advice or undertaking had been given. Therefore in denying a remedy in a case like *Michael* the court was not extending an immunity, but rather applying the normal tort law.

He rejected an argument that the specific problems associated with either domestic violence or potential liability under the HRA should affect the tort law application. On the latter point it was emphasized that the two had a different purpose: 'Whereas civil actions are designed essentially to compensate claimants for losses, Convention claims are intended to uphold minimum human rights standards and to vindicate those rights.'

Lord Kerr and Lady Hale dissented, seeing proximity as the key issue surrounding a duty of care. Lord Kerr argued:

Should someone in a vulnerable state, fearing imminent attack, who believes that an assurance of timeous assistance has been made when, through negligence on

---

[184] *OLL Ltd v Secretary of State for Transport* [1997] 3 All ER 897.
[185] *Kent v Griffiths* [2001] QB 36.   [186] [1997] QB 1004, para. 97.
[187] Ibid., para. 101.

the part of the police, that impression has been wrongly created, be treated differently from another who has in fact received an explicit assurance of immediate help, if both have relied on what they believed to be a clear promise that police would attend and avert the apprehended danger? The fact that an easily imagined example such as this can demonstrate the anomaly of the current state of the law in relation to voluntary assumption of responsibility indicates that a more expansive (or, at least, a more nuanced) approach is warranted. But it does more than that. It also illustrates the undesirability of creating a set of rules that may at first sight appear reasonable but which bring about incongruous results when applied to cases even slightly different from those in contemplation at the time of their conception.

Discussion

The recognition that human rights not only prevent the state from inflicting harm on citizens but also require the state to protect citizens from violence from another citizen is highly significant. It has particularly gendered consequences. As Edwards explains, limiting human rights protection from violence to state on citizen violence limits the effectiveness of human rights to cases of public violence:

On a practical level, the effect of distinguishing between the public and the private has 'rendered invisible', or at least less important, the many violations that women suffer in private. In this way, it leaves the private or family realm, where the majority of women spend the bulk of their lives, unregulated, unprotected, and susceptible to abuse.[188]

The extension of human rights to citizen on citizen violence ensures that all the violence experienced by women is covered, including rape and domestic abuse.[189] It brings an acceptance that torture has for too long been seen as based on a model around 'Jack Bauer' torture: the American hero using unpleasant violence on a terrorist to find out where they have put the bomb. That is an image of torture which has little relevance to women's lives and is often presented in a way which makes the torture more easily justified than if we were looking at, for example, rape as torture.

---

[188] A. Edwards, 'The Feminizing of Torture Under International Human Rights Law', (2006) 19 *Leiden Journal of International Law* 349.

[189] C. A. MacKinnon, 'On Torture: A Feminist Perspective on Human Rights', in K. E. Mahoney and P. Mahoney (eds), *Human Rights in the Twenty-First Century: A Global Challenge* (Amsterdam, Nijhoff 1993), 21; R. Copelon, 'Recognising the Egregious in the Everyday: Domestic Violence as Torture', (1994) 25 *Columbia Human Rights Law Review* 291.

The limitations of a human rights based approach

This chapter has attempted to consider how human rights can be used to create a more interventionist approach by the law into the protection of vulnerable people. It need hardly be added that there are limits to human rights analysis. As already indicated, there is a danger that rights too easily take a 'snapshot' approach to a problem, examining the rights of the parties at the particular time, and avoiding viewing the issue as part of what might be an ongoing relationship between the parties. It can also overlook the relationships the parties may have with other people in their lives. The rights parties may claim at a particular point in time are one thing, but, viewed in the context of a longer relationship, may not appear so straightforward. As argued above, there is a danger that the protection of a victim's autonomous decision not to obtain state protection at one point in time will lead to a continuation of the erosion of her autonomy through the abusive relationship. It has been claimed by some commentators that the kind of strongly interventionist approach emphasized in this article promotes a 'patriarchal kind of thinking' in that it promotes individual rights and isolation, rather than working with relationships.[190] Some even claim that such policies can work against the interests of some victims, particularly those in ethnic minority groups.[191]

Another danger with human rights and legal analysis in general is the assumption (often made) that once the court has made an order sentencing the defendant, there is victory: the victim has been protected. However, in a recent survey only 36 per cent of victims of domestic violence stated that prosecution had led to the violence ceasing, and 39 per cent stated it had not had any impact on the violence at all.[192] This emphasizes that the law must not only offer protection to the victim, but also, insofar as it is possible to do so, prevent or deter the abuser from re-offending. And of course, as has often been stated, the law can be but only one part of the battle against domestic violence.[193] And in so far as the disadvantages of vulnerability are a result of social provision these will continue to impact on the vulnerable adult.

---

[190] L. Mills, *Insult to Injury: Rethinking our Responses to Intimate Abuse* (New York, Princeton University Press 2003).

[191] D. Coker, 'Crime Control and Feminist Law Reform in Domestic Violence Law: A Critical Review', (2001) 4 *Buffalo Criminal Law Review* 801–60.

[192] C. Humphreys and R. Thiara, 'Neither Justice nor Protection; Women's Experiences of Post Separation Violence', (2003) 25 *Journal of Social Welfare and Family Law* 195.

[193] R. Lewis, 'Making Justice Work', (2004) 44 *British Journal of Criminology* 204.

Article 12, para. 1 of the Istanbul Convention acknowledges the broader measures that are needed:

Parties shall take the necessary measures to promote changes in the social and cultural patterns of behaviour of women and men with a view to eradicating prejudices, customs, traditions and all other practices which are based on the idea of the inferiority of women or on stereotyped roles for women and men.

The Convention goes on to require awareness-raising campaigns or programmes,[194] education,[195] general support services,[196] shelters,[197] and telegraph helplines[198] to combat domestic violence. All of these are essential, in addition to the legal measures, if there is to be a resolute response to domestic violence.

There is much to welcome in the approach taken by the courts. There is an acknowledgement that the state has a responsibility to protect the rights of all citizens from violence and abuse. Human rights do not only come into play when a state abuses a citizen but are as much in play when one citizen abuses another. If you are tortured, your human rights are seriously infringed, whoever is doing the torturing. It is therefore entirely right that the state has duties to protect their citizen's human rights, whatever the source of the interference.

What, however, is of particular interest for this book is the enhanced duties the state faces when a citizen is regarded as vulnerable or part of a group of vulnerable people. The question which the courts have largely avoided is why this is so? One answer may be that vulnerable people are less able to protect their rights than others, but that must be questioned. Domestic violence, a particular focus of this chapter, is a good example of this.

Conclusion

Despite the complexity, this chapter has provided, I hope, some structure for moving the legal response forward. I have argued that the starting point must be to recognize that elder abuse constitutes a grave interference in the rights of older people and one which amounts to, and perpetuates age discrimination. Recognition of these rights compels a state response. This requires both ensuring there is a legal framework to provide protection and that it is used to combat elder abuse. In doing so there needs to be a balance

---

[194] Article 13.   [195] Article 14.   [196] Article 22.   [197] Article 23.
[198] Article 24.

between rights of protection and rights of autonomy. This chapter has out-lined some more specific reforms it might entail. The road to an effective legal response to elder abuse has been a long one, but hopefully its destina-tion is not far away. Far more difficult will be reaching a society in which the causes of elder abuse, ageism, and the social disadvantages of older people are removed.[199]

Properly understood, a rights-based response mandates the state to take reasonable steps to protect victims of domestic abuse. This article has argued that, looking at the Istanbul Convention and the European Convention on Human Rights, victims have a right to protection in all cases of domestic vio-lence. This requires the state to take effective measures to protect the victim and requires proper investigation and effective prosecution in all cases. Even where the victim opposes the intervention it has been argued that unless the violence is at a low level prosecution should take place. The state must also have a range of civil law remedies for those who want to use them and a system of state investigation and protection for vulnerable adults. Adopting a sound legal framework and enforcing it, however, is only the start of the effort necessary to combat domestic violence. Changing beliefs and practices about gender roles and the nature of family life is essential if a truly effective response to domestic abuse is to be achieved.

---

[199] I. Doron, S. Alon, and N. Offir, 'Time for Policy: Legislative Response to Elder Abuse and Neglect in Israel', (2004) 16 *Journal of Elder Abuse and Neglect* 63.

6

Public Authorities and Vulnerable Adults

Introduction

As awareness of the abuse of vulnerable adults has increased, so the calls for the state to intervene to protect have become more powerful. In 2014 the Care Act was passed which put in statutory form the responsibilities of public authorities towards safeguarding adults from abuse. It is striking it has taken this long. The Children Act 1989 set out detailed provisions on the responsibilities of local authorities in relation to children who were facing abuse or otherwise in need. It was not until some twenty-five years later that the equivalent was provided in relation to adults. In part this was due to a failure to appreciate the significance of adult abuse.

One of the first major reports of abuse in recent times was in 1969, with the Ely Hospital Inquiry uncovering abuse in residential settings of people with learning disabilities.[1] In 1993 Action on Elder Abuse was formed to highlight the abuse of older people. The issue was first clearly acknowledged as a matter of government policy in Killick, published by the Department of Health and Home Office in 2000.[2] For the first time there was a national policy aimed at directing the protection of vulnerable adults. This led to a flow of guidance directed to encourage local authority to lead multi-agency responses to 'adults at risk'.[3] This led to increased statutory reform, crystallized in the Care Act 2014.

---

[1] G. Howe, *Report of the Committee of Inquiry into Allegations of Ill-Treatment of Patients and other Irregularities at the Ely Hospital, Cardiff* (Stationary Office, 1969) (Cm 3975).

[2] Department of Health, *Safeguarding Adults: Report of the Consultation on the Review of 'No Secrets'* (Stationery Office, 2009).

[3] Association of Directors of Social Services, *Safeguarding Adults: A National Framework of Standards for Good Practice and Outcomes in Adult Protection Work* (ADASS, 2005); Association of Directors of Social Services, *Standards for Adult Safeguarding* (ADASS, 2010); Department of Health, *Safeguarding Adults: Report of the Consultation on the Review of 'No Secrets'* (Stationery Office, 2009); Department of Health, *Caring for our Future: Reforming Care and Support* (Stationery Office, 2012).

The Care Act 2014 provides a new legal framework for the safeguarding of vulnerable adults. Prior to that legislation the Law Commission described the law as 'neither systematic nor co-ordinated, reflecting the sporadic development of safeguarding policy over the last 25 years'.[4] The previous law was a messy combination of law: NHS and community care legislation and guidance, mental health legislation, and common law. Before exploring the detail of the Care Act I will discuss the notion of abuse.

Definition of abuse

The definition of abuse is by no means straightforward. In recent years the most influential definition has been that in the Department of Health's *No Secrets*: 'Abuse is a violation of a person's human and civil rights by another person or persons.' However, that definition has a number of difficulties with it.

First, it seems too wide. A breach of contract might be a violation of a civil right, but not necessarily amount to abuse. Similarly, discriminating against a person who has applied for a job might breach their human rights, but would not normally be seen as abuse.

Second, it has been objected that the definition does not distinguish between a justified and unjustified violation.[5] Mikey Dunn[6] gives the example of a person sent to prison. That would violate their rights and fall into the definition of abuse, but that cannot be right. One response is simply to say that a right is not violated or even breached if the interference is justified. Hence the person sent to prison is not being abused because there was no violation of their rights, in that the interference of their rights was justified. There is certainly room for arguments about the nature of a 'breach of a right' but Dunn's point at least highlights a potentially misleading aspect of the definition.

Third, Dunn[7] believes the notion of abuse contains a relational element, at least in the context of adult safeguarding. A one off incidence of pickpocketing or even assault is not per se abuse, he suggests. Rather:

[t]he concept of abuse ... connects harm not just to an enduring relationship between two or more people, but to the particular features of relationships that cause harm to be brought about. The claim here is that the concept of abuse that ought to be

[4] Law Commission, *Adult Social Care, Report 326* (Law Commission, 2010), para. 9.1.
[5] M. Dunn, 'Rehabilitating the Concept of Abuse in Adult Safeguarding Policy and Practice', (2012) 6 *Journal of Care Services Management* 140.
[6] Ibid.   [7] Ibid.

articulated within adult safeguarding policy and practice is one that is focused on the *wrongful behaviours within relationships that cause harm.*

Dunn certainly has a good point here. Viewing abuse simply as a breach of a right might exclude awareness of the relational context in which a series of acts, none of which might on their own be particularly harmful, but together combine to constitute a serious wrong. Dunn gives the example of restricting access to money, which might be abusive in some relationships (if used, say, by an abusive husband to control his wife) but not in others (to ensure a person with learning difficulties is not financially exploited). Further, an act's abusive nature might depend on the role the perpetrator is performing. A nurse or care worker acting in a particular way may be committing abuse, when we would not say the same thing if a stranger acted in that way. For example, ignoring someone's cry for help might not be abusive if a stranger 'walks by on the other side', but may be if done by a person who has special responsibility for the person in trouble. Similarly acts of intimate care performed properly by a carer would not be abuse, but might well be abusive if done by a stranger.

Other definitions of abuse carry problems of their own. Some simply require proof that harm was caused. For example, *Action Against Elder Abuse* suggest this definition:[8] '[A] single or repeated act or lack of appropriate action occurring within any relationship where there is an expectation of trust, which causes harm or distress to an older person.' While this would capture anything we are likely to want to label abuse it is far too wide. It could cover for example a gay man coming out to his parents. Or perhaps even an adult child failing to telephone his mother as promised.

This brief discussion has highlighted the problem in seeking a definition of abuse. However, as Phillipson and Biggs argue in relation to elder abuse: 'Attempts to define and map the extent of elder abuse indicate that it should not be seen as a single monolithic phenomenon, but that it takes a variety of forms in different settings and in different kinds of relationships.'[9] As this quote indicates, we should be a little wary about seeking a single definition which captures all cases of abuse. First, so much depends on the context the definition is to be used in. If we are seeking to define the kind of behaviour which justifies a local authority investigation and potential intervention we would be using a very different understanding than if we were seeking to do a survey to find out how many harmful or unpleasant experiences a group of

---

[8] The definition was adopted in World Health Organization, *The Toronto Declaration on the Prevention of Elder Abuse* (WHO, 2002).

[9] C. Phillipson and S. Biggs, *Elder Abuse in Perspective* (London, Open University Press 1995), 202.

people had suffered. It may not, therefore, be helpful to identify a single definition; rather some themes about the concept can be drawn to use a definition in a particular context. With that in mind, rather than produce a single definition, it is more helpful to explore some of the markers of abuse.

First, abusive behaviour is behaviour which harms. But harm can cover physical, emotional, and financial harm. *No Secrets* usefully gives some examples of abuse:

- physical abuse: including hitting, slapping, pushing, kicking, misuse of medication, restraint or inappropriate sanctions
- sexual abuse: including rape and sexual assault or sexual acts to which the adult at risk has not consented, or could not consent or was pressured into consenting
- psychological abuse: including emotional abuse, threats of harm or abandonment, deprivation of contact, humiliation, blaming, controlling, intimidation, coercion, harassment, verbal abuse, isolation or withdrawal from services or supportive networks
- financial or material abuse: including theft, fraud, exploitation, pressure in connection with wills, property or inheritance or financial transactions or the misuse or misappropriation of property, possessions or benefits
- neglect and acts of omission: including ignoring medical or physical care needs, failure to provide access to appropriate health, social care or educational services, the withholding of the necessities of life such as medication, adequate nutrition and heating
- discriminatory abuse: including racist, sexist, that based on a person's disability, and other forms of harassment, slurs or similar treatment.[10]

Second, as already mentioned, the abuse should be understood in its relational context. Is this a single one off act or part of a series of acts which sets out to coercively control the victim? Is there a special responsibility or trust imposed by the victim?[11]

Third, we need to be aware that while abuse is often seen as the behaviour of wicked individuals, that would be an unduly narrow understanding of the concept. Loneliness, social exclusion, inadequate social facilities or support may all contribute to abuse, but not be directly the responsibility of

---

[10] Department of Health, *No Secrets: Guidance on Developing and Implementing Multi-Agency Policies and Procedures to Protect Vulnerable Adults From Abuse* (Department of Health, 2000), para. 2.

[11] M. Madden Dempsey, 'What Counts as Domestic Violence? A Conceptual Analysis', (2006) 12 *William and Mary Journal of Women and the Law* 301.

identified individuals. Further, even where there is a specific person abusing another, the act may take on added significance if it reflects wider societal attitudes towards elder people, people with learning difficulties, and others. So an assault in the street on an older person takes on added significance in a society which often puts barriers in the way of older people using public spaces. Similarly, the way that society arranges the care of adults with needs enables and to some sense causes abusive behaviour. This is not to excuse or justify the abuse, but to argue that given the way care of people with needs is approached in our society, abuse is a predictable, maybe even inevitable, result.[12] As Daniel and Bowes put it: '[I]nstead of focusing on individual vulnerability (or indeed resilience) state intervention should instead focus upon the structural factors that elevate the risks for particular groups and communities.'[13]

These three themes: the extent of the harm, the relational context, and the societal environment form a useful way of looking at adult abuse. The most serious kinds of adult domestic abuse will be those where serious harms are caused in the context of unequal relationships, reinforcing (and reinforced by) a negative social context about the individual and the group which they are identified with.

Statistics on abuse

It is only comparatively recently that data has been collected on the abuse of adults. One of the first major studies was in 2007, looking at the abuse and neglect of older people, carried out for Comic Relief and the Department of Health.[14] It found that 2.6 per cent of people aged sixty-six or over who were living in their own private household reported mistreatment involving a family member, close friend, or care worker in the past year. If the sample is an accurate reflection of the wider older population it would mean 227,000 people aged over sixty-six suffering mistreatment in a given year. The figures rise

---

[12] B. Taylor, C. Killick, M. O'Brien, E. Begley, and J. Carter-Anand, 'Older People's Conceptualization of Elder Abuse and Neglect', (2014) 26 *Journal of Elder Abuse and Neglect* 223.

[13] B. Daniel and A. Bowes, 'Re-thinking Harm and Abuse: Insights From a Lifespan Perspective', (2011) 41 *British Journal of Social Work* 820.

[14] M. O'Keeffe, A. Hills, M. Doyle, C. McCreadie, S. Scholes, R. Constantine, A. Tinker, J. Manthorpe, S. Biggs, and B. Erens, *UK Study of Abuse and Neglect of Older People Prevalence Survey Report* (Department of Health, 2008). See also A. Mowlam, R. Tennant, J. Dixon, and C. McCreadie, *UK Study of Abuse and Neglect of Older People: Qualitative Findings* (Department of Health, 2008) and C. Cooper, A. Selwood, and G. Livingston, 'The Prevalence of Elder Abuse and Neglect: A Systematic Review', (2008) 37 *Age and Ageing* 151.

if including incidents involving neighbours or acquaintances to 4 per cent or 342,400 people.[15] Three quarters of those interviewed said that the effect of mistreatment was either serious or very serious. The researchers believed these figures to be on the conservative side as they did not include care home residents in their survey and some of those most vulnerable to abuse lacked the capacity to take part. Also, even among those interviewed there may have been those who, for a variety of reasons, did not wish to disclose abuse.[16] Indeed one of the major barriers to collecting accurate statistics in this field is that some people do not acknowledge themselves as victims. As one victim of domestic abuse put it to Donovan and Hester:

> I'd never really thought of myself as a victim of domestic abuse … I don't feel like a victim, cos I think victim is very passive, allowing it to happen, although at the time I was, in that relationship. So it might be the right term for that, but it almost suggests you can't do anything about it.[17]

A recent literature review looking at evidence of elder abuse around the world concluded that 6 per cent of older people had suffered significant abuse in the past month, 5.6 per cent of older couples had experienced physical violence in their relationships, and 25 per cent of older people had suffered significant psychological abuse.[18]

The most useful set of data on vulnerable adults generally can be found in the Health and Social Care Information Centre,[19] which found that for 2013–14 there were safeguarding referrals for 104,050 people. A safeguarding referral indicates that professionals believed that an adult was suffering or was likely to suffer abuse. 60 per cent of those referred were female and 63 per cent were over the age of 65. 51 per cent had some kind of physical disability, frailty, or sensory impairment. Neglect was the most common cause of concern (30 per cent) and physical abuse close behind (27 per cent). Where the location of the abuse was known, it was the home of the adult in 42 per cent of cases and a care home in 36 per cent of cases. In 49 per cent of cases the referral indicated the source of the risk was someone known to the alleged victim, with social care employees being responsible for 36 per cent of cases. In only 15 per cent of cases was the source someone not known to the victim.

---

[15] M. O'Keeffe, A. Hills, M. Doyle, C. McCreadie, S. Scholes, R. Constantine, A. Tinker, J. Manthorpe, S. Biggs, and B. Erens, *UK Study of Abuse and Neglect of Older People Prevalence Survey Report* (Department of Health, 2008), 4.

[16] Ibid., para. 7.4.

[17] C. Donovan and M. Hester, ' "I Hate the Word Victim": An Exploration of Recognition of Domestic Violence in Same Sex Relationships', (2010) 9 *Social Policy and Society* 279, 285.

[18] C. Cooper, A. Selwood, and G. Livingston, 'Prevalence of Elder Abuse', (n. 14).

[19] Health and Social Care Information Centre, *Safeguarding Adults Return, Annual Report, England 2013–14* (HSCIC, 2014).

Statistics on those who are in need but not as a direct consequence of abuse are harder to come by. The best guide is looking at those who use social care services. For 2013–14, approaching 1.3 million older people and younger disabled and mentally ill adults used social care services in England, and 3.2 million were cared for informally, by their families and friends.[20]

Some studies have sought to produce a list of the kinds of adults most at risk of abuse. These typically include the following:

- People with learning difficulties.[21]
- People with social skill difficulties.[22]
- Old age.[23]
- Being female.[24]
- Being in receipt of, or in touch with, social services.[25]

Reports of abuse

Here I will examine some reports of abuse to give a clearer picture of what kinds of abuse are occurring. Many examples could be used and this is just a selection.

Care Quality Commission Report

Between March and June 2011 the Care Quality Commission (CQC) undertook one hundred unannounced inspections of acute NHS hospitals in England.[26] These focused on the standards of dignity and nutrition on wards caring for older people. Of the one hundred hospitals, two were found to be putting people at unacceptable risk of harm. Less than half the hospitals (forty-five) were fully compliant with the standards required for nutrition or

---

[20] T. Burchardt, P. Obolenskava, and P. Vizard, *The Coalition's Record on Adult Social Care: Policy, Spending and Outcomes 2010–2015* (LSE, 2015).

[21] C. Bruder and B. Kroese, 'The Efficacy of Interventions Designed to Prevent and Protect People with Intellectual Disabilities from Sexual Abuse: A Review of the Literature', (2005) 7 *The Journal of Adult Protection* 13.

[22] A. Hollomotz, 'Beyond Vulnerability: An Ecological Model Approach Conceptualising Risk of Sexual Violence Against People with Learning Disabilities', (2009) 39 *British Journal of Social Work* 99.

[23] N. Choi and J. Mayer, (2000) 'Elder Abuse, Neglect, and Exploitation—Risk Factors and Prevention Strategies', (2000) 33 *Journal of Gerontological Social Work* 5.

[24] M. O'Keeffe, A. Hills, M. Doyle, C. McCreadie, S. Scholes, R. Constantine, A. Tinker, J. Manthorpe, S. Biggs, and B. Erens, *UK Study of Abuse and Neglect of Older People Prevalence Survey Report* (Department of Health, 2008).

[25] Ibid.

[26] Care Quality Commission, *Dignity and Nutrition for Older People* (Care Quality Commission, 2011).

dignity. Thirty-five met the standards in both, but needed to improve on one or both. Twenty did not meet one or both standards.

The picture painted in the report was grim, particularly what the report noted about the standard of nursing care for older people. It is worth quoting from the introduction by Dame Jo Williams at length:

> Time and time again, we found cases where patients were treated by staff in a way that stripped them of their dignity and respect. People were spoken over, and not spoken to; people were left without call bells, ignored for hours on end, or not given assistance to do the basics of life—to eat, drink, or go to the toilet.
>
> Those who are responsible for the training and development of staff, particularly in nursing, need to look long and hard at why 'care' often seems to be broken down into tasks to be completed—focusing on the unit of work, rather than the person who needs to be looked after. Task-focused care is not person-centred care. It is not good enough and it is not what people want and expect. Kindness and compassion costs nothing.[27]

In fairness, it is worth quoting what Dame Williams went on to say about resources.

> … resources have a part to play. Many people told us about the wonderful nurses in their hospital, and then said how hard pressed they were to deliver care. Having plenty of staff does not guarantee good care (we saw unacceptable care on well-staffed wards, and excellent care on understaffed ones) but not having enough is a sure path to poor care. The best nurses and doctors can find themselves delivering care that falls below essential standards because they are overstretched.
>
> Staff must have the right support if they are to deliver truly compassionate care that is clinically effective. In the current economic climate this is easy to say and far harder to deliver, but as the regulator our role is to cast an independent eye over care and reflect on what we see. There are levels of under-resourcing that make poor care more likely, and those who run our hospitals must play their part in ensuring that budgets are used wisely to support front line care staff.[28]

What is particularly chilling about this report is there is little that is new here. We have known for a long time that too many older people are infantilized or ignored in hospital, that too often they fail to receive adequate hydration or nutrition, and that their dignity is not protected. In the report a long list of inappropriate conduct is listed, including:

- call bells being out of patient's reach;
- curtains not being properly closed when personal care was being given;

---

[27] Ibid., 3.   [28] Ibid., 4–5.

- staff speaking to patients in a rude or condescending manner;
- patients not being given the help to eat;
- patients being interrupted during meals and having to leave their food unfinished; and
- patients not being able to clean their hands before meals.

The report noted the following comments from patients and their relatives:

- The patient constantly called out for help and rattled the bedrail as staff passed by … We noted that 25 minutes passed before this patient received attention. When we spoke with the patient we observed that their fingernails were ragged and dirty.

- We saw a staff member taking a female patient to the toilet. The patient's clothing was above their knees and exposed their underwear. The staff member assisted them to the toilet in full view of other patients on the ward, only closing the door when they left the toilet room.

- When we spoke to one member of staff about how they managed to meet the needs of people on the ward, they said that they did not have enough time to care for patients. They said that when they are rushed they cannot always meet people's needs and some things have to be delayed as a result.

Alzheimer's Society Report

A report from the Alzheimer's Society[29] investigated the treatment of those suffering from dementia in hospital, noting that up to a quarter of hospital beds are occupied by people with dementia. The report finds a very mixed picture, with some excellent care, but also some neglectful care. The report found that:

- 47% of carer respondents said that being in hospital had a significant negative effect on the general physical health of the person with dementia, which wasn't a direct result of the medical condition.

- 77% of nurse managers and nursing staff said that antipsychotic drugs were used always or sometimes to treat people with dementia in the hospital environment.

- 77% of carer respondents were dissatisfied with the overall quality of dementia care provided.

[29] Alzheimer's Society, *Counting the Cost: Caring for People with Dementia on Hospital Wards* (Alzheimer's Society, 2009).

Centre for Policy on Aging

The Centre for Policy on Aging was commissioned to produce reviews of the literature on age discrimination in the areas of primary and community health care, social care, mental health services, and secondary health care.[30] The reports note the difficulties in ascertaining when there is discrimination. In relation to primary care the report notes:

There is evidence that older people are subject to covert, indirect discrimination. Stereotyping people on the basis of chronological age which can led to older people being excluded from treatments that are shown to be beneficial is a form of indirect discrimination ... Evidence of covert discrimination is shown in limited preventative care for older people; reluctance to refer older people to specialist services; poor quality of care for conditions associated with ageing, which includes under treatment for conditions. Covert discrimination is demonstrated in shortfalls in receipt of basic recommended care by adults aged 50 or more with common health conditions.

In relation to secondary care the report found very few instances of explicit policy based age discrimination, but noted it was difficult to assess the extent to which there might be indirect discrimination as a result of subconscious ageist attitudes on behalf of staff. The report notes that older patients are less likely than middle-aged ones to describe their care as excellent and that older people are most likely to report 'being talked over as if they weren't there'. The report also found some evidence that policies concerning mixed sex wards and food provision operate particularly harshly for older people. Older patients are less likely to be referred for surgical interventions for cancer, heart disease, and stroke, although that could be explained on the basis of an assessment of chances of survival. The report's conclusion on cancer was that:

Evidence of the under-investigation and under-treatment of older people in cancer care, cardiology and stroke is so widespread and strong that, even taking into account confounding factors such as frailty, co-morbidity and polypharmacy we must conclude that ageist attitudes are having an effect on overall investigation and treatment levels.[31]

Mid Staffordshire

In 2010 and 2013 the Francis Reports into the treatment of patients at Stafford hospital, a relatively small hospital in Staffordshire, produced

---

[30] Centre for Policy on Aging, *Age Discrimination* (CPA, 2015).
[31] Ibid., para. 11.2.

shockwaves.[32] It found that between January 2005 and March 2009 between 400 and 1,200 patients had died as a result of poor care. The report concluded that 'For many patients the most basic elements of care were neglected.' It found that 'The standards of hygiene were at times awful, with families forced to remove used bandages and dressings from public areas and clean toilets themselves for fear of catching infections.' The first inquiry heard harrowing personal stories from patients and patients' families about the appalling care received at the Trust. On many occasions, the accounts received related to basic elements of care and the quality of the patient experience. These included cases where:

- Patients were left in excrement in soiled bed clothes for lengthy periods.
- Assistance was not provided with feeding for patients who could not eat without help.
- Water was left out of reach.
- In spite of persistent requests for help, patients were not assisted in their toileting.
- Wards and toilet facilities were left in a filthy condition.
- Privacy and dignity, even in death, were denied.
- Triage in A&E was undertaken by untrained staff.
- Staff treated patients and those close to them with what appeared to be callous indifference.

These failures could not be put down to the acts of isolated individuals and the causes of the problems were complex. The report found they included:

- A culture focused on doing the system's business—not that of the patients.
- An institutional culture which ascribed more weight to positive information about the service than to information capable of implying cause for concern.
- Standards and methods of measuring compliance which did not focus on the effect of a service on patients.
- Too great a degree of tolerance of poor standards and of risk to patients.
- A failure of communication between the many agencies to share their knowledge of concerns.

[32] R. Francis, *The Final Report of the Mid Staffordshire NHS Foundation Trust Public Inquiry* (Department of Health, 2013); R. Francis, *Report of the Mid-Staffordshire NHS Foundation Trust Public Inquiry* (Department of Health, 2011).

- Assumptions that monitoring, performance management, or intervention were the responsibility of someone else.
- A failure to tackle challenges to the building up of a positive culture, in nursing in particular but also within the medical profession.
- A failure to appreciate until recently the risk of disruptive loss of corporate memory and focus resulting from repeated, multi-level reorganization.

Deaths of people with learning difficulties

A study in 2013[33] looked at the deaths of people with learning difficulties in the South West, focusing on 233 adults and fourteen children. It was found that in 20 per cent of cases there had previously been safeguarding concerns raised. The report found that in 37 per cent of cases deaths could have been avoided had good quality intervention been provided. The report found: 'People with learning disabilities had a considerable burden of ill-health at the time of their death. Key issues that appeared to be problematic were the lack of coordination of care across and between the different disease pathways and service providers, and the episodic nature of care provision.'[34]

Some general themes

Turning to how the public law has responded to the issues raised by vulnerable adults, it is helpful to explore some of the general themes of policy which emerge, before discussing the more detailed legal provisions.

Terminology: From abuse to vulnerability to wellbeing

How are we to define the group of people who are in need of particular intervention? In 2000, *No Secrets* stated that the focus of state protection was on vulnerable adults and ensuring their protection from abuse. The primary approach is set out in the opening paragraphs of that report:

1.1 In recent years several serious incidents have demonstrated the need for immediate action to ensure that vulnerable adults, who are at risk of abuse, receive

---

[33] P Heslop et al., *Confidential Inquiry into Premature Deaths of People with Learning Disabilities Final Report* (University of Bath 2013).
[34] Ibid., 6.

protection and support. The Government gives a high priority to such action and sees local statutory agencies and other relevant agencies as important partners in ensuring such action is taken
wherever needed . . .

1.2. The aim should be to create a framework for action within which all responsible agencies work together to ensure a coherent policy for the protection of vulnerable adults at risk of abuse and a consistent and effective response to any circumstances giving ground for concern or formal complaints or expressions of anxiety. The agencies' primary aim should be to prevent abuse where possible but, if the preventive strategy fails, agencies should ensure that robust procedures are in place for dealing with incidents of abuse . . .

Paragraph 2.3 defined a vulnerable adult as a person 'who is or may be in need of community care services by reason of mental or other disability, age or illness; and who is or may be unable to take care of him or herself, or unable to protect him or herself against significant harm or exploitation'. In *Safeguarding Adults* in 2005[35] the government sought to shift the focus away from the language of vulnerability. The Law Commission had expressed concern that the term vulnerable adult was 'stigmatising, dated, negative and disempowering'.[36] People may be deterred from seeking assistance if they reject the label. The focus instead was on risks to independence. This sees independence as the norm and the role of the state to enable independence. The report sees safeguarding adults as 'all work which enables an adult "who is or may be eligible for community care services" to retain independence, wellbeing and choice and to access their human right to live a life that is free from abuse and neglect'.[37] The report explains that vulnerability 'can be misunderstood, because it seems to locate the cause of abuse with the victim, rather than in placing responsibility with the actions or omissions of others'.[38] While there are welcome aspects of this approach, particularly in its acknowledgement of social provision as generating vulnerability, there are two major grounds for concern. First, there is the focus on independence as a goal. As argued in Chapter 2, I do not think that is a desirable or realistic goal for anyone. Second, the grouping together of abuse and anything that restricts independence is in danger of downplaying the wrongfulness of abuse. Indeed there is a danger that the concept becomes so watered down as to become meaningless.

[35] Association of Directors of Social Services, *Safeguarding Adults* (Association of Directors of Social Services, 2005).
[36] Law Commission, *Adult Social Care, Report 326* (Law Commission, 2010), para. 9.24.
[37] Ibid.   [38] Ibid.

The 2005 approach to safeguarding has been amended again in the 2014 Care Act. The Statutory Guidance for the Care Act 2014[39] explains the Act is focussed on those who need care and support:

The core purpose of adult care and support is to help people to achieve the outcomes that matter to them in their life ... The wellbeing principle applies in all cases where a local authority is carrying out a care and support function, or making a decision, in relation to a person. For this reason it is referred to throughout this guidance. It applies equally to adults with care and support needs and their carers.

It is noticeable here that the language is not of vulnerability, nor primarily in terms of protection nor even independence. Rather the focus is on wellbeing: assisting a person to achieve the outcomes that matter to them. Quite what that means will be discussed later in this chapter. The difficulty with this approach is that it uses as its descriptor 'those who need care and support' terminology that looks like a conclusion, rather than a definition. How do we know who needs care and support to achieve their goals? Perhaps the answer to that is, as suggested in Chapter 2, everyone.

The source of vulnerability

Dunn, Holland, and Clare[40] have emphasized the difference between inherent and situational vulnerability. They explain the difference in this distinction:

[A]dults are at risk of harm if they have a disability, illness, or are of an age which limits their ability to safeguard their own welfare, *and* their life circumstances render them at an identifiable and increased risk of being abused. Understanding adults' risk of being abused with reference to their inherent vulnerability alone would be discriminatory, whereas only taking situational factors into account, without an inherent vulnerability threshold, would mean that adult safeguarding would be potentially infinite in scope and application, and likely to conflict with other legislation designed to protect adults at risk of, for example, domestic violence (*Domestic Violence, Crime and Victims Act 2004*) or forced marriage (*Forced Marriage (Civil Protection) Act 2007*).

This is a helpful distinction in some respects. Identifying whether the source of the risk is due to factors inherent in the individual or from the factors outside of them will be important in determining the correct response to their situation. Obviously if the risks have external causes it may be easier for intervention to tackle them. The approach does have drawbacks, however. Some

---

[39] Department of Health, *Care Act 2014: Statutory Guidance* (Department of Health, 2014).
[40] M. Dunn, A. Holland, and I. Clare, 'The Duty to Safeguard Adults From Abuse', (2009) 8 *Psychiatry* 484.

inherent factors only become the cause of a risk in certain circumstances. Or, putting it the other way round, some situations are only threatening to some because of their internal features. This is just to say the distinction should not be seen as a watertight one.

Personalization

A key theme in modern approaches to adult care has been the move towards personalization. The focus should be on the goals and wishes of the individual (P). P should be involved in determining what their goals are and be helped to achieve them.

At first sight that seems to be a very sensible approach. Who else better to decide what is in P's best interests than P themselves. It avoids the state or another person determining how people should live their lives. P will know which kinds of services benefit them and which do not. However, personalization is not without its problems.

The problems and benefits of personalization are well illustrated by the issue of personal budgets. These are pots of money given to people who have care needs. The idea is that P will use them to purchase the services they need. They are put in control of their care provision.[41] The Guidance for the Care Act 2014 cites research it says shows that, if implemented well, personal budgets can provide better care and value for money.[42] Although personal budgets have been used for a while, the Care Act puts personal budgets into legalization for the first time and makes 'them the norm for people with care and support needs'.[43] The Guidance states it will provide great choice and allow people to 'take control' over how their needs are met. This might include how often they receive the care (some people might, for example, prefer a smaller number of longer visits), or when they receive visits (if they need care at particular times they can contract to ensure that occurs), who provides the care (they may select people known to them), or ensure care meets personal preferences (e.g. that they are provided by a religious organization). Most importantly they can control the kind of care they receive.

The personal budget will give clear guidance as to how much money has been allocated to meet identified needs. The budget will be based on the care and support plan that is drawn up with P's involvement and indeed 'it should be made clear that the plan "belongs" to the person it is intended for, with the

---

[41] H. Carr and C. Hunter, 'Are Judicial Approaches to Adult Social Care at a Dead-end? Care as a Problem Space', (2012) 21 *Social and Legal Studies* 73.

[42] C. Glendinning et al., *Evaluation of the Individual Budgets Pilot Programme* (IBSEN, 2008).

[43] *Care Act 2014: Statutory Guidance*, (n. 39), para. 11.2.

local authority role to ensure the production and sign-off of the plan to ensure that it is appropriate to meet the identified needs'.[44] P can determine what set of services will best meet their needs, who would be the best provider of those services, and the details about when and how the services should be provided.

The example given in the Code is that 'the personal budget should not assume that people are forced to accept specific care options, such as moving into care homes, against their will because this is perceived to be the cheapest option'.[45] The budget must set out what is sufficient to meet the person's care and support needs.[46] It may be that some needs will be met through the budget and other needs through local authority provision.

There are three main ways in which a personal budget can be deployed:

- as a managed account held by the local authority with support provided in line with the person's wishes;
- as a managed account held by a third party (often called an individual service fund or ISF) with support provided in line with the person's wishes; and
- as a direct payment.

Generally needs will be met through services, but in some cases needs might be met by putting an individual in touch with a voluntary sector organization. Certain services are not provided and indeed must not be provided, such as health services provided by the NHS or Housing Act 1996.

There are however concerns. One is that it assumes that P is best placed to determine what their needs are and how they are best met. However, it is common for people to hide from their weaknesses and be overly optimistic. Is P really in a position to understand the market for care services and know which provider to select? For some with care needs, arranging their own care needs may be stressful and complex. Are those with care needs well placed to follow matters up with providers if the care is inadequate?

There is also a danger that P may not be able to find service providers to meet their needs using their budget, in which case the state might seek to lay the blame for the failure to meet the needs of individuals at their own feet. If they have chosen to spend their budget in a particular way or have identified different goals from those others would have chosen, they cannot complain about the gap in services. Further, there is evidence that some people find it highly stressful having the responsibility of organizing their own budget.[47] Mandelstam[48]

---

[44] Ibid., para. 10.2.   [45] Ibid., para. 11.7.   [46] Ibid., para. 11.10.

[47] C. Glendinning, *Evaluation of the Individual Budgets Pilot Programme: Final Report* (York, University of York 2008).

[48] M. Mandelstam, *Safeguarding Vulnerable Adults and the Law* (York, Jessica Kingsley 2009), 54.

suggests individuals may be overwhelmed at the task of arranging their care and at increased risk, stating 'there may, however, be a tension between this notion of people as active consumers of social care services and safeguarding adults'.

Janet Leece is concerned that personal budgets are part of a broader picture with 'social care provision is treated progressively as a commodity to be bought and sold'.[49] Indeed other provisions in the legislation show an open acknowledgement of this marketization. Section 5 deals with market shaping and commissioning. It puts a duty on a local authority to achieve a vibrant, responsive market of service providers. Sections 19 and 48–57 provide detailed guidance on the responsibilities of local authorities where there is a business failure impacting on the provision of services. These provisions reflect the fact that although social care is the responsibility of local authorities, 'few … are now involved in the direct delivery of care and support services', with most services operated by private providers.[50]

Personalization can have benefits in relation to adult safeguarding too. As one recent report noted, 'people are more likely to maintain a safer life if they have been involved in a safeguarding process and empowered to take measures to protect themselves'[51] than if the safeguarding solution is imposed upon them.[52] Sir James Munby captured this approach well:

What does all this mean? It surely requires that in all our dealings with the vulnerable or incapacitated we must show our respect for them as a human being, as a unique individual, requiring of us understanding, empathy and compassion. Moreover, any attempt to control is likely to be nothing but counter-productive when it comes to a local authority 'working together', as it must, with family carers.[53]

One benefit from the move away from the language of vulnerability in this context is that it encourages people to focus on the things they can do, rather than the things they cannot.[54] So rather than the focus of the intervention being negative (what are the risks that P faces and how can we mitigate them?), the focus becomes: what would P like to do with their life and how can we help them achieve that. This might help remove the stigma that some people see as attached to vulnerability and put P in control of their life. The

---

[49] J. Leece, 'Money Talks, But What Does it Say? Direct Payments and the Commodification of Care', (2004) 16 *Practice: Social Work in Action* 211.

[50] D. Kelly, 'Editorial: Reflecting on the Implications of the Care Act 2014 for Care Providers', (2013) 7 *Journal of Care Services Management* 74, at 74.

[51] Local Government Association, *Making Safeguarding Personal 2013/14* (LGA, 2014).

[52] Ibid.

[53] J. Munby, 'Safeguarding, Capacity and the Law'; speech to Local Government Association, 2013.

[54] B. Fawcett, 'Vulnerability Questioning the Certainties in Social Work and Health', (2009) 52 *International Social Work* 473.

danger, however, is that it can overlook the impact on P's understanding of their well-being of the abuse. This is particularly so where P is currently living in an abusive relationship.

An overview of the Care Act 2014

The Department of Health explains that the Care Act 2014 'creates a single, consistent route to establishing an entitlement to public care and support for all adults with [relevant] needs'.[55] While the Act seeks to prevent or delay care and support needs arising in the first place,[56] it is clear that is not always possible.[57] At the heart of the Care Act 2014 are two principles: the well-being principle[58] and the aim of 'putting people and their carers in control of their care and support'.[59] However, as we shall see, a degree of vagueness surrounds both these principles; for example, there is no set standard of well-being to which the legislation aspires.[60] The statutory guidance explains that the apparent vagueness is a reflection that the Act is designed to let people decide for themselves what they need. This is reinforced by the fact the Act puts personal budgets on a statutory footing for the first time.[61] Despite these grand principles it should be noted that the government has admitted that the well-being principle is 'designed to set out the overarching purpose of care and support into which specific duties … fit, rather than require a[n] [local authority] to undertake any particular action in … itself'.[62] The well-being principle, at the heart of the Act, is more about changing attitudes than creating legally enforceable duties. Another major theme in the Care Act 2014 is that it sets out a clear legal framework for how local authorities and other parts of the system should protect adults at risk of abuse or neglect.[63] We shall now look at some of the specific aspects of the Act in more detail.

---

[55] Department of Health, *Factsheet 2* (Department of Health, 2014), 1.

[56] Care Act 2014, s. 2.

[57] D. Kelly, 'Reflecting on the Implications of the Care Act 2014 for Care Providers', (2013) 7 *Journal of Care Services Management* 74, at 74.

[58] Department of Health, *Care Act 2014: How Should Local Authorities Deliver the Care and Support Reforms? Please Give Us Your Views: Wellbeing* (Department of Health, 2014).

[59] Ibid.

[60] C. Slasberg and P. Beresford, 'Government Guidance for the Care Act: Undermining Ambitions for Change?', (2014) 29 *Disability & Society* 1677.

[61] Care Act 2014, s. 26; See, generally, C. Needham and J. Glasby, *Debates in Personalisation* (Bristol, Policy Press 2014).

[62] Department of Health, *Response to the Consultation on Draft Regulations and Guidance* (Department of Health 2014), 11.

[63] Care Act 2014, ss 42–7.

The well-being principle

The Care Act 2014, s. 1 sets out the general duty to promote the well-being of people. Sub-section (2) sets out factors to consider:

(2) 'Well-being', in relation to an individual, means that individual's well-being so far as relating to any of the following—
   (a) personal dignity (including treatment of the individual with respect);
   (b) physical and mental health and emotional well-being;
   (c) protection from abuse and neglect;
   (d) control by the individual over day-to-day life (including over care and support, or support, provided to the individual and the way in which it is provided);
   (e) participation in work, education, training or recreation;
   (f) social and economic well-being;
   (g) domestic, family and personal relationships;
   (h) suitability of living accommodation;
   (i) the individual's contribution to society.
(3) In exercising a function under this Part in the case of an individual, a local authority must have regard to the following matters in particular—
   (a) the importance of beginning with the assumption that the individual is best-placed to judge the individual's well-being;
   (b) the individual's views, wishes, feelings and beliefs;
   (c) the importance of preventing or delaying the development of needs for care and support or needs for support and the importance of reducing needs of either kind that already exist;
   (d) the need to ensure that decisions about the individual are made having regard to all the individual's circumstances (and are not based only on the individual's age or appearance or any condition of the individual's or aspect of the individual's behaviour which might lead others to make unjustified assumptions about the individual's well-being);
   (e) the importance of the individual participating as fully as possible in decisions relating to the exercise of the function concerned and being provided with the information and support necessary to enable the individual to participate;
   (f) the importance of achieving a balance between the individual's well-being and that of any friends or relatives who are involved in caring for the individual;
   (g) the need to protect people from abuse and neglect;
   (h) the need to ensure that any restriction on the individual's rights or freedom of action that is involved in the exercise of the function is kept to the minimum necessary for achieving the purpose for which the function is being exercised.

This opening section of the statute indicates the emphasis on care services being about the promotion of well-being. That concept involves consideration of a range of factors listed in the legislation:

The individual aspects of wellbeing or outcomes above are those which are set out in the Care Act, and are most relevant to people with care and support needs and carers. There is no hierarchy, and all should be considered of equal importance when considering 'wellbeing' in the round.[64]

The Department of Health guidance states 'the language used in the Act is intended to be clearer, and focus on the outcomes that truly matter to people, rather than using the relatively abstract term "independent living"'.[65] That is because authorities should start 'with the assumption that the individual is best-placed to judge the individual's wellbeing'.[66] However, the statutory definition reveals the tensions between protecting well-being as objectively understood and well-being as understood by the individuals. The Code of Practice issued with the Act is helpful. It states in the opening paragraph:

The core purpose of adult care and support is to help people to achieve the outcomes that matter to them in their life. Throughout this guidance document, the different chapters set out how a local authority should go about performing its care and support responsibilities. Underpinning all of these individual 'care and support functions' (that is, any process, activity or broader responsibility that the local authority performs) is the need to ensure that doing so focuses on the needs and goals of the person concerned.

Despite the suggestion there that it is P's views about their well-being which are paramount, the Guidance goes on to say that at the end of the day the council will have to be 'satisfied that the individual's self-assessment has accurately captured their needs' (para. 6.58). This might be caricatured as saying 'you can decide your care needs as long as you decide in the way we think'.

That is perhaps a little unfair. The Act and Guidance does seem to create at least a presumption that the individual should set the agenda, set out their own goal for well-being, and determine what needs they have. The council does have the power to override that, but it seems only if there is good reason to doubt it. That seems entirely appropriate. It could not be that the legislation required councils to fund clearly inappropriate care packages. The council in making that determination should remember 'an assessment must be person centred, involving the individual'.[67] This is not inconsistent with giving the council the power to determine needs. The concern is that the

---

[64] *Care Act 2014: How Should Local Authorities Deliver,* (n. 58).   [65] Ibid., 1.18.
[66] Ibid., 1.13.   [67] *Care Act 2014: Statutory Guidance,* (n. 39), para. 6.7.

emphasis in the legislation and some of the rhetoric surrounding the Act will give the false impression that P and P only gets to determine what services they need.

The best reading of the Act, I suggest, is that it takes a middle path between taking an objective and subjective understanding of well-being. P selects the goals (the 'outcomes that matter to them') but the local authority seeks to provide them with what they need. This gives some scope for a local authority to depart from P's decision if they do not think that, in fact, it will promote their goals. P may believe, for example, that eating lots of pizza will improve their depression, but the council is entitled to determine that would be an improper way to achieve their goal. However, it leaves little room for a local authority to determine that P's goals are inappropriate. So, P may conclude they wish to leave an independent life. Even if the authority determines that P cannot live alone they should be seeking to provide as independent a life as possible within a residential care setting.

Similarly, I would suggest, the wording in the legislation gives the authority room to determine that P is not representing their own goals, but the views of others who have dominance over them. If P is merely repeating the views of a person who dominates, those will not be P's views and so the authority is not required to respect them.

Finally it is important to note that included in the notion of well-being is the 'need to protect people from abuse and neglect' and that will surely carry considerable weight, whatever P's views. The legislation seems to assume, correctly I suggest, that P will never conceive of being abused and neglected as an aspect of their well-being. That is not to say P may determine that they would rather remain in an abusive relationship, as the alternative is even worse. However, in deciding what to do in a case where P is facing abuse but does not want protection, proportionality is key. It is well worth recalling the views of Munby J in *Local Authority X v MM*:[68]

The emphasis must be on sensible risk appraisal, not striving to avoid all risk, whatever the price, but instead seeking a proper balance and being willing to tolerate manageable or acceptable risks the price appropriately to be paid in order to achieve some other good—in particular to achieve the vital good of the elderly or vulnerable person's happiness. What good is it making someone safer if it merely makes them miserable.[69]

The well-being principle in the Act is designed to encourage councils to see their work as a shift away from providing 'services' and towards promoting

---

[68] [2007] EWHC 2003 (Fam).
[69] *Care Act 2014: Statutory Guidance*, (n. 39), para. 102.

well-being. There are a number of benefits behind this approach. First, it promotes a more tailored approach. Rather than the local authority understanding its role as providing services and the question then being which of its packages it should give to a person, the approach now starts with the needs and goals of the individual and asking what will help achieve these. These may, or may not, involve the kind of services traditionally offered by a council. Helping someone attend the matches of their favourite football team may do more to promote their well-being than enabling them to attend a day centre, for example. Second, the well-being approach emphasizes a shift in power. As already mentioned, the services are not determined by the local authority and provided to P. Instead, P's goals and wishes are to be the starting point. The person is involved in assessing their own needs and deciding what will help achieve them. 'Co-production'[70] is mentioned in the Code as an important principle: 'an individual influences the support and services received, or when groups of people get together to influence the way that services are designed, commissioned and delivered'. Third, it correctly identifies the goal of the local authority as the meeting of needs rather than the provision of good services. A service which is well provided but does not meet the needs of the individual is hardly a success. Fourth, it emphasizes that well-being should not be seen simply as a matter of physical health. The term is wide enough to include emotional, spiritual, social, and relational welfare.

The well-being approach can be justified in terms of some of the points about vulnerability in Chapter 2. It acknowledges that both providers of services and receivers are vulnerable and it is wrong to assume there is a strong party who has wisdom over the other party. It encourages a relational approach where the authority and P work together to determine what will work between them. Allowing P a degree of choice over services through personal budgets can encourage them to form relationships with others, which include enabling financial recognition to those who have been giving care without payment (although there are restrictions on who can be paid under personal budgets).

However, there are also some concerns about the emphasis on well-being from a vulnerability perspective. One is that the concept could be considered in a highly individualistic way, with the interests of P being considered in isolation from the network of relationships within which they live. The Guidance indicates that is not supposed to happen: 'People should be considered in the context of their families and support networks, not just as isolated individuals with needs. Local authorities should take into account the

---

[70] Ibid., para. 2.21.

impact of an individual's need on those who support them, and take steps to help others access information or support.'[71] Nevertheless, this might not go far enough. It seems to imply that while the interests of others can be taken into account the interests of P are still the primary focus. This is short of the focus on relationships advocated in Chapter 2.

There is also a danger that, with all the emphasis on involving P in the decision making, those who do not want to be involved or cannot be involved in the decision making will be side-lined. Or perhaps worse, they will be pressurized into being involved in the process against their will, or give views which do not genuinely reflect their wishes. Subsection 2(3) emphasizes the importance of listening to P's views and it is suggested that should include the possibility that P has no views or wants other people to make decisions on their behalf.

Independent living

One phrase that used to play an important role in this area, but is not mentioned in the legislation, is the concept of 'independent living'.[72] However, the Code suggests that independent living is 'a core part of the wellbeing principle'.[73] It argues that by referring to an 'individual's control of their day-to-day life, suitability of living accommodation, contribution to society' and considering a person's views, wishes, and feelings, the 'key components of independent living' are included.

I would question the Code's suggestion that 'supporting people to live as independently as possible, for as long as possible, is a guiding principle of the Care Act'. This is not what the Act says. The Act certainly suggests that for someone who wishes to live independently, where that would promote their dignity and meet their needs, then we should allow them to do so. However, it would be wrong to suggest that we should assume that to be a goal or a need for everyone. Indeed I would question why it is assumed that independent living is seen as a good in and of itself. Many people do not choose to live independently but in families or with friends. Few students I teach choose when seeking accommodation to live 'independently'. They prefer an environment with friends where they can share resources or receive emotional and financial support. Independent living should only be seen as a goal for those who seek it.

---

[71] Ibid., para. 1.14.
[72] The idea that a person should be able to live without the assistance of others.
[73] Ibid., para. 1.18.

The Code[74] also talks about the importance of 'supporting people to live as independently as possible for as long as possible'. Again it is not clear that this is provided for in the legislation. I am not saying that in many cases that is not an appropriate goal; the point of the legislation is to work with P to determine what will promote well-being for them. That may, or may not, involve independence.

Prevention

Section 2 of the Care Act 2014 in the first two subsections deals with preventing needs arising:

(1) A local authority must provide or arrange for the provision of services, facilities or resources, or take other steps, which it considers will—
    (a) contribute towards preventing or delaying the development by adults in its area of needs for care and support;
    (b) contribute towards preventing or delaying the development by carers in its area of needs for support;
    (c) reduce the needs for care and support of adults in its area;
    (d) reduce the needs for support of carers in its area.
(2) In performing that duty, a local authority must have regard to—
    (a) the importance of identifying services, facilities and resources already available in the authority's area and the extent to which the authority could involve or make use of them in performing that duty;
    (b) the importance of identifying adults in the authority's area with needs for care and support which are not being met (by the authority or otherwise);
    (c) the importance of identifying carers in the authority's area with needs for support which are not being met (by the authority or otherwise).

This is an important set of provisions which is designed to ensure that the Act is not only about responding to crises, but also seeks to avoid crises arising. The Act deliberately does not limit the kinds of interventions available, but rather focuses on the aims of any intervention.

The Code suggests that prevention can be seen as primary, secondary, or tertiary.[75] Primary prevention is designed at individuals who have no current needs. These tend to be services available to everyone, and include providing access to information, developing safe neighbourhoods, promoting health lifestyles, and the like. A specific example is s. 4 of the Care Act which requires local authorities to establish and maintain information and advice services for care and support for all people in their area. The aim is to enable

---

[74] Ibid., para. 1.20.   [75] Ibid., para. 2.6 et seq.

people, carers, and families to make informed choices about the care and how it can be funded. This helps prevent or delay the need for care.

Secondary intervention is aimed at those who 'who have an increased risk of developing needs'.[76] These might be designed to prevent a person who is seen as in danger of 'tipping into crisis'. This might include, for example, those living in the community with mental health issues, who are currently able to cope, but need support to ensure they continue to do so. The Code suggests ensuring that these interventions can be used to support carers, who may themselves be at risk of developing a need for care.

Tertiary prevention is directed at a person who has identified needs and is designed to limit or reduce them. They are typically directed at people with progressive conditions or seek to rehabilitate people with impairments.[77]

Core duties to assess

One of the aims of the Care Act 2014 was to set out clearly the duties of a local authority in relation to the assessment of needs for people and whether they were eligible for publicly funded care. The Act makes it clear that the assessment must be provided for all who appear to require care and support, even where it seems unlikely they will be entitled to state-funded care. The Guidance explains:

The aim of the assessment is to identify what needs the person may have and what outcomes they are looking to achieve to maintain or improve their wellbeing. The outcome of the assessment is to provide a full picture of the individual's needs so that a local authority can provide an appropriate response at the right time to meet the level of the person's needs.[78]

Section 9 of the Care Act 2014 sets out the core duty to assess an adult with support needs:

(1) Where it appears to a local authority that an adult may have needs for care and support, the authority must assess—
    (a) whether the adult does have needs for care and support, and
    (b) if the adult does, what those needs are.
(2) An assessment under subsection (1) is referred to in this Part as a 'needs assessment'.

---

[76] Ibid., para. 2.7.
[77] A. Faulkner and A. Sweeney, *Prevention in Adult Safeguarding: A Review of the Literature* (SCIE, 2014).
[78] Ibid., para. 6.

(3) The duty to carry out a needs assessment applies regardless of the authority's view of—
  (a) the level of the adult's needs for care and support, or
  (b) the level of the adult's financial resources.
(4) A needs assessment must include an assessment of—
  (a) the impact of the adult's needs for care and support on the matters specified in section 1(2),
  (b) the outcomes that the adult wishes to achieve in day-to-day life, and
  (c) whether, and if so to what extent, the provision of care and support could contribute to the achievement of those outcomes.
(5) A local authority, in carrying out a needs assessment, must involve—
  (a) the adult,
  (b) any carer that the adult has, and
  (c) any person whom the adult asks the authority to involve or, where the adult lacks capacity to ask the authority to do that, any person who appears to the authority to be interested in the adult's welfare.
(6) When carrying out a needs assessment, a local authority must also consider—
  (a) whether, and if so to what extent, matters other than the provision of care and support could contribute to the achievement of the outcomes that the adult wishes to achieve in day-to-day life, and
  (b) whether the adult would benefit from the provision of anything under section 2 or 4 or of anything which might be available in the community.
(7) This section is subject to section 11(1) to (4) (refusal by adult of assessment).

Section 10 makes a similar provision for assessments of carers. This assessment 'must seek to establish not only the carer's needs for support, but also the sustainability of the caring role itself, which includes both the practical and emotional support the carer provides to the adult'.[79]

In line with the well-being principle, the assessment must focus on P's needs and the impact of their needs on their wellbeing. P and their carer or a person nominated by P can be involved in the assessment. It may be appropriate for P to have access to an independent advocate. The assessment may involve face-to-face interviews[80] but the Code suggests that in some cases there could be online or phone assessments or even a degree of self-assessment. The aim is it to be flexible and respond to P's needs.

The assessment will be performed by a social worker or other appropriately trained assessor.[81] Its focus should be on whether P is able to meet their goals and needs. This will involve practical questions such as whether P needs help getting dressed, whether they feel lonely and would like to meet people, and whether they need help getting to work.[82] However, it

---

[79] Ibid., para. 6.18.   [80] Ibid., para. 6.2.
[81] Department of Health, *Care Act 2014: Factsheet* (Department of Health, 2014), 1.
[82] Ibid.

will also involve broader questions about what things P enjoys doing, what their goals are in life, and what they would like to be able to do that they currently cannot. The extent of the investigation into a person's life should be proportionate to the concerns about their case. An intrusive assessment may not be appropriate if there are only a few minor concerns about an individual or they have a clearly identifiable need. Having considered their needs, the focus will be on the extent to which the needs can be met by public care and support.

As Tim Spencer-Lane explains, it is '[o]nly once needs have been identified should they be evaluated against an eligibility framework and a decision made about whether the person is entitled to care and support'.[83] This is a rejection of the view under the old law expressed by Lord Brown in *R (McDonald) v Kensington and Chelsea Royal London Borough Council* that resources were relevant to the needs assessment.[84] As Spencer-Lane emphasizes, the new cap on care costs may well mean that 'people and their families will have a significant economic interest in establishing that they have eligible needs [by requesting an assessment] because that is when the meter starts ticking for … free care and support'.[85] Hence there may well be a significant increase in those seeking an assessment.[86]

Refusal to be assessed

It is important to appreciate that the duty to assess can arise even if there is not a specific request from P. In any case where a local authority is aware of potential or actual abuse or neglect of a person who may have care and support needs then the assessment duties will be triggered. Less straightforward are cases where P refuses to be assessed. Section 11(1) states that if P refuses an assessment 'the local authority is not required to carry out the assessment' unless the case falls in to one of two scenarios set out in subs. (2). The first of those is that P lacks capacity to refuse and the assessment would be in P's best interests. The second is that P 'is at risk of abuse or neglect'.

No doubt in cases where P is refusing to consent the assessment and supplying of care becomes harder, but this statutory provision is important. The very worst cases of abuse may well be those where the individual does not recognize the need for assessment. There is ample literature on domestic abuse which highlights the ways that the perpetrator so dominates the victim that

---

[83] T. Spencer-Lane, *Care Act Manual* (London, Sweet and Maxwell 2014), [1-100].
[84] [2011] UKSC 33, para. 8.   [85] T. Spencer-Lane, (n. 83), [1-093].
[86] *Care Act 2014: Statutory Guidance*, (n. 39), paras. 23, 43.

the victim comes to accept that their treatment is appropriate and in fact their own fault.[87]

But what if P is refusing to consent to the assessment, but neither of the conditions in s. 11(2) applies? The statute simply says that authority is not required to perform the assessment. That seems to imply that the authority may, if it wishes, perform the assessment. That said, it is worth remembering that the exception that covers those 'at risk of experiencing abuse or neglect' is potentially very broad. Indeed it might be suggested that everyone falls within that group. The question of whether an assessment should be made of a person without their consent who does not fall into s. 11(2) is therefore very unlikely to arise.

Eligibility

The eligibility criteria set out a minimum threshold for the care and support needs that local authorities must meet. These are found in the Care and Support (Eligibility Criteria) Regulations 2015.[88] The Code summarizes the three cases where needs must be met:

- The adult's needs arise from or are related to a physical or mental impairment or illness.

- As a result of the adult's needs the adult is unable to achieve two or more of the specified outcomes.[89]

- As a consequence of being unable to achieve these outcomes there is, or there is likely to be, a significant impact on the adult's wellbeing.

If the assessment finds no eligible needs then the local authority should provide information and advice on what can be done to meet or reduce needs. This might be through support in the community. Just because needs are found does not mean that the local authority must meet them. The local authority must discuss this with the individual and:

[a]gree with the adult which of their needs they would like the local authority to meet. The person may not wish to have support in relation to all their

---

[87] J. Herring, 'The Serious Wrong of Domestic Abuse and the Loss of Control Defence' in A. Reed and M. Bohlander (eds), *Loss of Control and Diminished Responsibility* (Aldershot, Ashgate 2011).

[88] SI 2015/313.

[89] They are: managing and maintaining nutrition, maintaining personal hygiene, being appropriately clothed, developing and maintaining family/other personal relationships, being able to make use of the home safely, maintaining a habitable home environment, accessing and engaging in work, training, education, or volunteering, 'making use of necessary facilities or services ... including public transport, and recreational facilities or services', and carrying out caring responsibilities for a child.

needs—they may, for example, intend to arrange alternative services themselves to meet some needs. Others may not wish for the local authority to meet any of their needs, but approach the authority only for the purposes of determining eligible needs.

An authority can choose to meet non-eligible needs, although given the straitened financial situation of most local authorities that will be rare.[90]

In exceptional cases a Human Rights Act claim may be available against a local authority who refuses to meet care needs. The leading case is the case of *R (McDonald) v Kensington and Chelsea*.[91] Elaine McDonald had a severe stroke and was unable to get to a commode in the night without the help of a carer. She had a bladder condition which required her to urinate several times a night. She was initially assessed under s. 47 of the National Health Service and Community Care Act 1990[92] by the local authority and carers were provided so she could reach the commode. The authority later decided she should use incontinence pads and absorbent bedding and withdrew the carers. The authority accepted this was proposed primarily to save the cost of providing the carers (some £22,000 pa). Ms McDonald argued the proposal was 'an intolerable affront to her dignity'.[93] Her claim that her Article 8 rights were improperly infringed was rejected in the Supreme Court and largely by the European Court of Human Rights.

In the Supreme Court it was accepted by the majority that '[t]here is no dispute that in principle [Article 8] can impose a positive obligation on a state ... to provide support [or] that the provision of home-based community care falls within the scope of the article'.[94] However, that was only if there was 'a direct and immediate link between the measures sought ... and [her] private life'[95] and 'a special link between the situation complained of and the particular needs of [her] private life'.[96] This was not shown in this case. Even if it had been present there was a wide margin of appreciation for local authorities, who were balancing budgets, and the needs of others to limit resources could be used to justify any breach of another's Article 8 rights.

---

[90] Care Act 2014, s. 19.

[91] *R (McDonald) v Kensington and Chelsea Royal London Borough Council* [2011] UKSC 33. See, H. Carr, '"Rational Men and Difficult Women". *McDonald v United Kingdom*', (2015) 60 *European Human Rights Review* 1.

[92] See also the duties owed by local authorities under the Chronically Sick and Disabled Persons Act 1970, s. 2(1).

[93] [2011] UKSC 33, para. 1.   [94] Ibid., para. 15.

[95] Ibid., para. 15, citing *Botta v Italy* (1998) 26 EHRR 241, paras 34–5.

[96] Ibid., para. 15, citing *Sentges v Netherlands* (2003) 7 CCL Rep. 400, at 405.

The Supreme Court referred to *R (Bernard) v Enfield London Borough Council*,[97] where it was noted that a breach of Article 8 was found when disabled parents were housed in accommodation that had no toilet facilities on the ground floor. The parents had to use their garden or the floor in the sitting room for toileting. Sullivan J held that following its assessment the local authority in *Bernard* 'was under an obligation ... to take positive steps, including the provision of suitably adapted accommodation, to enable the claimants and their children to lead as normal a family life as possible, bearing in mind the second claimant's severe disabilities'.[98] Their living conditions were making it 'virtually impossible for them to have any meaningful private or family life'.[99] Lord Brown contrasted *McDonald*, where he believed the authority had 'sought to respect as far as possible her personal feelings and desires, at the same time taking account of her safety, her independence and their own responsibilities towards all their other clients', and 'respected [her] human dignity and autonomy, allowing her to choose the details of her care package within their overall assessment of her needs'.[100] He held that the claimant's Article 8(1) rights had not even been interfered with, so that there was no need to justify the decision under Article 8(2), except for the period where the care provided was not in accordance with its own care plan.

Baroness Hale dissented. At the heart of her response was that the local authority proposal of pads and sheeting was an appropriate response to a person who suffered from incontinence, but Ms McDonald was not incontinent.

The European Court of Human Rights was 'prepared to approach the ... case as ... involving an interference with the ... right to respect for ... private life, without entering into the question whether ... art 8(1) imposes a positive obligation on ... states to put in place a[n equivalent] level of entitlement'.[101] However, it accepted that 'the interference pursued a legitimate aim, namely the economic well-being of the state and the interests of ... other care-users'.[102] It then considered whether 'the decision not to provide ... a night-time carer ... was "necessary in a democratic society" ... and ... proportionate to the legitimate aim'.[103] It concluded that both of those criteria were met having regard to the wide margin of appreciation, and was 'satisfied that the national courts adequately balanced the applicant's personal interests against the more general interest of the ... [local authority] in carrying out its social responsibility' of care provision 'to the

---

[97] [2002] EWHC 2282 (Admin).   [98] Ibid., para. 33.   [99] Ibid., para. 34.
[100] [2011] UKSC 33, para. 19.   [101] (2015) 60 EHRR 1, para. 49.
[102] Ibid., para. 53.   [103] Ibid., para. 53.

community at large'.[104] This litigation does not close the door on Human Rights Act claims being made in cases where care and support is not provided, but indicates that in cases where the local authority pleads a lack of resources, only cases of serious degradation are likely to succeed.

One of the trickiest issues concerning eligibility determination is the extent to which 'informal carers' such as family members are meeting P's needs. In making the determination of eligibility the fact that needs are being met by an informal carer is to be taken into account.[105] A key point is in para. 10.26 of the Code:

Local authorities are not under a duty to meet any needs that are being met by a carer. The local authority must identify, during the assessment process, those needs which are being met by a carer at that time, and determine whether those needs would be eligible. But any eligible needs met by a carer are not required to be met by the local authority, for so long as the carer continues to do so. The local authority should record in the care and support plan which needs are being met by a carer, and should consider putting in place plans to respond to any breakdown in the caring relationship.

This is an unfortunate provision. In short it means that although P has needs which should be provided for by the state, if they are provided by a carer then the state is left off the hook. While this might be appropriate if carers received appropriate remuneration and acknowledgement for their work, in fact carers receive little support.[106] The fear is that this reinforces the historical practice of shifting to carers, predominantly women, the costs of care that would otherwise fall on the state. That said, remember that the carer themselves is entitled to an assessment in their own right.

Safeguarding

One of the major themes of the Care Act 2014 was to provide a sound footing for adult protection. As the Commission for Social Care Inspection put it: 'The existing legal framework for adult protection is neither systematic nor coordinated, reflecting sporadic development of safeguarding policy over the last 25 years.'[107] A major issue in the consultation was whether there should be joint responsibilities and duties over adult protection on local authorities, health services, and the police. The Law Commission rejected such a view and

---

[104] Ibid., para. 57.   [105] *Care Act 2014: Statutory Guidance*, (n. 39), para. 6.119.
[106] J. Herring, *Caring and the Law* (Oxford, Hart 2013).
[107] Commission for Social Care Inspection, quoted in Department of Health, *Factsheet 7* (Department of Health, 2014).

believed that social service authorities should be in charge of co-ordinating and have the responsibility for safeguarding. This conclusion led to the decision that rather than produce a stand alone safeguarding statute, it would be more appropriate to add a Care Act 2014 generally dealing with adult social care. Clearly there are forces pulling in two directions here. On the one hand putting a single agency in charge of adult protection may undermine the sense that the problem must be regarded as a multiagency one. On the other hand, not having a single body with oversight runs the risk that each agency will see it as someone else's responsibility to respond to a particular issue. The government explained the balance between having a lead agency (local authorities) while recognizing that several agencies will be involved:

This should frame the responsibility as being the lead co-ordinating agency, as other agencies also need to contribute to adult safeguarding in their day-to-day work within their existing statutory duties (for example, within healthcare for the delivery of NHS services and within law enforcement and crime prevention for the police).[108]

Local authorities are required to co-operate with other bodies involved with adults who may have needs, as described in section 6(7) of the Care Act. Those bodies must co-operate with the local authority. The Guidance refers to the following kinds of bodies which may be involved:

NHS England;
Clinical Commissioning Groups;
NHS trusts and NHS Foundation Trusts;
Department for Work and Pensions;
the Police;
Prisons; and
Probation services.

This is by no means an exhaustive list and one can imagine general practitioners, housing associations, and others being involved.

The notion of Safeguarding is explained in the Guidance in this way:

Safeguarding means protecting an adult's right to live in safety, free from abuse and neglect. It is about people and organisations working together to prevent and stop both the risks and experience of abuse or neglect, while at the same time making sure that the adult's wellbeing is promoted including, where appropriate, having regard to their views, wishes, feelings and beliefs in deciding on any action. This must recognise that adults sometimes have complex interpersonal

---

[108] Department of Health, *Reforming the Law of Adult and Care Support* (Stationary Office, 2012), para. 9.8.

relationships and may be ambivalent, unclear or unrealistic about their personal circumstances.[109]

The safeguarding duties apply to an adult who:

- has needs for care and support (whether or not the local authority is meeting any of those needs); and
- is experiencing, or at risk of, abuse or neglect; and
- as a result of those care and support needs is unable to protect themselves from either the risk of, or the experience of abuse or neglect.

The key safeguarding duties imposed on a local authority are the following (as summarized in the Guidance).

- **lead a multi-agency local adult safeguarding system** that seeks to prevent abuse and neglect and stop it quickly when it happens;
- **make enquiries, or request others to make them,** when they think an adult with care and support needs may be at risk of abuse or neglect and they need to find out what action may be needed;
- **establish Safeguarding Adults Boards**, including the local authority, NHS and police, which will develop, share and implement a joint safeguarding strategy;
- **carry out Safeguarding Adults Reviews** when someone with care and support needs dies as a result of neglect or abuse and there is a concern that the local authority or its partners could have done more to protect them;
- **arrange for an independent advocate** to represent and support a person who is the subject of a safeguarding enquiry or review, if required.[110]

The aims of adult safeguarding are also set out in the Guidance:[111]

- stop abuse or neglect wherever possible;
- prevent harm and reduce the risk of abuse or neglect to adults with care and support needs;
- safeguard adults in a way that supports them in making choices and having control about how they want to live;
- promote an approach that concentrates on improving life for the adults concerned;
- raise public awareness so that communities as a whole, alongside professionals, play their part in preventing, identifying and responding to abuse and neglect;

---

[109] *Care Act 2014: Statutory Guidance*, (n. 39), para. 14.7.   [110] Ibid.
[111] Ibid., para. 11.41.

- provide information and support in accessible ways to help people understand the different types of abuse, how to stay safe and what to do to raise a concern about the safety or well-being of an adult; and address what has caused the abuse or neglect.

The Guidance also sets out the six principles which it is said to underpin all adult safeguarding work:[112]

- **Empowerment**—People being supported and encouraged to make their own decisions and informed consent.
  'I am asked what I want as the outcomes from the safeguarding process and these directly inform what happens.'
- **Prevention**—It is better to take action before harm occurs.
  'I receive clear and simple information about what abuse is, how to recognise the signs and what I can do to seek help.'
- **Proportionality**—The least intrusive response appropriate to the risk presented.
  'I am sure that the professionals will work in my interest, as I see them and they will only get involved as much as needed.'
- **Protection**—Support and representation for those in greatest need.
  'I get help and support to report abuse and neglect. I get help so that I am able to take part in the safeguarding process to the extent to which I want.'
- **Partnership**—Local solutions through services working with their communities. Communities have a part to play in preventing, detecting and reporting neglect and abuse.
  'I know that staff treat any personal and sensitive information in confidence, only sharing what is helpful and necessary. I am confident that professionals will work together and with me to get the best result for me.'
- **Accountability**—Accountability and transparency in delivering safeguarding.
  'I understand the role of everyone involved in my life and so do they.'

I shall now explore some of the key themes in the law on safeguarding.

Safeguarding adults boards

One of the issues which has bedevilled adult safeguarding (as it has with child protection) is the difficulty integrating the work of different organizations and teams who may interact with, have information about, or are

---

[112] *Care Act 2014: Statutory Guidance,* (n. 39).

in contact with an adult about whom there are concerns.[113] One of the patterns which has emerged, particularly in the area of child protection, is that different agencies (say a school, a hospital, a social work team, a health visitor) might all have pieces of information which on their own indicate some mild cause for concern, but do not indicate a major risk of abuse, but once these pieces of information are put together a picture is painted of a serious risk of harm which would have justified major intervention.[114] Safeguarding boards are designed to bring together the different bodies who interact with potential victims of abuse and ease communication and the sharing of information. This gives the authority the best chance of seeing the overall picture.

The Care Act 2014 seeks to integrate the approach to adult safeguarding through the creation of Safeguarding Adults Boards (SAB). These boards existed informally before the legislation[115] but the Act puts them on a statutory footing and requires local authorities to set them up.[116] The legislation states that the SAB must include the local authority, the NHS, and the police. Other bodies can be involved as necessary (e.g. educational bodies). These organizations must develop shared plans for safeguarding and deciding how to protect adults in vulnerable situations. In the Guidance[117] the role of the SAB is said to be to 'oversee and lead' adults safeguarding across the locality. It has three core duties. These are:

1. To publish a strategic plan as to how it will meet its objective and what its members will do to achieve this.

2. To publish an annual report setting out what it is has done to meet its objectives and implement its plan.

3. To conduct any Safeguarding Adults Reviews.

Other obligations include to:

- 'establish ways of analysing and interrogating data on safeguarding notifications that increase the SAB's understanding of prevalence of abuse and neglect locally that builds up a picture over time';

- 'develop preventative strategies that aim to reduce instances of abuse and neglect in its area'; and

---

[113] E. Stevens, 'Safeguarding Vulnerable Adults: Exploring the Challenges to Best Practice Across Multi-agency Settings', (2013) 15 *Journal of Adult Protection* 85.

[114] See J. Herring, *Family Law* (7th edn, Harlow, Pearson 2015), ch 11 for a discussion and examples.

[115] S. Braye et al., *The Governance of Adult Safeguarding* (Brighton, University of Bedfordshire and University of Sussex 2010).

[116] Section 43.   [117] *Care Act 2014: Statutory Guidance*, (n. 39), para. 14.105.

- 'formulate guidance about the arrangements for managing adult safeguarding, and dealing with complaints, grievances and professional and administrative malpractice in relation to safeguarding adults'.[118]

Safeguarding enquiries

The Care Act 2015 also requires local authorities to make enquiries if there is an adult who may be at risk of abuse or neglect in their area and to find out what, if any, action may be needed. That applies to all adults and is not limited to the adults receiving care and support services from a local authority. This is found in s. 43:

(1) This section applies where a local authority has reasonable cause to suspect that an adult in its area (whether or not ordinarily resident there)—
    (a) has needs for care and support (whether or not the authority is meeting any of those needs),
    (b) is experiencing, or is at risk of, abuse or neglect, and
    (c) as a result of those needs is unable to protect himself or herself against the abuse or neglect or the risk of it.
(2) The local authority must make (or cause to be made) whatever enquiries it thinks necessary to enable it to decide whether any action should be taken in the adult's case (whether under this Part or otherwise) and, if so, what and by whom.
(3) 'Abuse' includes financial abuse; and for that purpose 'financial abuse' includes—
    (a) having money or other property stolen,
    (b) being defrauded,
    (c) being put under pressure in relation to money or other property, and
    (d) having money or other property misused.

This is the first time that English law has created a core duty to undertake an adult safeguarding enquiry. This duty sits alongside the duties in ss 9 and 10 to assess an adult with support needs and their carer. In cases of a person at risk of abuse or neglect then there may be both a duty under s. 42 to make enquiries and a duty to assess under s. 9. It is also important to note that under s. 19(3) temporary services must be provided before the needs assessment can be completed in cases of urgency. It might well be questioned whether s. 42 is needed, given s. 9. A person suffering abuse is very likely to be in need of care and support and the s. 9 assessment will consider what steps should be taken to stop the abuse or neglect. The issue was considered by the Law Commission which explained:

---

[118] Ibid., para. 14.110.

Enquiries into abuse and neglect often amount to a more formal process than a community care assessment, and may tend to focus less on the need for services and more on establishing the facts and validity of the allegations, especially if police inquiries are also taking place. The most common outcomes of a safeguarding investigation is not the provision of care and support services but increased monitoring. Furthermore, an adult protection investigation may need to consider compulsory forms of intervention.[119]

This indicates that although there may in the language of the statute not be much of a difference between a needs assessment and an abuse enquiry, there is a difference in the style and atmosphere of the investigation. The abuse enquiry will focus on establishing whether or not there is abuse, based on objective evidence, while the needs assessment will be more pragmatic in nature and consider how needs can be met. This might well mean, for example, that a safeguarding enquiry might want to interview P on her own, separately from her family. However, a needs assessment is likely to involve all those who are important figures in P's life.

The objectives of an enquiry into abuse or neglect are to:

- establish facts;
- ascertain the adult's views and wishes;
- assess the needs of the adult for protection, support and redress and how they might be met;
- protect from the abuse and neglect, in accordance with the wishes of the adult;
- make decisions as to what follow-up action should be taken with regard to the person or organisation responsible for the abuse or neglect; and
- enable the adult to achieve resolution and recovery.[120]

If the local authority determines that a different body should make the enquiry, then it must set out a clear timescale and what will be done by the other body and prepare a course of action if it is not done.[121] This means the local authority still retains responsibility for protection, even though a third party is to provide the intervention. If it is suspected that a criminal offence has been committed the police should be involved at the earliest opportunity.[122]

---

[119] Law Commission, *Adult Social Care, Report 326* (Law Commission, 2010), para. 9.11.
[120] Department of Health, *Care Act 2014: Statutory Guidance* (Department of Health, 2014), para. 14.78.
[121] Ibid., para. 14.65.
[122] Ibid., para. 14.70

Despite the detailed provisions governing an enquiry it is important to note that the legislation requires the authority to determine how to respond to the abuse or neglect, but it does not compel the local authority to meet those needs. This might be surprising, but that mirrors the provision in the Children Act 1989 in relation to child abuse. It might be explained by the fact that a local authority may be dealing with many cases of abuse to which it must respond and it will focus resources on the most serious cases. Those kinds of resourcing decisions will need to be made free of pressure of a statutory duty. The omission is not as concerning as it might be because if the local authority determines that P is suffering abuse or neglect and needs care services, but decides not to provide them, it could well face a claim under the Human Rights Act 1998 (see Chapter 4) or for judicial review. It is submitted that these remedies mean the failure to put a specific duty to intervene is less concerning than it would otherwise be.

'Reasonable cause to suspect'

An abuse enquiry is triggered if there is reasonable cause to suspect that there has been abuse or neglect. But what does 'reasonable cause to suspect' mean? Of course we have no case law on the Care Act 2014 yet, but s. 47 of the Children Act 1989 has a duty to investigate in cases of children, relying on reasonable cause to suspect and the case law on that which may be used as a precedent. This has emphasized that there is a difference between having a reasonable cause to suspect and a reasonable cause to believe. Requiring merely a reasonable cause to suspect means the standard is 'quite low'.[123] It certainly does not require proof that the authority believes it is more likely than not that the abuse occurred. Tim Spencer-Lane suggests the following as examples of what might in general be 'reasonable' causes to suspect:

- past evidence, such as previous allegations of abuse or neglect and court proceedings;[124]
- a report from a clinician;[125] and
- accusations made by the victim to their social worker.[126]

However, it would be wrong to say there is no barrier here. The authority will need to point to objective reasonable grounds on which the facts are based. It is not enough to think they have reasonable grounds, they need to show that objectively they are reasonable. That said, in connection with s. 47 Lady Hale,

---

[123] *R (S) v Swindon BC* [2001] EWHC Admin 334, para. 36.
[124] Ibid., para. 36.   [125] *A v Enfield LBC* [2008] EWHC 1886 (Admin).
[126] *Gogay v Hertfordshire CC* [2001] 1 FLR 280.

in *Gogay v Hertfordshire CC*,[127] held that the courts should be 'slow indeed' to find a local authority did not have reasonable grounds for suspicion which justified further enquiries.

Abuse or neglect

Abuse is generally understood to involve acts, either isolated or a pattern of abuse, which cause harm to another. Neglect is seen to refer to omissions, where a person's care and support needs are being ignored or not met. This might range from not giving the person the medication they need to not giving the food or necessities of life.

Deliberately the Act avoids the terms 'significant or serious harm'[128] and rather uses abuse or neglect. This highlights the fact that the focus is on the acts and omissions of others, rather than P's current state. The Department of Health explained:

Our preference would be to define the scope of safeguarding in law with clearer concepts of 'abuse' and 'neglect'. This is where the core work of adult safeguarding should sit—where adults in vulnerable situations are hurt because of the actions or lack of action of others. In our view, this would be a more straightforward description of the policy showing explicitly that safeguarding is a response to the actions and ommissions of others in a way that 'harm', however defined, cannot capture alone.[129]

There appear to be two primary reasons driving this approach. The first is to exclude cases where the disadvantages P is suffering are a result of poverty or social exclusion, rather than the conduct of identifiable individuals.

The second is to exclude cases where a person has adopted a lifestyle which others may believe to be harmful to them. One might, for example, imagine a clutterer, who has filled their house with rubbish. While some might believe they are suffering harm, it would not be able to identify an abuser or neglecter. Indeed it seems that self-neglect will not be covered, with the Guidance stating:

For similar reasons, we do not intend to set out 'self-harm' as a specific example of the situation where an adult safeguarding response might be required. Adult safeguarding should be focused on cases where a person is at risk as a result of the act or omission another person. Cases of self-harm or self-neglect may raise professional concerns, but we do not believe they should be specifically set out as examples of

---

[127] [2000] EWCA Civ 288.

[128] In relation to child abuse the Children Act 1989, s. 31, uses the term 'significant harm'.

[129] Department of Health, *Government Response to the Law Commission* (Department of Health, 2012) para. 9.15.

where a safeguarding response would always be necessary. This, of course, would not stop Safeguarding Adults Boards local decisions to consider activity in this area, if that is thought to be a local priority.[130]

It is not clear, however, that the statutory words which refer to experiencing neglect cover self-neglect, nor indeed that the word abuse includes self-abuse.[131] It is suggested it would be better to interpret the Act so that it does include self-neglect and self-abuse, but to recognize that in many of those cases intervention is not necessary. While it may well be that there are cases where a person has chosen a lifestyle which others will feel is self-neglect, that may not be a fully autonomous choice or the result of previous abuse.

But what do neglect and abuse mean? Surprisingly perhaps these concepts are not defined in the Act. The government[132] has taken the view that it is best to allow the courts to use the natural meaning of the words, to keep the duty flexible.

Those seeking a definition of abuse might turn to Council of Europe Resolution (2005) on safeguarding adults and children with disability against abuse:[133]

[A]ny act or failure to act, which results in a breach of a vulnerable person's human rights, civil liberties, physical and mental integrity, dignity or general well-being, whether intended or through negligence, including sexual relationships or financial transactions to which the person does not or cannot validly consent, or which are deliberately exploitative.

The Guidance lists the following as examples of abuse:[134]

- **Physical abuse**—including assault, hitting, slapping, pushing, misuse of medication, restraint or inappropriate physical sanctions.

- **Domestic violence**—including psychological, physical, sexual, financial, emotional abuse; so called 'honour' based violence.

- **Sexual abuse**—including rape, indecent exposure, sexual harassment, inappropriate looking or touching, sexual teasing or innuendo, sexual photography, subjection to pornography or witnessing sexual acts, indecent exposure and sexual assault or sexual acts to which the adult has not consented or was pressured into consenting.

---

[130]   *Care Act 2014: Statutory Guidance*, (n. 39), para. 9.16.
[131]   T. Spencer-Lane, (n. 83), 274.
[132]   Baroness Northover, Hansard HL, July 22, 2013, vol 747 col 1115.
[133]   Council of Europe, Resolution on safeguarding adults and children with disability against abuse (Council of Europe, 2005), 12.
[134]   *Care Act 2014: Statutory Guidance*, (n. 39), para. 6.17.

- **Psychological abuse**—including emotional abuse, threats of harm or abandonment, deprivation of contact, humiliation, blaming, controlling, intimidation, coercion, harassment, verbal abuse, cyber bullying, isolation or unreasonable and unjustified withdrawal of services or supportive networks.

- **Financial or material abuse**—including theft, fraud, internet scamming, coercion in relation to an adult's financial affairs or arrangements, including in connection with wills, property, inheritance or financial transactions, or the misuse or misappropriation of property, possessions or benefits.

- **Modern slavery**—encompasses slavery, human trafficking, forced labour and domestic servitude. Traffickers and slave masters use whatever means they have at their disposal to coerce, deceive and force individuals into a life of abuse, servitude and inhumane treatment.

- **Discriminatory abuse**—including forms of harassment, slurs or similar treatment; because of race, gender and gender identity, age, disability, sexual orientation or religion.

- **Organisational abuse**—including neglect and poor care practice within an institution or specific care setting such as a hospital or care home, for example, or in relation to care provided in one's own home. This may range from one off incidents to on-going ill-treatment. It can be through neglect or poor professional practice as a result of the structure, policies, processes and practices within an organisation.

- **Neglect and acts of omission**—including ignoring medical, emotional or physical care needs, failure to provide access to appropriate health, care and support or educational services, the withholding of the necessities of life, such as medication, adequate nutrition and heating.

- **Self-neglect**—this covers a wide range of behaviour neglecting to care for one's personal hygiene, health or surroundings and includes behaviour such as hoarding.

The Guidance goes on to emphasize that abuse might be a one off incident or a series of incidents. In some cases it will be 'opportunistic' abuse, for example where a stranger takes advantage of someone else. In other cases there may be 'serial abuse', where there perpetrator has set out to befriend and take advantage of someone. Sexual abuse following grooming would fall within this category. Long term abuse where the abuse is ingrained into the relationship, such as with domestic abuse, is thought to fall into a third category.

Unable to protect him or herself

This is a very important limitation on the s. 42 duty. It means if a person on their own or with others can protect themselves from abuse or neglect then the duty does not arise. There will be no difficulty in determining that a person who lacks mental capacity is unable to safeguard themselves nor that a person in an abusive relationship and cannot see a way out their situation. Much trickier is a case where a person is suffering serious abuse and could leave the relationship, but decides not to. It might also be thought that cases of self-neglect or self-abuse can be prevented by the individual. Are they 'unable to protect' themselves? Consider, for example, the couple in *DL v A Local Authority*,[135] who were being abused by the son they were living with, but did not want to move away from him. In a physical sense they were able to protect themselves by moving out, but they lacked the emotional capacity to move out. It is suggested that the term 'unable to protect him or herself' should be interpreted broadly, to include those facing external or internal emotional or psychological pressure not to take steps to protect themselves.

Need for care and support

The s. 42 duty applies to any adult who 'has need for care and support'. There is no need to show that the person is receiving services or even meets the eligibility criteria to be entitled to receive services. The Guidance to the Act states: 'Safeguarding enquiries should be made on the understanding of the risk of neglect or abuse, irrespective whether the individual would meet the criteria for the provision of services.'[136] There is some dispute over whether the duty is applicable to carers who are at risk of harm as a result of their caring role. The Law Commission had proposed that the duty apply to them, but in the statute s. 42 is limited to those with care or support needs who are facing abuse or neglect. It may well be replied that carers can be seen as in need of care and support. Even if they fall outside s. 42, it may be argued that carers have a right to be assessed under s. 10 and this can deal with concerns about them. One reason why that may not be entirely sufficient is that under s. 11(5) a carer can refuse to have a needs assessment and only if it was found they lacked capacity to refuse could the local authority perform the assessment. Perhaps the inherent jurisdiction could be used to protect a carer if they refused to be assessed under s. 10.

Case conference

A common outcome following a safeguarding enquiry is a case conference. The purpose of a conference is to look at the evidence from all the different bodies who have interacted with P. It must decide if a plan is necessary

---

[135] [2012] EWCA Civ 253.   [136] *Care Act 2014: Statutory Guidance*, (n. 39).

and what to do to protect P from abuse or neglect. The conference should look at current and future risks and whether a plan needs to be reviewed or monitored.

While the primary meeting of the conference is to protect vulnerable adults and prevent abuse, there is a duty to ensure that its procedures are fair and comply with natural justice. In *Davies v West Sussex CC*[137] it was held the case conference treated the owner of a care home where there were concerns over alleged abuse in a deplorable way. The owner of the care home was herself an elderly woman and the meeting continued for eight hours. She had had little notice of the proceedings and conclusions were drawn about her credibility and fitness over issues on which she had no personal knowledge.

Enquiries

If the criteria in s. 42(1) are met then the local authority is required to make or cause to be made the enquiries that are necessary to enable it to decide (a) whether any action should be taken in the adult's case and (b) if so what and (c) by whom. The use of the term 'cause to be made' indicates that although the local authority may have the lead responsibility for ensuring the actions are undertaken it is a multi-agency task, and the correct agency to undertake the work may not be the local authority. That said, the use of the words 'cause to be undertaken' indicates the local authority has the lead on this and ensures that the enquiry is dealt with by the other agency and, if it is not, ensures the enquiry is performed by someone.

One controversial issue during the debates was whether the local authority should have power to enter P's property without consent in order to conduct an enquiry. The government consulted on the issue. Opinions were deeply divided and the government concluded that the evidence in favour of giving the power was not strong enough. The police do have a range of powers available if a person is at risk of harm and the local authority could ask the police to use these powers.

If the abuse is in a regulated care setting, such as a care home, hospital, or college, then the employer of the institution must co-operate with the investigation. If an employer is aware of abuse or neglect they are under a duty to correct this and protect the adult from harm. However the local authority is still under a duty to make enquiries, if it has reasonable cause to suspect that an adult may be experiencing or is at risk of abuse or neglect. The Guidance indicates that in some cases the local authority will be persuaded by the

---

[137] [2012] EWHC 2152 (Fam).

employer's response that no further action was necessary if that was sufficient to deal with the issue.[138]

Action

The duty under subsection 43(1)(a) is to decide whether any action should be undertaken. It is perhaps surprising that there is no explicit duty to then undertake that action. It seems that is designed to offer some protection to a local authority where scarcity of resources means that it is unable to provide the services needed in cases of low level abuse. That said, it would require particularly strong reasons to justify not making provision where a person is suffering, or is at risk of suffering, abuse or neglect. The most common response will be to provide care and support under Part 1 of the Care Act. However in other cases it may be that bringing proceedings under the Mental Capacity Act 2005 or the inherent jurisdiction are needed. That will be where it is necessary to remove a person from an abusive situation and they are not co-operating in that. In other cases it may be that NHS services are an appropriate response.[139]

If the investigation reveals a criminal offence has been committed the police should take over the investigation. Otherwise the local authority must determine the response. This will normally focus on steps that can be taken to protect P from further abuse. The Guidance suggests the following factors to be considered in determining what intervention is necessary:

- the adult's needs for care and support;
- the adult's risk of abuse or neglect;
- the adult's ability to protect themselves or the ability of their networks to increase the support they offer;
- the impact on the adult, their wishes;
- the possible impact on important relationships;
- potential of action and increasing risk to the adult;
- the risk of repeated or increasingly serious acts involving children, or another adult at risk of abuse or neglect;
- the responsibility of the person or organisation that has caused the abuse or neglect; and
- research evidence to support any intervention.[140]

The most difficult cases will be those where P does not want any intervention. The Guidance is somewhat vague on that issue:

---

[138] *Care Act 2014: Statutory Guidance*, (n. 39), 14.57.
[139] *Re Z* [2004] EWHC 2817 (Fam).
[140] *Care Act 2014: Statutory Guidance*, (n. 39), 14.83.

Practitioners should wherever practicable seek the consent of the adult before taking action. However, there may be circumstances when consent cannot be obtained because the adult lacks the capacity to give it, but it is in their best interests to undertake an enquiry. Whether or not the adult has capacity to give consent, action may need to be taken if others are or will be put at risk if nothing is done or where it is in the public interest to take action because a criminal offence has occurred. It is the responsibility of all staff and members of the public to act on any suspicion or evidence of abuse or neglect and to pass on their concerns to a responsible person or agency.[141]

The Code quotes the BMA Adult safeguarding toolkit:

… where a competent adult explicitly refuses any supporting intervention, this should normally be respected. Exceptions to this may be where a criminal offence may have taken place or where there may be a significant risk of harm to a third party. If, for example, there may be an abusive adult in a position of authority in relation to other vulnerable adults [sic], it may be appropriate to breach confidentiality and disclose information to an appropriate authority. Where a criminal offence is suspected it may also be necessary to take legal advice. Ongoing support should also be offered. Because an adult initially refuses the offer of assistance he or she should not therefore be lost to or abandoned by relevant services. The situation should be monitored and the individual informed that she or he can take up the offer of assistance at any time.

Although it does not say so explicitly, presumably the Code supports such an approach.

I respectfully suggest that this fails to take into account adequately the obligations on local authorities to protect people from abuse under the Human Rights Act (see Chapter 3). The Guidance refers to criminal offences where it believes a protection may be necessary even if P objects. However, it should be remembered that something which is not a criminal offence may still cause considerable harm. It may be, for example, that no crime is committed because the abuser lacks the *mens rea* to be guilty of a crime or has a defence based on a mental condition. Indeed, with that in mind it is not entirely clear why whether or not the act is a criminal offence is particularly relevant in the balance between protection from harm and respect for autonomy. In striking the balance the amount of harm involved seems more significant than the blameworthiness of the abuser. I suspect the reference to criminal charges was meant to indicate that only in cases where the level of harm is very low should P's objections be taken into account so as to not intervene to protect. It would have been better to state that explicitly. It should not be forgotten

---

[141] Ibid., 14.79.

that the Code states: 'The first priority should always be to ensure the safety and well-being of the adult.'[142]

The most difficult cases are those where it is alleged that a family member is abusing P. The Code states:

Any intervention in family or personal relationships needs to be carefully considered. While abusive relationships never contribute to the wellbeing of an adult, interventions which remove all contact with family members may also be experienced as abusive interventions and risk breaching the adult's right to family life if not justified or proportionate. Safeguarding needs to recognise that the right to safety needs to be balanced with other rights, such as rights to liberty and autonomy, and rights to family life. Action might be primarily supportive or therapeutic, or it might involve the application of civil orders, sanctions, suspension, regulatory activity or criminal prosecution, disciplinary action or de-registration from a professional body.[143]

In such a case the human rights analysis in Chapter 3 provides a helpful way of weighing up the importance to attach to family life and the need to be protected from violence. In cases where the family relationship is marked by persistent abuse the weight to attach to family life becomes much weaker. Munby J, writing extrajudicially, has made some useful observations. He argues:

[W]e need to consider very carefully whether a vulnerable or incapacitated adult who has been looked after within their family will not be better off if they continue to be looked after within the family rather than by the State. Often they will be, sometimes they will not be. It all depends. Similarly we need to consider very carefully whether vulnerable or incapacitated adults will not be better off if they live with a family (or something approximating to a family) rather than in an institution—however benign and enlightened the institution may be, and however well integrated into the community. We have to be conscious of the limited ability of public authorities to improve on nature … And we should not lightly interfere with family life. On the other hand, we need to recognise that removal from the family home may be required, not only where there is abuse, ill-treatment or neglect but if it is necessary, for example, to enable P to extend her social and community networks or to give her the independence which all young adults need as they 'grow away' from their families. The key consideration, as always, is welfare. What is it, in all the circumstances, that is truly in P's best interests?

Safeguarding adult reviews

A failure in safeguarding should result in a Safeguarding Adults Review if an adult with care and support needs dies as a result of abuse or neglect and there are concerns about how the SAB or its members acted. Under s. 44

---

[142] Ibid., 14.79.   [143] Ibid., 14.82.

(1) An SAB must arrange for there to be a review of a case involving an adult in its area with needs for care and support (whether or not the local authority has been meeting any of those needs) if—
  (a) there is reasonable cause for concern about how the SAB, members of it or other persons with relevant functions worked together to safeguard the adult, and
  (b) condition 1 or 2 is met.
(2) Condition 1 is met if—
  (a) the adult has died, and
  (b) the SAB knows or suspects that the death resulted from abuse or neglect (whether or not it knew about or suspected the abuse or neglect before the adult died).
(3) Condition 2 is met if—
  (a) the adult is still alive, and
  (b) the SAB knows or suspects that the adult has experienced serious abuse or neglect.
(4) An SAB may arrange for there to be a review of any other case involving an adult in its area with needs for care and support (whether or not the local authority has been meeting any of those needs).
(5) Each member of the SAB must co-operate in and contribute to the carrying out of a review under this section with a view to—
  (a) identifying the lessons to be learnt from the adult's case, and
  (b) applying those lessons to future cases.

These reviews are designed to look back at cases where there has been serious failure in safeguarding cases. Importantly, the aim of the review is not to apportion blame but to learn lessons and, in particular, seek to improve local practices and procedures. Prior to the Act reviews of this kind did occur but they were not based on a statutory model and were not consistently performed.[144]

Conclusion

This chapter has explored the responsibilities of local authorities in relation to the provision of care and support under the Care Act 2014. It is striking how the legislation has moved away from using the category of 'vulnerable adults' to use the terminology of those who are in need of care and support services. In part this reflects a negative attitude towards vulnerability, which was criticized in Chapter 2. However, it also reflects a refocusing of approach so that care and support services are given to meet the goals and

---

[144] T. Spencer-Lane, (n. 83), 280.

aspirations of the person concerned, rather than being restricted to limiting risks they face. This ties in with a broader move towards giving personalized services which are driven by the hopes of the individual, rather than determined by the local authority. While these are desirable developments in this area of the law, they are not without concern. It is noticeable that although there are strong duties on local authorities to assess the needs of individuals and to enquire if they are at risk, there are no enforceable duties in the Act to provide care or protection. There are also the financial payments that will be required by all bar the worse off. In part this is an acknowledgement of the limited resources that public authorities have. However, it does mean there is a danger that the legislation will offer false hope to individuals by identifying their needs but then failing to meet them. The solution to that dilemma is essentially political in increasing funding for social care. The driver for that might be an acknowledgement of our mutual vulnerability and dependence by all of us on the services of public authorities.

7

Criminal Law and the Protection of Vulnerable Adults

Introduction

The criminal law is a recognition that we are all vulnerable. We might all suffer attacks on our interests at the hands of others from which we cannot defend ourselves. The criminal law offers a deterrence against such attacks and, on conviction, a public acknowledgement of the wrong done and a holding to account of the person who has caused the harm.

There are some offences which are designed to protect those regarded as particularly vulnerable. Indeed this can be highlighted as a particularly important role of the criminal law. A typical comment comes from the then Home Secretary in 2009: 'The mark of any civilized society is how it protects the most vulnerable.'[1] However, generally vulnerable adults, like anyone else, are protected by the criminal law. The offences of murder, manslaughter, assault, and the like apply whether the victim is classified as a vulnerable adult or not. However, as we shall see, that apparently benign role is controversial. What from one perspective may be regarded as protection, from another is an interference in liberty. This issue has already been raised in this book, but it comes to the fore in this chapter.

This is not the place to go through all the different criminal offences, which are discussed in detail elsewhere.[2] Instead, this chapter will look at a number of themes that arise when the criminal law seeks to protect vulnerable people. It will start by looking at what significance, if any, should be attached to the fact that a particular victim is a vulnerable person. It will then turn to the difficult balance between protection and paternalism in the

---

[1] Jacqui Smith, during the second reading of the Policing and Crime Bill, Hansard House of Commons Debates, 19 January 2009, col 524, regarding provisions on prostitution. Available at <http://www.publications.parliament.uk/pa/cm200809/cmhansrd/cm090119/debtext/90119-0010.htm>, col 524, last accessed September 2012.

[2] For example J. Herring, *Criminal Law* (Oxford, Oxford University Press 2014).

criminal law context. The chapter will move on to examine the ways that protection of vulnerable adults can end up criminalizing other vulnerable adults. The chapter will conclude by considering offences that are specifically designed to protect vulnerable adults.

The protection of vulnerable adults in the criminal law

What is the relevance of the fact that the victim of a crime is a vulnerable adult? This section will explore four reasons that might be given for why a crime might be regarded as more serious if the victim is a vulnerable adult.

First, it is commonly said that criminal law should be used as a 'last resort'. In many contexts we expect people to take care of themselves and protect themselves from harm. The criminal law is an expensive, invasive, and cumbersome procedure and we do not want the criminal law to be involved unless there is a good reason for doing so. Michelle Madden Dempsey and I have suggested that criminalization should be seen as a 'prima facie wrong': something that requires justification.[3] There is no particular need for the criminal law to protect those who are perfectly able to take reasonable steps to prevent themselves from being harmed. If someone does suffer a loss when they could have easily prevented that occurring we assume that that is their choice or they are in some other way responsible for their misfortune.

However, such an approach might not apply in relation to a vulnerable adult. An obvious example may be a financial transaction. We might think that generally it is reasonable to expect people to make their own enquiries and determine whether or not it is appropriate to purchase a particular item. If they buy a car and it turns out to be a bad deal, well, they only have themselves to blame. However, in the case of a vulnerable adult it might be argued that the normal presumption cannot apply. We cannot expect the vulnerable adult to look after their own interests in the way we do others.

A second argument may be that there is an especial wrong done to vulnerable people. The harm done to the vulnerable person is particularly serious because of its impact upon them. Their failure to understand fully what has happened; their impaired ability to protect themselves from repetition; and the impact of the crime combined with other social and legal disadvantages may all magnify the wrong done to them. Crimes against vulnerable adults may lead them to be dominated by others in a way which is less likely for

---

[3] M. Madden Dempsey and J. Herring, 'Why Sexual Penetration Requires Justification', (2007) 27 *Oxford Journal of Legal Studies* 467.

other people. Philip Petit,[4] discussing his theory of republicanism, makes some insightful comments on the nature of the wrong from the perspective of the vulnerable adults:

The republican theory of suitable protection emphasizes the need to guard against domination, not just interference. You will enjoy suitable protection in a particular choice just to the extent that other individuals or groups do not have access to means of non-deliberative control over that choice. Others may be able to deliberate with you on the basis of sincere, take-it-or-leave-it reasons and influence what you do. But they should not be allowed a power of interfering with the choice, without exposing themselves to an inhibiting risk of punishment; they should not be able to block, burden, or deceptively redirect the choice with any degree of impunity. In short, they should not have 'dominating control' over what you choose.

A third argument is that if someone else is then taking advantage of another's wrong there is a social harm committed. Where a person is unable to meet their own needs and becomes dependent on others to meet their needs, it is important for society that it is done in an effective way. Where people dealing with vulnerable adults take advantage of their needs then the social task in meeting the needs of all citizens is impeded.

Finally, a defendant who takes advantage of a vulnerable person may be committing the particular wrong of exploitation. By exploiting the vulnerability of another the defendant is using that person as a means to an end. They are not genuinely respecting the vulnerable person's autonomy, but manipulating the vulnerable person to act in a way which benefits the defendant. This final point needs much more discussion.

Exploitation

One of the key roles of the criminal law is to protect people from exploitation. This leaves open the question of how we are to understand the concept of exploitation. A starting definition may be as follows: 'Exploitation is a special kind of moral wrong and arises where a defendant who takes advantage of a person's vulnerability for the defendant's personal gain and/or the victim's loss.' This captures the essence of exploitation, but it requires quite a bit of unpacking and is far from straightforward.

---

[4] P. Petit, 'The Basic Liberties' in M. Kramer, C. Grant, B. Colburn, and A. Hatzistavrou, *The Legacy of HLA Hart: Legal, Political and Moral Philosophy* (Oxford, Oxford University Press 2008), 67.

Vulnerability

It is generally accepted that exploitation involves taking advantage of another's vulnerability. But what is meant by vulnerability in this context? Robert Goodin[5] argues: 'If A's interests are vulnerable to B's actions and choices, B has a special responsibility to protect A's interests; the strength of this responsibility depends strictly upon the degree to which B can affect A's interests.' This is an interesting analysis of vulnerability because it focuses on the extent to which B is in a position to affect A's interests, rather than any inherent characteristic of B. This is a broad concept of vulnerability because in many transactions one party can affect the interests of the other.

I am sympathetic to Goodin's approach but it raises a number of queries. First, is vulnerability to be limited to cases where someone's essential needs are involved? My love of chocolate may make me particularly susceptible to succumbing to a two-for-one deal on my favourite chocolate bar but that does not seem to be exploitation. Tea Logar[6] suggests that vulnerability should be limited to cases where the person is in real need: 'vulnerabilities considered relevant for exploitation are usually those that are more or less directly connected to our essential needs, while taking advantage of mere desires is generally not considered exploitative'. In response to this it should be noted that Goodin is clear that the extent of the vulnerability, and the corresponding responsibility of the other party, depends on the depth of the need. So Goodin can easily say that the person desiring chocolate has far less vulnerability and is owed a far lower responsibility than the person needing, say, essential medical treatment. The difficulty with Logar's approach is much then turns on what is an 'essential need'. That seems such a fluid concept that it may not be helpful. It also seems to overlook the human nature of being powerfully influenced by desires that are not 'essential needs'.

Second, there is a debate in the literature over whether the concept of vulnerability includes disadvantages a person has due to background injustices, caused generally by the distribution of resources in society and the operation of the market. For Marxists, for example, workers give more through labour than they receive from wages and the goods the wages can buy, and so are taken advantage of.[7] Not everyone will agree with that, but even free marketeers accept there are distortions in the market that can work against individuals and groups of individuals. This occurs at both national and international levels.

---

[5] R. Goodin, *Protecting the Vulnerable* (Chicago, University of Chicago Press 1985).

[6] T. Logar, 'Exploitation as Wrongful Use: Beyond Taking Advantage of Vulnerabilities', (2010) 25 *Acta Analytica* 329.

[7] For a critique and discussion see J. Roemer, *A General Theory of Exploitation and Class* (Cambridge, Harvard University Press 1982).

Does that make any transaction in our society potentially exploitative? If it does there is a danger that the term will lose a particular meaning and will be hard to avoid.[8] Indeed, seeking to live life in a typical western democracy without engaging in transactions which might be said to take advantage of another's weak place in the market might be difficult, if not impossible. This leads some writers to suggest that exploitation only arises where there is a departure from the market prices as they would normally be, given the inequalities that exist.[9] So something no more than simply coming across a person who is in particular need as a result of socio-economic forces and entering a deal with them will not be exploitation. Indeed if that was taken as exploitation then that might hinder the needs of those who are vulnerable, because people would be deterred from entering into any deals with them.[10] However, excluding such background disadvantages seems to leave some of the most vulnerable outside the scope of exploitation. It is also very difficult in many cases to determine precisely the cause of a person's needs, which in many cases will be a complex interplay between personal and social causes. Further, if a person is wrongfully taking advantage of another's needs, it seems to matter little whether that comes from general societal power structure or some personal characteristics. So, I suggest that vulnerability should include background disadvantages. As Ruth Sample argues, 'if we gain advantage from an interaction with another, and that advantage is due in part to an injustice he has suffered, we have failed to give him appropriate respect'.[11] A third issue is whether we exclude from the concept of exploitation those situations where a person has brought about their own misfortune. If a person is responsible for their situation, does that make it less blameworthy to charge an unduly high price for a service they need than it would if that need was produced or caused by forces outside the person's control? A person who takes advantage of another's learning disability to make financial gain would by most definitions be exploiting; but what of the person who takes advantage of the paedophile's addiction to child pornography? This had led some to question whether exploiting a character flaw is not exploitation.[12] Feinberg[13] interestingly suggests that such behaviour (he gives the example of taking advantage of another's greed) may be exploitation, but

---

[8] E. Malmqvist, 'Taking Advantage of Injustice', (2013) 39.4 *Social Theory and Practice* 557.

[9] A. Wertheimer, *Exploitation* (Princeton, NJ, Princeton University Press 1996).

[10] That might be taking for granted the legitimacy of the current economic system; however if we are seeking to identify the kind of conduct which involves the criminal law, we need to limit it in such a way and doing so does not prevent us from seeking to challenge inequalities in other ways.

[11] R. Sample, *Exploitation: What it is and Why it is Wrong* (Lanhamn, MD, Rowman and Littlefield 2003), 76.

[12] Logar (n. 6).

[13] J. Feinberg, The Moral Limits of the Criminal Law (New York, Oxford University Press 1983), 206.

least blamable; indeed, it may contain a 'pleasing element'. The trickiness here is to assess the extent to which a person is to blame for their sexual preferences or their smoking habit or whatever is in question. That is notoriously difficult. I think it is simply too difficult to separate out blameworthy and unblameworthy conditions. Further, it assumes there is a consensus on what position people would be in if there was a just system. You might believe that a just society would ensure free health care for all citizens. In this case you might assess a society which did not provide free health care as an unjust society and a person charging for health care in such a society as taking advantage of that injustice. However, if you did not think a just society would necessarily pay for all health care, you would see no underlying injustice here. This highlights the difficulty in determining whether there is an underpinning injustice of which another person is taking advantage.

So, although at first sight Goodin's proposal that A is vulnerable in relation to B if B can affect A's interests seems too broad, it is suggested that it is correct. Any further limitation creates enormous difficulties in drawing distinctions between serious or less serious need, or needs for which a person is or is not responsible.

Content

Generally an exploitative transaction will lead to the victim suffering a loss. But can transactions which are fair in their content be exploitative? Robert Mayer argues that the unfair content is an essential element of exploitation. He argues that 'to say that wrongful exploitation has occurred always implies that an undeserved loss of a relative sort has been inflicted'.[14] I suggest that is not correct. Exploitation can occur even if a fair price is paid for the goods or service; or the terms of the contract would be regarded as objectively reasonable.

If A's vulnerability is manipulated so that gain is made without that being A's autonomous decision, it matters not whether the amount paid was fair or not. It was a non-autonomous transaction. As Robert Goodin argues in relation to exploitation: 'It is not a matter of how things end up at all. It is instead a matter of how you get there. The essence of exploitation must be sought in some characteristic of the process, rather than in some characteristic of the end results.'[15] Imagine a case where a door-to-door sales person is selling their gardening services for £20 per hour, which at an objective level (or at least market level) is a fair price. He persuades an older man to engage in his service through a range of devices, taking advantage of the frail person's

---

[14] R. Mayer, 'What's Wrong with Exploitation', (2007) 24 *Journal of Applied Philosophy* 137, 141.
[15] R. Goodin, 'Exploiting a Situation and Exploiting a Person' in A. Reeve (ed.), *Modern Theories of Exploitation* (London, Sage Publications 1987), p. 181.

vulnerability. The fact the price is fair does not seem very relevant. The gardener has breached the well-known Kantian imperative that people should not be treated as mere means. The sales person has used the older person simply to obtain money and has shown no regard for their autonomy. Ruth Sample argues that exploitation can arise from failing to respect others by ensuring that their needs are met when we do choose to interact with them and instead pursue our own advantage. That can arise whether the terms of the contract are fair or not.[16]

Consent

One major issue is whether or not a transaction is exploitative if it is consensual.[17] Stephen Wilkinson[18] argues that a transaction between A and B 'amounts to A's exploiting B if and only if: (a) the distribution of benefit and harm between A and B is (other things being equal) unjust (in A's favour); and (b) B does not validly consent'. The basis of this argument is that otherwise exploitation opens the door to paternalism. Wilkinson claims that it is easy for others to believe that, for example, a person who sells their kidney for £20,000 must be being 'exploited'. Without the consent exception, he suggests, we are in danger of undermining the autonomy of people. I would argue against this.

First, exploitation may in its nature undermine autonomy, even if there is consent. There is only autonomy, according to Raz, if the choices are 'free from coercion and manipulation by others'.[19] Many forms of exploitation will, therefore, negate autonomy, even if there is consent for legal purposes. This argument was developed in Chapter 2 and will not be repeated there.

Second, the exploiter is showing the wrong attitude towards consent. If we take the principle of autonomy seriously, we should require people to show respect for other's autonomy. A person who takes unfair advantage of another's vulnerability to obtain a consent may be failing to show due respect for their autonomy.[20] As I have written elsewhere:[21]

[W]hen D is going to do an act which is a prima facie wrong against V, D needs good reasons for committing the act. The consent of V can provide that good reason, but D has a responsibility to ensure that the consent is sufficient to authorize him to do

---

[16] M. Fleurbaey, 'The Facets of Exploitation', (2014) 26(4) *Journal of Theoretical Politics* 653–76.

[17] A. Werthmeimer, *Exploitation* (Princeton, Princeton University Press, 1996).

[18] S. Wilkinson, 'The Exploitation Argument Against Commercial Surrogacy', (2003) 17 *Bioethics* 163, 173.

[19] J. Raz, The Morality of Freedom (OUP, 1986), p. 373.   [20] Ibid., p. 74.

[21] J. Herring, 'Consent in the Criminal Law: The Importance of Relationality and Responsibility' in A. Reed and M. Bohlander (eds), *General Defences in Criminal Law* (Ashgate 2014).

the act. It should always be remembered that D has no right to commit a prima facie wrong against another person and is always free to walk away or wait until any uncertainty is resolved. In relying on consent D has the responsibility of giving V the time, information, and freedom from pressure to provide that consent. Where D has used deceptions, pressure, manipulation or exploitation in order to obtain consent, this is inconsistent with D properly relying on consent as an expression by V of their assessment of their well-being. He has not been respecting the right to bodily integrity that gives V the right to determine for themselves whether an act is in their well-being.

Taking advantage

At the heart of exploitation is the concept of taking advantage as key, but what does that mean?[22] Goodin argues that power-holders have a 'moral responsibility to protect the weaker'. This is notable because it is not limited to acts which might be seen as wrongful, but a failure to positively take steps to protect a vulnerable person. Contrast, for example, Alisa Carse and Margaret Little's[23] definition of exploitation as 'an exchange that involves wresting benefit from a genuine vulnerability in a way or to a degree one ought not'.[24] Goodin's understanding is clearly broader than the notion of 'wrestling' but would include simply taking something from a willing victim, without ensuring their interests are duly protected.

Jennifer Collins,[25] applying Goodin's approach, gives some examples of what taking advantage might involve:

Such circumstances could be occasions where D plays for advantage against those who have renounced playing for advantage themselves or against those who are unfit to play. Alternatively, it could be taking advantage if those who D plays against are no match for him, or where D's relative advantage derives from others' grave misfortunes. The power-holder is examined on the basis of whether they have engaged in 'fair play' in the context of the norms of the particular relationship.

Conclusion on exploitation

It has proved surprisingly difficult to define exploitation. It is clear there are several elements at play. Most definitions include some combination of the following elements:

---

[22] A. Wood, 'Exploitation' (1995) 12 *Social Philosophy and Policy* 136.
[23] A. Carse and M. Little, 'Threats and Offers' in T. Honderich (ed), *Encyclopedia of Philosophy*. (New York, Oxford University Press 2005).
[24] R. Sample, *Exploitation: What It Is and Why It's Wrong* (Lanhamn, MD, Rowman & Littlefield 2003).
[25] J. Collins, 'The Contours of Vulnerability' in J. Wallbank and J. Herring (eds), *Vulnerabilities, Care and Family Law* (Abingdon, Routledge 2013).

One party being able to influence the interests of the other party.

One party improperly taking advantage of the other party.

There not being an adequate sharing of the gains and losses flowing from the transaction.

It may be that the difficulty of definition arises because the exploitation arises from a combination of all three of these, but there is no one level at which these can be set. So in a case where one party has considerable power over another, a relatively small degree of inequality in the sharing of the gains and losses is sufficient to make the transaction exploitative. Where, however, there is relatively little power one party has over the other, a more significant inequality in the sharing of the gains and losses needs to be shown.

It is suggested that what may be the most helpful approach is to ask whether the parties showed each other due respect for the vulnerability of the other. Where one party is aware that the other is vulnerable in some sense, that may require them to take special steps to ensure the transaction is fair. We should ask: to what extent was the stronger party legitimately able to say 'I am confident that the other party was able to make a reasonable assessment of whether the transaction was in their best interests'? The greater the pressures, the mistakes, and the incapacities of the other party, the harder it will be persuade the court of that. A party who contributes to these will find it all the harder to claim they were properly seeking a justification for the transaction.

Criminalizing exploitation in practice

I have been exploring some of the difficulties in defining exploitation. The proposed definition in the previous paragraph will strike many as being vague and not useful in a legal setting. The difficulty is exacerbated because if we define exploitation too narrowly there is a risk that people will be left without protection from exploitation, but if we define it too broadly, both victims and defendants have their autonomy interfered with by the court. Can my proposed approach of asking whether due respect was paid for the vulnerability of the other provide any kind of clear guidance? In this next section I will show how it can, discussing a controversial area of the law: sexual exploitation.[26]

---

[26] See also J. Herring, 'Rape and the Definition of Consent', (2014) 26 *National Law School of India Review* 46.

How can we draw the line between sexual behaviour which is exploitative and deserving of criminal sanction and that which is not? There are
some cases of rape where it is obvious that there is no consent. The difficult
cases turn on whether the exploitative techniques employed by a defendant
mean there is no genuine consent, even though there may have been words
or behaviour indicating consent.

To understand the issue it is necessary to say a little more about consent.[27] You do need a person's consent to perform an act unless you are
doing something that harms them. You do not normally need permission
to look at someone because looking at them causes them no harm. Consent
becomes relevant when D's act wrongfully harms another person (V)'s well-
being thereby rendering the act a prima facie wrong. Where an act is a
prima facie wrong the actor (D) must provide a reason justifying acting in
the way they did. Consent operates as providing a justifying reason. Where
V consents to the act D is entitled to assume that the act is not all things
considered contrary to the wellbeing of the victim (V). That is because D is
permitted to rely on V's assessment that the act is overall in V's best interests. Madden Dempsey explains that in effect, where consent is effective D
is entitled to say:

> This is [V]'s decision. He's an adult and can decide for himself whether he thinks
> the risk is worth it. In considering what to do, I will assume that his decision is
> the right one for him. After all, he is in a better position than I to judge his own
> well-being. And so, I will not take it upon myself to reconsider those reasons.
> Instead, I will base my decision of whether to [harm] him on the other relevant
> reasons.[28]

This approach only operates where there is full consent. That means that D
can reasonably take V to be making an effective assessment of V's best interests. This means that where V is mistaken or pressurized or their thinking
is impaired, then their apparent consent will not be sufficient to entitle D to
assume that V has made an effective assessment of their best interests. This
important point can be developed further.

If V is consenting to an act which is prima facie wrongful, but is doing
so under pressure or under a mistake, D cannot be confident the act will
promote V's best interests. So if V is, for example, agrees to have sex with D
or agrees to give D her car, but is doing so because V believes D is a former
lover she has not seen for many years, whereas in fact D is someone else, D

---

[27] M. Madden Dempsey, 'Victimless Conduct and the Volenti Maxim: How Consent Works',
(2013) 7 *Criminal Law and Philosophy* 11.
[28] Ibid., 20.

cannot take V's consent as an assessment of her well-being, because it is an assessment based on an error of the factual scenario.

There is a further important point about this model of consent. It reinforces the idea that if D is to wrong V, D has responsibilities to ensure that they have good reasons for so acting. V's consent might provide that but D has to take reasonable steps to ensure that the consent can be taken as an assessment by V of their well-being. This is why the mere word 'yes' is not enough for consent. Even though, for example, an intoxicated V may be saying 'yes', it will not give D warrant to assume that V has made an effective assessment of her well-being.

When the court is considering whether V's consent provides D with a defence, this involves looking at the encounter between the two people, how they understood and negotiated the act. This involves not looking just at the moment of sex but also at the context of the relationship and the broader social environment. Does the interaction indicate that D was seeking to let or enable V to make a free, informed decision about what was in her best interests or was D lying, threatening, pressurizing V? The use of deceptions, pressures, manipulations, and the like indicate that D was not seeking to use consent as an assessment by V of their wellbeing. Was D given time and space to make the decision, ensuring they were not labouring under any mistake? I believe this provides a sufficiently clear approach to identifying sexual exploitation and one which better protects the sexual rights of everyone.

Rule of law and exploitation

Earlier I mentioned the concerns that the model of exploitation mentioned here may be seen as excessively vague. The difficulty here is that, particularly in the area of exploitation, the more precisely defined the offence, the greater the danger a defendant will get around the 'letter of the law' to make a gain. The practice of tax avoidance shows this well. The obvious answer, to rely on vaguely worded laws capturing the spirit of exploitation, risks the danger of being too vague to comply with the rule of law. In brief, the rule of law requires that the criminal law should be clear and predictable so that a citizen seeking to comply with the law should know exactly what they do or do not have to do to remain lawful. That is why much ink is spilt in academic criminal lawyers complaining about apparent ambiguities in the law. This issue particularly comes to the fore in relation to offences around exploitation.

It is important to remember that the rule of law, while an important value, is not the only value of significance in the law.[29] As Joseph Raz remarks:

Conflict between the rule of law and other values is just what is to be expected. Conformity to the rule of law is a matter of degree, and though, other things being equal, the greater the conformity the better—other things are rarely equal. A lesser degree of conformity is often to be preferred precisely because it helps the realization of other goals.[30]

Raz promotes the rule of law as valuable for reducing arbitrariness, promoting freedom and protecting human dignity.

One way of responding to this issue may be to rely on the 'thin ice principle' developed in *Knuller v DPP*. There it was stated 'those who skate on thin ice can hardly expect to find a sign which will denote the precise spot where [they] will fall in'. The argument is that if a person realizes that their behaviour is border-line illegal then they must take the risk that they will be found criminally liable. Where the behaviour is harmful and is blameworthy, the defendant realizes they are on thin ice. A defendant who realizes that what they are doing may well be criminal can hardly complain if it turns out that the activity was criminal. So, to use an example which we will return to later, if a defendant dishonestly exploits their relationship with someone else, they cannot complain if the court interprets s. 4 of the Fraud Act 2006 to cover their conduct. By exploiting another and acting dishonestly they were skating on thin ice. That is the kind of behaviour you should realize might get you into trouble with the criminal law, even if the law is somewhat unclear in that area.

A good example of the debate is that over *Hinks*, in which a defendant exploited a vulnerable man in a way which was dishonest but which was, according to many commentators, not generally thought to be criminal. The House of Lords found the transaction was theft. It may have been a valid gift in terms of property law, but that did not prevent it being a criminal offence. Many commentators found that a surprising conclusion and complained that it breached the rule of law.[31] In response to such claims Alan Bogg and John Stanton-Ife[32] note the defendant in that case 'cannot say that she suffered

---

[29] This section owes a great deal to A. L. Bogg and J. Stanton-Ife, 'Protecting the Vulnerable: Legality, Harm and Theft', (2003) 23 *Legal Studies* 402.

[30] J. Raz, *The Authority of Law* (Oxford, Oxford University Press 1979) p. 228.

See Raz, n. 18 above, pp. 219–23, 408.

[31] J.C. Smith, who condemns the decision as, with all respect, 'contrary to common sense' ([2001] Crim LR 163, p. 164); A.P. Simester and G.R. Sullivan, *Criminal Law, Theory and Doctrine* (Hart, Oxford 2000), who argue that the decision 'must be undone' (p. 455); and M. Allen, *Textbook on Criminal Law* (6th edn, Oxford, Oxford University Press, 2001), who describes the decision as incredible (p. 404), 'almost surreal' (p. 405), and 'ridiculous' and 'bizarre' (p. 415).

[32] A.L. Bogg and J. Stanton-Ife (n. 29).

from uncertainty, since *ex hypothesi* she had no belief in the legality of her actions and had by contrast a belief that they were dishonest by the standards of ordinary and decent people'. They also argue that protecting vulnerable people from dishonest exploitation promotes the dignity and autonomy of those vulnerable people. So in determining how the rule of law balances against the other values it is by no means clear that 'legal certainty' must always win out. That last point is developed by John Gardner, writing in the context of offences against the person. He argues that too great a precision in the definition of offences can allow defendants to

enjoy a bizarre kind of mastery over their own normative situation. They could evade a moral or legal rule which is means-specific simply by adopting different means ... So there is good reason, other things being equal, to withdraw some or all of the means-specificity from a moral or legal rule where its violation consists in the intentional pursuit or achievement of some result.[42]

It is indeed striking that the majority of commentators who have criticized Hinks seem to assume that certainty is more important than protecting people from exploitation. The primary concern seems to be protecting the market freedoms of the strong and the capable, rather than protecting the vulnerable from exploitation.

Protection and paternalism

One of the major themes in the debates concerning the response of the criminal law to 'vulnerable people' is the balance between protection and paternalism. On the one hand criminalizing offences which are seen to harm vulnerable people can be seen as a benefit to them, in that it recognizes harms that previously went under acknowledged. Victims can receive the help they need, the public are informed about the dangers of these crimes for vulnerable people, people know to look out for friends and relatives who may be victims, and there is a public acknowledgement and response to the wrong behavior. On the other hand, a law which might be designed to protect a vulnerable group may at the same time restrict the freedom of members of that group. It may also reinforce stigmatizing attitudes towards them. I will look at two issues which illustrate these difficulties well: prostitution and prosecution of domestic abuse.

Prostitution

A central problem with the use of the criminal law to protect the vulnerable is the danger of over breadth. The issue is well illustrated by the fierce debates over whether prostitute use should be made illegal. There is a widespread agreement among commentators that the prostituted women should not be criminalized and social support needs to be offered to enable those who wish to leave the profession to do so.[33] Further, there is agreement that if a prostitute user is aware that a woman has been forced into prostitution and still has sex he should be guilty of rape.[34] The debates turn on whether prostitute use should be a crime.

The 'Nordic Model',[35] developed in Scandinavia, has been particularly influential. This promotes the decriminalization of prostituted women and provides comprehensive social support for those seeking to exit prostitution. At the same time prostitute users, pimps, and traffickers face criminal sanctions. The approach has recently been supported by the European Parliament which has called on national parliaments to adopt the Nordic model.

Arguments in favour of criminalizing prostitute use include that prostitute users cannot know (unless they know the prostitutes very well) whether the prostituted woman is acting freely. Therefore a prostitute user is always taking a risk in using a prostitute that he is committing rape. There may be cases where a person is doing something which risks harm to others but this is justified because the activity has a considerable social benefit. The driving of cars may be an example. However, it is argued that prostitute use carries no social benefits, or certainly none sufficient to justify the risk of rape.

Other arguments in favour of the Nordic model place much weight on vulnerability. Supporters claim that criminalizing prostitute use will protect vulnerable women who are forced, trafficked, or coerced into prostitution. Fiona Taggart MP in the debates on prostitution stated that those engaged in prostitution are 'vulnerable young women with disturbed backgrounds' and insisted that 'it is all too easy for such a person to fall under the influence of a dominant male, who exploits that vulnerability for financial gain'.[36] The Home Office explains that vulnerability is a key route into prostitution and that 'for adults, economic vulnerability is likely to play as significant a part as emotional vulnerability'.[37]

Some feminist arguments also draw on language which might be linked to vulnerability. It is argued that prostitution is the epitome of

---

[33] M.M. Dempsey, 'Decriminalizing Victims of Sex Trafficking', (2015) 52 *American Criminal Law Review* 207.

[34] Sexual Offences Act 2003, s. 53A. Paying for sexual services of a prostitute subjected to force etc.

[35] Countries such as Sweden, Norway, Finland, and Iceland.

[36] Hansard HC vol 486 col 548 (1996).

[37] Home Office, *Paying the Price* (London, Home Office, 2004), 33.

patriarchal commodification of women.[38] The fact women turn to prostitution, even if apparently willingly, is due to the societal pressures on women which leave them with so few options. Persistent abuse of women, reinforced by broader social attitudes towards women, creates the market for prostitution.

Opponents argue that making prostitute use illegal would interfere in the rights of women who choose to enter prostitution. The Wolfenden Report concluded that criminalization of prostitute use was beyond the proper scope of a liberal criminal law system. This conclusion was based on the assumption that the 'great majority of prostitutes ... choose this life because they find in it a style of living which is to them easier, freer and more profitable than would be provided by any other occupation'.[39] Opponents claim supporters of the Nordic model assume all prostitutes are 'vulnerable', whereas for many it is a free choice, which deserves respect.[40] Sharon Cowan argues:

I argue that law and policy makers presume vulnerability (often alongside deviance) on the basis of normative conceptions of risky behaviour, or ascription of normative identity categories such as prostitute, sado-masochist and so on (a similar critique has also been made of the psychoanalytic categorisation of sexual deviance, or 'paraphilias'). This is not to argue that individual sex workers or BDSM participants can never be vulnerable; rather, that vulnerability is all too often assumed and projected, and then used as a basis for criminalisation, regardless of the lived realities of sexual subjects who constantly negotiate power, identities and relationships in their daily lives. Rather than mark out individuals or particular identity categories as victims or irresponsible sexual subjects, there is potential for the broader recognition of vulnerability as a product of social and institutional interactions, which can be experienced in a variety of ways by all, to be, as McRobbie suggests, 'productive of new forms of sociability', and 'conducive to developing wider modes of commonality and co-operation'.

Cowan is certainly right that there are dangers in describing prostitutes as a vulnerable group.[41]

Sharon Cowan complains that supporters of criminalizing prostitute use claim that prostitutes are vulnerable and in need of protection as a mask

---

[38] S. Jeffreys, *The Idea of Prostitution* (Melbourne, Spinifex Press 1997).

[39] Lord Wolfenden, *Committee on Homosexual Offences and Prostituion* (London, Home Office, 1957)

[40] S. Day, 'Wolfenden 50: Revisiting State Policy and the Politics of Sex Work in the UK' in V. Munro and M. Giusta (eds), *Demanding Sex: Critical Reflections on the Regulation of Prostitution* (London, Ashgate 2008).

[41] V. Munro and J. Scoular, 'Abusing Vulnerability? Contemporary Law and Policy Responses to Sex Work in the UK', (2012) 20(3) *Feminist Legal Studies* 189.

for their moral dislike of prostitution.[42] While no doubt some who support criminalizing prostitute use do solely based on their moral objection, many do not and so I am not sure that point gets us very far. Michelle Madden Demspey agrees that the feminist cause seeking to promote the criminalization of prostitute use has 'strange bed fellows'. She sees that as not necessarily problematic. Many good causes may be supported by people who support it for strange reasons, but that does not make the cause improper. However, she recognizes the dangers that the powers the law creates might be used by police, prosecutors, and judges who are not committed to feminist goals.

Some observations can be made about the debate. The first is that it is quite possible, indeed almost inevitable, that it is true that there are some sex workers who are not 'vulnerable' and make a full free decision to do this work, and others from whom there is coercion and a lack of freedom. There is a fierce debate over which is the larger of these groups. Indeed, the division into those who are trafficked and 'professional sex workers' is clearly not straightforward and there are plenty of cases which fall between such classifications.[43] A Home Office study found that 50 per cent of prostituted women started being paid for sex before they were 18 years old and 95% of women engaged in street prostitution are 'problematic drug users'.[44] Further, there is strong evidence that many prostituted women are subject to violence from their pimps and coercion.[45] So while it is difficult to put a precise figure on how many prostituted women are autonomously choosing to be prostitutes, it is clear many are.[46]

In fact, the exact percentages of how many prostituted women are acting autonomously may not be that significant for the debate. The argument mentioned earlier, that the prostitute user cannot know whether or not the prostitute is freely consenting or not, does not depend very much on the exact percentages of prostitutes who are non-autonomous as long as there is a number of some significance. In light of the severe gravity of the harm at issue (namely rape), the likelihood that this harm occurs systematically (rather than in isolated cases), the low social value (if any) in prostitute use,

---

[42] S. Cowan, 'To Buy or Not to Buy? Vulnerability and the Criminalisation of Commercial BDSM', (2012) 20 *Feminist Legal Studies* 263.

[43] V. Munro and M. Giusta (eds), *Demanding Sex: Critical Reflections on the Regulation of Prostitution* (London, Ashgate 2008).

[44] Home Office, *Paying the Price: A Consultation Paper on Prostitution* (London, Home Office, 2004).

[45] M. O'Neill, 'Prostitute Women Now' in G. Scambler and A. Scambler (eds), *Rethinking Prostitution: Purchasing Sex in the 1990s* (Routledge, London 1997), pp. 15, 17; J. Phoenix, *Making Sense of Prostitution* (MacMillan Press, London 1999), p. 121.

[46] V. E. Munro and J. Scoular (n. 41).

the case for criminalization seems strong, regardless of the precise percentage of non-autonomous prostituted women.[47]

The second observation on the debate is that the legal intervention can create vulnerabilities as well as protect them. One of the arguments that is used against criminalization of prostitute use is that it will drive the practice underground and mean that sex workers are at greater risk of abuse. Alternatively women currently undertaking sex work may, if it is prohibited, find even more exploitative and dangerous work to undertake.[48] There is also a concern that prosecution of sex workers might be combined with attempts to 'rehabilitate' former prostitutes with pressure being used to place them in other jobs. Whether this is true or not is debatable. Madden Dempsey[49] emphasizes research suggesting that in Sweden, following an implementation of this model, there was a decline of over 50 per cent in prostitute use and that there was no evidence to suggest that prostitution had been hidden or driven underground. It has provided, she argues, an effective tool against sex trafficking. Not everyone is convinced, but the fear that legal interventions designed to protect prostituted women may end up harming them is an important concern that must always be borne in mind.

The third observation is that the issue highlights well the difficulty in identifying which acts harm vulnerable people. Madden Dempsey[50] has made a powerful case in favour of criminalizing prostitute use. She notes that even in a case where the prostituted woman is acting freely, the prostitute user is encouraging a market in prostitution, a market that inevitably includes prostituted women who are not acting autonomously. She argues: '[T]he harm suffered by forced prostitutes can be fairly imputed to all prostitute-users, due to their role in creating the demand for the prostitution market.' These points, it is argued, make a powerful case for criminalizing prostitute use. This argument demonstrates that the actions between two people, even if deemed non-vulnerable, can have an impact on others who would be deemed vulnerable. Not everyone will be convinced by this argument, although I am, but it does demonstrate that the task of protection of vulnerable people may not be limited to prohibiting acts directly targeted at vulnerable people themselves.

Fourth, one of the dangers of identifying prostituted women as liable to manipulation and coercion in the sexual area may be that it suggests that

---

[47] M.M. Dempsey, 'How to Argue About Prostitution', (2012) 6 *Criminal Law & Philosophy* 65.

[48] Although it may be questioned whether any such work could be found that would not be similarly prohibited.

[49] M.M. Dempsey, 'Decriminalizing Victims of Sex Trafficking', (2015) 52 *American Criminal Law Review* 207.

[50] Ibid.

other people are not. Catherine Mackinnon and other radical feminists have emphasized that women are commonly subjected to coercive pressure and force in relation to sex.[51] The concern is that once one group is labelled vulnerable it may be assumed that others outside that group are not vulnerable.

Fifth, it is striking how both sides of the debate can rely on autonomy based arguments.

Given that it is clear that sex trafficked women make up a proportion of prostituted women and other sex workers are acting voluntarily, it might be thought that we must choose between a law which protects the autonomy of women choosing to work in prostitution but interferes in the autonomy of those who are coerced into prostitution; or a law which protects the autonomy of those not freely choosing prostitution, but interferes with those who have chosen that profession.[52] I would argue against that approach. Those sex workers acting voluntarily have a range of options open to them if prostitute use is criminalized. They can, of course, have sex without payment in all cases of consensual sex. There are many other forms of employment open to them. The interference in their autonomy is, therefore, limited. For the non-consenting prostituted women, if the law does not prevent their abuse then they are stuck in prostitution with no other options. Further, repeatedly being raped is a far bigger invasion of their rights than being denied the choice of entering sex work.[53]

Prosecution of domestic abuse

There is little dispute that domestic abuse should be treated as a crime. But should prosecutions proceed even where the victim opposes the prosecution? In some jurisdictions, for example, prosecution authorities are encouraged or even required to prosecute cases of domestic violence, even where the victim fails to co-operate or even opposes the use of such procedures.[54] Such a policy is commonly known as mandatory prosecution.

---

[51] C. MacKinnon, *Towards a Feminist Theory of the State* (Cambridge MA, Harvard University Press 1989).

[52] L. Kelly and L. Regan, *Stopping Traffic: Exploring the Extent of and Response to Trafficking of Women for Sexual Exploitation in the UK* (Home Office, 2000), p. 22

[53] M. Farley, 'Prostitution, Trafficking, and Cultural Amnesia: What We Must Not Know in Order to Keep the Business of Sexual Exploitation Running Smoothly', (2006) 18 *Yale Journal of Law and Feminism* 109.

[54] A. Gruber, 'The Feminist War on Crime', (2007) 92 *Iowa Law Review* 741, 813 (describing the historical development of this phenomenon in the domestic violence context). Others might argue that the shift is not to disempower victims, but perpetrators.

Supporters of mandatory prosecution policy often refer to vulnerability of victims of domestic abuse. They claim that if victims are able to veto the bringing of proceedings then pressure will be put upon them by perpetrators. There are also concerns that if the victim is saying they do not want the prosecution to proceed that may be because they are still under the control of the abuser and fail to appreciate the position they are in.[55] Mandatory prosecution is also supported on the basis that it sends a clear message about the unacceptability of domestic abuse[56] and ensures that children who are suffering living in a household marked by domestic violence are protected, regardless of the wishes of the direct victim.[57]

Opponents of the policy object that mandatory policies in practice are used in a way which discriminates against victims of domestic violence who are particularly vulnerable through being in a disadvantaged group by being of minority race or in a low socio-economic class.[58] Hence it is claimed that mandatory prosecution policies tend to be given effect by police officers against poor black men, and overlooked in other cases.[59] The policy is also said to reinforce a stereotype of victims of domestic abuse as lacking capacity and being unable to make decisions for themselves.[60] Rather than the abuser dominating the victim and making decisions about her life, now the state is taking on the same role.[61] Naomi Kohn, writing in the context of elder abuse, suggests:

by allowing the state to act without the active participation of victims—and even over their objections—and by differentiating among victims based on chronological age, the criminal justice system response is poised to further victimize elder abuse victims, promote negative stereotypes about older adults, and undermine efforts to provide services to elder abuse victims.[62]

---

[55] D. Epstein, 'Effective Intervention in Domestic Violence Cases: Rethinking the Roles of Prosecutors, Judges, and the Court System', (1999) 11 *Yale Journal of Law & Feminism* 3, 17.

[56] D. Epstein, M. E. Bell, and L. A. Goodman, 'Transforming Aggressive Prosecution Policies: Prioritizing Victims' Long-Term Safety in the Prosecution of Domestic Violence Cases', (2003) 11 *American University Journal of Gender, Social Policy & the Law* 465, 466 (describing no-drop policies as sending 'a strong symbolic message that the community will not tolerate domestic violence').

[57] S. Choudhry and J. Herring, 'Righting Domestic Violence', (2006) *International Journal of Law, Policy and the Family* 95.

[58] L. G. Mills, *Violent Partners: A Breakthrough Plan for Ending the Cycle of Violence* (New York, Oxford University Press 2009) 31–3.

[59] A. Gruber, 'The Feminist War on Crime', (2007) 92 *Iowa Law Review* 741, 813.

[60] L. Goodmark, 'Autonomy Feminism: An Anti-Essentialist Critique of Mandatory Intervention in Domestic Violence Cases', (2009) 37 *Florida State University Law Review* 1, 45.

[61] D. Epstein, 'Effective Intervention', (n. 55), 17 ('[W]here the bulk of control was ceded to the perpetrator under the old automatic drop system, it is now ceded to the prosecutor.').

[62] N. Kohn, 'Elder (In)Justice: A Critique of the Criminalization of Elder Abuse', (2012) 49 *American Journal of Criminal Law* 1.

We see in these arguments over the prosecution of domestic abuse some of the tensions already highlighted. As with prostitution, we have a group of women (victims of domestic abuse) some of whom are able to make decisions and some of whom are not able to act autonomously. If we are not able to identify who falls within which group, we have the difficulty of disempowering one part of the group in the name of empowering another. There are the concerns that policies designed to protect vulnerable people end up depriving them of power even further. There is also the tension in the interference in the autonomy of some members of the group being justified in the name of protecting others.[63]

Shared vulnerabilities

One of the dangers with the use of the criminal law to protect vulnerable people is that vulnerable people can end up being prosecuted. We have already seen in Chapter 3 that the state has a duty to protect vulnerable adults, although it often fails in that regard. Where a vulnerable adult is injured the criminal law currently is in danger of blaming others around them who are equally vulnerable, rather than acknowledging the state and societal responsibilities for what has happened. I will use two examples to illustrate this point.

Manslaughter

The controversial decision of *R v Stone and Dobinson*[64] is a fine example of the issue in the context of manslaughter. Stone and Dobinson were an unmarried couple. Stone was described as almost blind and of low intelligence. Dobinson, his partner, was described as 'ineffectual and inadequate'. Stone's sister was unwell and appeared to have suffered from anorexia nervosa and was infirm. The sister had not been able to access medical help and went to live with the defendants. They struggled enough to look after themselves, let alone to look after her. She was placed in a room with no ventilation or a toilet, and only a bucket to wash herself. Stone and Dobinson were encouraged by neighbours to seek the help of social services, but the sister refused to give the name of her doctor. Stone tried to get his own doctor to attend without success. After several weeks the sister died.

---

[63] L. G. Mills, *Violent Partners* (n. 58), 31–3.   [64] [1977] 2 All ER 341.

The Court of Appeal upheld the conviction of Stone and Dobinson for manslaughter. The defendants had undertaken a duty to care for the sister and failed to provide an appropriate level of care. The jury had found this to be a reckless disregard for the health and safety of another person.

The case is controversial for several reasons. First, it seems that the defendants could be classified as 'vulnerable adults' themselves. They seem barely able to care for themselves, let alone be held legally accountable for the care of another. Second, it seems the real failures were the lack of support from the social services and medical professionals. One could imagine a very different telling of this story where the focus was on the failing of the different public authorities to support Stone, Dobinson, and the sister. Indeed in terms of resources, knowledge, and expertise, were not the authorities in a far better position to intervene than Stone and Dobinson?[65] Was this a case where laws designed to protect one vulnerable person left another vulnerable person open to abuse?

To be fair, it should be emphasized that it is not clear whether the same decision would be reached today. Nowadays the case would be charged as one of gross negligence manslaughter and the jury would need to decide whether the behaviour of the defendants fell so far below the standard expected that they deserved a criminal conviction.[66] Whether using this direction a jury would convict is hard to predict.

Causing or allowing the death of a child or vulnerable adult

Another example of the way a criminal offence designed to protect vulnerable people can, in fact, end up being used to prosecute vulnerable people is the offence of familial homicide. The offence was created to deal with a difficulty that arose in cases where a child or vulnerable adult was killed in a house where two defendants lived. The Law Commission[67] put the issue in this way:

[In many cases] ... it cannot be proved which of two or more defendants was directly responsible for the offence and it cannot be proved that whichever defendant was not directly responsible must have been guilty as an accomplice ... The present law is that there is no prima facie case against either and therefore both defendants must be acquitted at the conclusion of the prosecution case.

---

[65] J. Herring, *Criminal Law*, (n. 2), ch 6.   [66] Ibid.
[67] The difficulty was summarized by the Law Commission Report *Children: Their Non-Accidental Death, or Serious Injury (Criminal Trials)* (2003) Law Com. No. 282; HC 1054), para. 2.

To deal with this an offence was created in s. 5 of the Domestic Violence Crime and Victim Act 2004:

(1) A person ('D') is guilty of an offence if—
  (a) a child or vulnerable adult ('V') dies or suffers serious physical harm as a result of the unlawful act of a person who—
    (i)   was a member of the same household as V, and
    (ii) had frequent contact with him,
  (b) D was such a person at the time of that act,
  (c) at that time there was a significant risk of serious physical harm being caused to V by the unlawful act of such a person, and
  (d) either D was the person whose act caused the death or serious physical harm or—
    (i)   D was, or ought to have been, aware of the risk mentioned in paragraph (c),
    (ii) D failed to take such steps as he could reasonably have been expected to take to protect V from the risk, and
    (iii) the act occurred in circumstances of the kind that D foresaw or ought to have foreseen.
(2) The prosecution does not have to prove whether it is the first alternative in sub-section (1)(d) or the second (sub-paragraphs (i) to (iii)) that applies.
(3) If D was not the mother or father of V—
  (a) D may not be charged with an offence under this section if he was under the age of 16 at the time of the act that caused the death or serious physical harm;
  (b) for the purposes of subsection (1)(d)(ii) D could not have been expected to take any such step as is referred to there before attaining that age.
(4) For the purposes of this section—
  (a) a person is to be regarded as a 'member' of a particular household, even if he does not live in that household, if he visits it so often and for such periods of time that it is reasonable to regard him as a member of it;
  (b) where V lived in different households at different times, '*the same household as V*' refers to the household in which V was living at the time of the act that caused the death or serious physical harm.
(5) For the purposes of this section an 'unlawful' act is one that—
  (a) constitutes an offence, or
  (b) would constitute an offence but for being the act of—
    (i)   a person under the age of ten, or
    (ii) a person entitled to rely on a defence of insanity.
  Paragraph (b) does not apply to an act of D.
(6) In this section—
  '*act*' includes a course of conduct and also includes omission;
  '*child*' means a person under the age of 16;
  '*serious*' harm means harm that amounts to grievous bodily harm for the purposes of the Offences against the Person Act 1861 (c. 100);

'*vulnerable adult*' means a person aged 16 or over whose ability to protect himself from violence, abuse or neglect is significantly impaired through physical or mental disability or illness, through old age or otherwise.

This offence means that in the problematic scenario the prosecution can allege that each defendant is guilty of the s. 5 offence. Either they committed the murder (or caused grievous bodily harm) or they failed to protect the child or vulnerable adult from death.

The point for this section is that it is noticeable how this offence has been used to prosecute victims of domestic abuse. Two cases are particularly concerning.

The first reported conviction concerned Sandra Mujuru, aged twenty-one, who 'allowed' her partner, Jerry Stephens, to murder their four-year-old baby (Ayesha).[68] The Court of Appeal justified her conviction in this way:

There was also evidence before the jury capable of supporting a finding that Miss M knew that S had broken A's arm, or had good reason to think that he might have done so, and that she was, or ought to have been, aware that there was a significant risk that he might deliberately harm A again. If they made those findings, the jury could go on to find that by leaving A in his care while she went to work Miss M failed to take such steps as she could reasonably have been expected to take to protect her.[69]

The Crown Prosecution Service (CPS), justifying the decision to prosecute, noted that Ms Mujuru was aware of Stephens' potential for violence because she had visited him while he was serving time in prison for an attack on his previous girlfriend.

These explanations fail to give sufficient weight to the circumstances in which Ms Mujuru found herself. She was an asylum-seeker escaping violence in Zimbabwe. In sentencing her the judge commented that she was a 'decent young woman in a vulnerable position'. The judge noticed that Stephens was twice her age and was a 'self-centered and dangerous man with a dangerously short fuse'. As a young asylum-seeker, should she really have been expected to know from which authorities to seek advice and how to access the appropriate services? Could she have done this without endangering her child and herself by igniting her partner's 'dangerously short fuse'? On the day the child's body was found, Stephens had assaulted his previous girlfriend, hitting her on the head with a frying pan and a vase. So, were her fears that she would be attacked if she sought help for her and her child really so ill-founded?

In May 2005 Rebecca Lewis, aged twenty-one, was sentenced for failing to prevent the murder of her baby, Aaron Gilbert, at the hands of her partner,

---

[68] *Stephens and Mujuru* [2007] EWCA Crim 1249.   [69] Ibid., para. 32.

Andrew Lloyd, with whom she had lived for six weeks.[70] She was sentenced to six years in prison. Lloyd was sentenced to twenty-four years in prison for murder. The court accepted that Lewis was largely absent during the attacks and was not present at the killing, but held she did know enough to be aware of a risk of death or serious harm. In particular Lewis knew that Lloyd had flicked Aaron's ears and feet when he cried; had picked him up by his ears and ankles; and had thrown him onto a bed. In sentencing her the judge said: 'You put your own interests first, above and beyond that of your vulnerable child. You could have stopped the violence that Lloyd was subjecting Aaron to. You could so easily have got the authorities to stop it.' Again this case seems to inadequately take account of the impact of the domestic violence. At the trial Lewis had explained that she did not summon help because Lloyd had said he would kill her if she left. For 'putting her interests first' she was given a sentence only a little shorter than the average given for rape. Of particular note is the fact that local services had been told by Lewis's cousin of concerns about the child. The social services wrote a letter asking to make an appointment, but it was sent to the wrong address. The authorities were aware of the dangers the child faced and, given their expertise, were in a better position than Lewis to foresee what might happen. More importantly, the authorities had the resources to respond to the problems and the freedom from fear of reprisals if they did so. Was it really Lewis who was to blame in this scenario?

These concerns have been noted by the Court of Appeal in *Khan*,[71] which stated:

We note the concern expressed by Jonathan Herring in *Familial Homicide, Failure to Protect and Domestic Violence: Who's the Victim* [2007] Crim. L.R. 923 that abused women, for example, may be prosecuted for allowing their violent partners to kill their child. However, s.5(1)(d)(ii) makes clear that the protective steps which could have been expected of the defendant depend on what reasonably could have been expected of him or her. In the present case, for example, if either of the female appellants had herself been subjected by her brother, Shazad, to serious violence of the kind which engulfed Sabia, the jury might have concluded that it would not have been reasonable to expect her to take any protective steps, or that any protective steps she might have taken, even if relatively minor, and although in the end unsuccessful to save the deceased, were reasonable in the circumstances.

Whether the reference to what could reasonably be expected of the defendant is sufficient to deal with these concerns is questionable, at least unless the jury are given expert advice on the impact of domestic abuse. I have argued

---

[70] BBC News online, 'Mother Allowed Baby Son's Murder', 15 December, 2006.
[71] *R v Khan* [2009] EWCA Crim 2, para. 33.

for a specific defence to be created to this offence to deal with cases where the defendant was themselves a victim of domestic abuse. Samantha Moreton[72] has provided a robust response:

> Providing for this group of vulnerable defendants in the legislation to the exclusion of other vulnerable defendants would be discriminatory. It would provide a defence for one pool of defendants in one type of case who are psychologically unable to perceive risk in the same way as those who are vulnerable due to domestic violence. It would not provide the same protection for defendants who are vulnerable to the same extent for equally blameless reasons such as due to age or mental illness. Yet these defendants could be at risk of familial homicide liability whilst those who were victims of domestic violence could have a possible defence if such a defence was introduced.

This point is well made. It may be that a more general defence needs to be created which deals with defendants who have sufficiently strong reasons for being unable to live up to the objective requirement.

So we have seen in these two examples that attempts by the authorities to protect vulnerable people who have been left to suffer serious harm have resulted in prosecutions of defendants who themselves are vulnerable. In these cases the networks of vulnerability and care have not adequately been taken into account. Further, the responsibilities of public authorities to vulnerable people have been sidelined by locating the blame on those least in a position to protect the victims.

Especial protection for the vulnerable

The criminal law has created a series of offences which are specifically designed to deal with vulnerable adults and we will explore these here.

Fraud by abuse of position

Section 4 of the Fraud Act 2006 appears particularly designed to protect vulnerable people. The offence is fraud by abuse of position, although there has been much debate over precisely what is the nature of the wrong at the heart of the offence. Section 4(1) of the Fraud Act 2006 states that it will be fraud if a person:

(a) occupies a position in which he is expected to safeguard, or not to act against, the financial interests of another person,

---

[72] S. Morrison, 'Should There Be a Domestic Violence Defence to the Offence of Familial Homicide?', [2013] *Criminal Law Review* 826.

(b) dishonestly abuses that position, and
(c) intends, by means of the abuse of that position—
    (i) to make a gain for himself or another, or
    (ii) to cause loss to another or to expose another to a risk of loss.

Further, s. 4(2) states that: 'A person may be regarded as having abused his position even though his conduct consisted of an omission rather than an act.' Much debate has, however, concerned what is meant by 'a position in which [the defendant] is expected to safeguard, or not to act against, the financial interests of another person'. There are some obvious examples where this is so: a solicitor acting for a client or a trustee acting for a beneficiary. However, it seems generally agreed that the provision is intended to apply to a broader category of cases than those. The Law Commission suggested the following situations should be covered:

> The necessary relationship will be present between trustee and beneficiary, director and company, professional person and client, agent and principal, employee and employer, or between partners. It may arise otherwise, for example within a family, or in the context of voluntary work, or in any context where the parties are not at arm's length. In nearly all cases where it arises, it will be recognised by the civil law as importing fiduciary duties, and any relationship that is so recognised will suffice. We see no reason, however, why the existence of such duties should be essential. This does not of course mean that it would be entirely a matter for the fact-finders whether the necessary relationship exists. The question whether the particular facts alleged can properly be described as giving rise to that relationship will be an issue capable of being ruled upon by the judge and, if the case goes to the jury, of being the subject of directions.[73]

This suggests that the class of relationships is not limited to those where there is a fiduciary relationship of the kind recognized by law, but more broadly covers relationships between family members and relationships where one person has a responsibility towards another. It also suggests that we are not talking only about legal responsibilities here, but generally about cases where a person has a legal or moral obligation to take care of another.

The key requirement is that the defendant was 'expected to safeguard or not act against the financial interests of another person'. As Jennifer Collins[74] notes, it is not clear from the Act whose expectation we are discussing. She argues it could not be enough for the victim to expect someone to look after their interests because otherwise a defendant may end up

---

[73] *Fraud,* Law Com. No. 276, para. 7.38.
[74] J. Collins, 'The Contours of Vulnerability' in J. Wallbank and J. Herring (eds), *Vulnerabilities, Care and Family Law* (Abingdon, Routledge 2013).

facing a responsibility which they did not intend to take on. Similarly it should not be an entirely subjective test for the defendant. It would be hard for the prosecution to show the defendant intended to accept responsibility for the financial interests of another. A more likely interpretation is that it is the expectation of a reasonable onlooker which is considered. Would a reasonable onlooker accept that in this situation and in the context of the relationship between the parties, the defendant could be expected to safeguard or not act against the financial interests of another person? That seems the correct test, although it is far from clear to what extent a person has an expectation to safeguard the financial interests of another person. Indeed, in the argument advanced earlier in this chapter it was suggested that we all have some obligation to treat others fairly and not improperly harm the interests of another. That seems to me a not improper reading of the offence. Should there be cases where D has dishonestly abused their relationship with another person for financial gain, but they should be not guilty on the basis they could not be expected to look out for the financial interests of the other?

The offence is committed if there is an abuse of that position. That can be done by an act or omission. According to Simester et al. the new s. 4 offence is partly targeted at:

[A]cquisitive family members, neighbours, or acquaintances who batten on vulnerable people who have lost their wits, or who never had any, and relieve them of their money or other property by inducing them to make them gifts or exorbitant payments for minor services, or otherwise financially abuse them.[75]

Jennifer Green suggests that: 'Loyalty creates in one a prima facie obligation to act in the best interests of a particular person or cause, even when doing so would be against one's own self-interest … To commit fraud by abuse of position is to be disloyal to those whose financial affairs are entrusted to you.'[76] Collins explains:

Disloyalty, on this account, is criminalised because it has a corrosive effect on an important basic value held by society: the importance of trust relationships where an individual is entrusted with the oversight of the financial affairs of another. The risk of harm to these trust relationships (in themselves a public good) passes the threshold for criminalisation. It is desirable that as citizens we can trust those who are entrusted with our financial affairs if the relevant expectation has arisen.

---

[75] A.P. Simester, G.R. Sullivan, J. Spencer, and G. Virgo, *Criminal Law, Theory and Doctrine* (Oxford, Hart 2014), 356.

[76] J. Collins, 'The Contours of Vulnerability' in J. Wallbank and J. Herring (eds) *Vulnerabilities, Care and Family Law* (Abingdon, Routledge 2013).

I would agree with Collins on this account of the wrong of the s. 4 offence. I would, however, suggest a wider reading than her, because I would impose a wider obligation to ensure we do not abuse our relationships with all we come across, out of recognition of our mutual vulnerability.

Causing or allowing the death of a child or vulnerable adult

We have already discussed this offence (see p. 203), but add two further observations at this point.

First, the offence imposes an obligation on people to take reasonable steps to protect vulnerable people who are at risk of violence, yet this is imposed on a limited number of people. As we have already seen, in practice this has too often been people who themselves are the victims of domestic abuse and are least well placed to take steps to protect them. The obligation is imposed on a person who is a member of V's household and had frequent contact with him.[77] That would exclude a social worker or other professional who has contact with the person. It is not clear that those living in a violent household are either in a position to foresee what the future holds or are readily able to protect others in the household.

Second, it is worth noting that the definition of 'vulnerable adult' provided in the 2004 Act is: 'a person aged 16 or over whose ability to protect himself from violence, abuse or neglect is significantly impaired through physical or mental disability or illness, through old age or otherwise'. In *Khan*[78] it was accepted that 'an adult who is utterly dependent on others, even if physically young or apparently fit, may fall within the protective ambit of the Act'. This makes it clear that the definition is not restricted to those who have a physical impairment. It should be remembered that we are dealing with cases where a person has decided to remain in a house where there is a risk of death or serious injury. It is hard to imagine a case where such a person must have some form of significant impairment in their ability to protect themselves. It should also be noted that the definition does not give sufficient weight to the fact that external factors may impede their ability to protect themselves. Should the offence not apply, for example, if the person at risk has the physical and mental resources to protect themselves, but the local authority does not supply shelters or accommodation and so their ability to protect themselves is limited for that reason?

---

[77] *R v Khan* [2009] EWCA Crim 2.   [78] Ibid.

Mental Health Act 1983

Section 117 of the Mental Health Act 1983 has a specific offence designed to protect those suffering from a mental disorder:

(1) It shall be an offence for any person who is an officer on the staff of or otherwise employed in, or who is one of the managers of, a hospital [F1, independent hospital or care home]—
 (a) to ill-treat or wilfully to neglect a patient for the time being receiving treatment for mental disorder as an in-patient in that hospital or home; or
 (b) to ill-treat or wilfully to neglect, on the premises of which the hospital or home forms part, a patient for the time being receiving such treatment there as an out-patient.
(2) It shall be an offence for any individual to ill-treat or wilfully to neglect a mentally disordered patient who is for the time being subject to his guardianship under this Act or otherwise in his custody or care (whether by virtue of any legal or moral obligation or otherwise).

This offence has been interpreted to mean that ill-treatment and wilful neglect are separate offences.[79] Ill-treatment has been defined as deliberate conduct. It does not require proof that it harms the patient.[80] So, degrading treatment of a patient in a coma, which does no direct harm to the patient, could still be seen as ill-treatment. Neglect is a failure to act when one is under a duty to do so.[81] Leaving a patient alone with no supervision could be neglect, even if fortunately no injuries occurred. The elements of the offence were well summarized in *R v Newington*:[82]

In our judgment, the judge should have told the jury that for there to be a conviction of ill treatment contrary to the Act of 1983, the Crown would have to prove: 1) deliberate conduct by the appellant which could properly be described as ill treatment irrespective of whether this ill treatment damaged, or threatened to damage the health of the victim and; 2) a guilty mind involving either appreciation by the appellant at the time that she was inexcusably ill-treating a patient or that she was reckless as to whether she was inexcusably acting in that way.[83]

It is interesting that this offence is restricted to patients receiving care under the Mental Health Act 1983, and not to patients more generally. As we shall see, an offence has been recently passed to protect patients more broadly. The legislation appears premised on the fact that patients with a mental disorder

[79] *R v Lennon* [2005] EWCA Crim 3530.
[80] *R v Newington* [1990] 91 Cr App R 247. [81] Ibid.
[82] (1990) 91 Cr App R at 247.
[83] *Regina v Shone* [2005] EWCA Crim 3662; *R v Salisu* [2009] EWCA Crim 2702.

are less able to protect their own interests than other patients. Following a series of recent scandals (see Chapter 6) it is now clear that patients generally can be subject to maltreatment and neglect.

Mental Capacity Act 2005 Offence

Section 44 Mental Capacity Act 2005 states:

(1) Subsection (2) applies if a person ('D')—
   (a) has the care of a person ('P') who lacks, or whom D reasonably believes to lack, capacity,
   (b) is the donee of a lasting power of attorney, or an enduring power of attorney (within the meaning of Schedule 4), created by P, or
   (c) is a deputy appointed by the court for P.
(2) D is guilty of an offence if he ill-treats or wilfully neglects P.

This criminal offence is designed to protect those who lack mental capacity from abuse.[84] Several features are notable. First, a defendant must 'have the care of' P. That term is not defined, but would include both employed and informal carers. Second, it applies to those who lack capacity. Interestingly, it also applies to those 'D reasonably believes to lack capacity'. This prevents D from arguing that although they believed P lacked capacity, in fact P had it. Technically this provision was not needed in that if D believed P lacked capacity, but in fact P did not, D could be charged with attempting to commit the offence. It may be that the drafting indicates that the wrong is failing to comply with one's duty towards a person seen as vulnerable, rather than the wrong being done to a particular victim. Third, the offence covers both active ill-treatment[85] but also wilful neglect. It is generally assumed that 'wilful' will be interpreted to mean to require proof of a deliberate decision not to help or that D did not care whether P needed help.[86]

One of the first cases under the provision was *Patel*,[87] which involved a nurse who failed to provide CPR (cardiac pulmonary resuscitation) on an elderly nursing home resident. The defence was based on evidence that the chance of survival, had CPR been administered, was very low and so the failure did not cause death. This argument failed as s. 44 does not require

---

[84] A. Brammer, 'Carers and the Mental Capacity Act 2005: Angels Permitted, Devils Prosecuted?', (2014) 8 *Criminal Law Review* 589.

[85] *R v Strong* [2014] EWCA Crim 2744.

[86] *R v Sheppard* [1981] AC 394 is the leading case on the meaning of the term 'wilfully' in the context of the Children and Young Persons Act 1933.

[87] *R v Patel* [2013] EWCA Crim 965, [2013] Med LR 507; *R v Nursing* [2012] EWCA Crim 2521, [2013] 1 WLR 1031.

proof of an adverse consequence to follow from the neglect. As Jackson LJ clearly stated: 'It seems to us that the actus reus of this offence is complete if a nurse or a medical practitioner neglects to do that which should be done in the treatment of a patient.' The defence raised the argument that the neglect was not wilful, but rather caused by panic. However, it was held this provided no defence to the charge, only mitigation. If the defendant neglected the patient the reason for this was not relevant to the conviction. Jackson LJ stated: '… neglect is wilful if a nurse or medical practitioner knows that it is necessary to administer a piece of treatment and deliberately decides not to carry out that treatment, which is within their power but which they cannot face performing.' The key difficulty in the interpretation of the offence is over the capacity issue. The offence refers to a person who lacks capacity. However, as the Court of Appeal in *Dunn*[88] explained, that is a problematic concept:

Bearing in mind the absolute requirement in s.2(1) of the Act for any assessment of capacity to be both *time specific and decision specific* ('a person lacks capacity in relation to a matter if at the material time he is unable to make a decision for himself in relation to the matter'). The question thrown up by the section creating the offence is this: in relation to which *matter* does a person need to lack capacity for the purpose of s. 44(1)(a) above. The section does not specify.

The Court went on to criticize the complexity resulting from this. The solution was to ask whether the residents were able to make decisions about their care. The Court of Appeal concluded:

Although … there is something of a disconnection between the simple criminal offence created by s.44 of the Act and the elaborate definition sections which are directed to the more general questions of mental capacity in the wide context of the legislation as a whole, nevertheless the stark reality is that it was open to the jury to conclude that the decisions about the care of each of these residents at the time they were subjected to ill-treatment were being made for by others, including the appellant, just because they lacked the capacity to make these decisions for themselves. For the purposes of section 2, this was the "matter" envisaged in the legislation.

In *Hopkins*, the Court of Appeal repeated the concerns about the provision in strong terms. Pitchford LJ stated:

Unconstrained by authority, this court would be minded to accept the submission made on behalf of the appellants that section 44(1)(a), read together with section 2(1) of the Mental Capacity Act 2005, is so vague that it fails the test of sufficient

---

[88] [2011] EWCA Crim 2935.

certainty at common law and under Article 7.1, ECHR. However this court has made a decision upon section 44 which binds this court.[89]

Certainly the question of whether P had capacity to make a decision about their 'care' is very vague.[90] Not only is there vagueness about what 'care' is in this context, there are also the difficulties referred to in Chapter 4 about the definition of capacity. This is particularly problematic in cases of patients with fluctuating capacity.

Interestingly, in *R v Nursing (Ligaya)*[91] it was held that a carer who was seeking to respect the autonomy of a person of borderline capacity under their care would not be constituting wilful neglect. The prosecution had relied on the neglect of the defendant to deal with issues about the victim's personal hygiene, the dirtiness of bed linen, and the uncleanliness of her rooms. There were also concerns about her taking medication and food. The defendant claimed that the victim had refused to accept her help and that she did not want to override the victim's clear wishes. The Court of Appeal held the offence had to be viewed in light of the Mental Capacity Act 2005 as a whole which made it clear that people should be given the greatest amount of autonomy possible:

It makes it an offence for an individual responsible for the care of someone who lacks the capacity to care for himself to ill-treat or wilfully to neglect that person. Those in care who still enjoy some level of capacity for making their own decisions are entitled to be protected from wilful neglect which impacts on the areas of their lives over which they lack capacity. However section 44 did not create an absolute offence. Therefore, actions or omissions, or a combination of both, which reflect or are believed to reflect the protected autonomy of the individual needing care do not constitute wilful neglect. Within these clear principles, the issue in an individual prosecution is fact-specific.[92]

Apart from the difficulties in the definition of the offence, I would highlight two matters. First, it must be questioned why the offence is limited to those who lack capacity. If an older patient cannot get to the toilet without help and is in a callous way without assistance so they soil themselves, is that not deserving of punishment?[93] The offence, in short, should apply to all those who are vulnerable, not just those who lack capacity.

---

[89] [2011] EWCA Crim 1513.

[90] J. Manthorpe and K. Samsi, 'Care Professionals' Understanding of the New Criminal Offences Created by the Mental Capacity Act 2005', (2015) 30 *International Journal of Geriatric Psychiatry* 384.

[91] [2012] EWCA Crim 2521.   [92] Ibid., para. 18.

[93] A Alghrani et al., 'Healthcare Scandals in the NHS: Crime and Punishment', (2011) 37 *Journal of Medical Ethics* 230.

Second, the focus of the prosecutions have been on individual care workers. Neil Allen writes:

Prosecutions have so far been successfully brought against hands-on carers and those who own or manage care homes. Few, if any, hospital managers have yet been convicted, despite managerial prosecutions being clearly envisaged by the MHA. Determining who should be held to account for criminal care standards is far from straightforward. Prosecutions have been brought against the staff members filmed at Winterbourne View but let us not forget that other individuals and organisations also held positions of responsibility. Those managing the private hospital, Castlebeck Care (Teesdale) Limited that ran it, the Primary Care Trust that arranged for the patients to be there, South Gloucestershire Council that took the safeguarding lead, and the Care Quality Commission that was responsible for regulating the care being provided: which, if any, of these could and should be held to account? And to whom should they be accountable? The criminal courts? The civil courts? The Health and Safety Executive? Parliament?[94]

As mentioned in the previous section, there are concerns prosecutions are being launched against low paid, over-worked nurses and care staff, while the real causes of the neglect may well be found higher up the management chain.

Mental disorder: sections 30–3

The Sexual Offences Act itself creates particular offences, including of sexual activity with a person with a mental disorder impeding choice:

(1) A person (A) commits an offence if—
    (a) he intentionally touches another person (B),
    (b) the touching is sexual,
    (c) B is unable to refuse because of or for a reason related to a mental disorder, and
    (d) A knows or could reasonably be expected to know that B has a mental disorder and that because of it or for a reason related to it B is likely to be unable to refuse.
(2) B is unable to refuse if—
    (a) he lacks the capacity to choose whether to agree to the touching (whether because he lacks sufficient understanding of the nature or reasonably foreseeable consequences of what is being done, or for any other reason), or
    (b) he is unable to communicate such a choice to A.
(3) A person guilty of an offence under this section, if the touching involved—
    (a) penetration of B's anus or vagina with a part of A's body or anything else,
    (b) penetration of B's mouth with A's penis,

---

[94] N. Allen, 'Criminal Care: Ill-treatment and Wilful Neglect', (2012) 2 *Elder Law Journal* 71.

    (c) penetration of A's anus or vagina with a part of B's body, or

    (d) penetration of A's mouth with B's penis,

        is liable, on conviction on indictment, to imprisonment for life.

(4) Unless subsection (3) applies, a person guilty of an offence under this section is liable—

    (a) on summary conviction, to imprisonment for a term not exceeding 6 months or to a fine not exceeding the statutory maximum or both;

    (b) on conviction on indictment, to imprisonment for a term not exceeding 14 years.

Section 31 goes on to criminalize causing or inciting a person with a mental disorder to engage in a sexual activity and s. 32 engaging in a sexual activity in the presence of a person with a mental disorder for the purpose of sexual gratification or causing a person with a mental disorder to watch a sexual act for the purposes of sexual gratification. There is also an offence in s. 38 concerning care workers engaging in sexual conduct with those with mental disorders.

These offences are in addition to equivalent offences committed against anyone without their consent, such as rape and sexual assault. This indicates that the legislation envisaged that there can be cases where a person with a mental disorder has consented to the conduct, but the conduct should still be criminal.

The leading case is *R v Cooper*[95] which involved a twenty-eight-year-old woman with schizoaffective disorder, emotionally unstable personality disorder, a low IQ, and harmful use of alcohol. One day she left the mental health team resource centre she was staying in in a distressed and agitated state. The defendant met her in a car park and offered to help her. He took her to his friend's house, gave her drugs, and then asked him to engage in a sexual activity with him, which she did. He was convicted of an offence of sexual touching of a person with a mental disorder impeding choice, contrary to s. 30. The victim gave evidence that at the time of the sex she was panicky, did not want to die, and did what the defendant asked. The appeal was based on whether it had to be shown the victim lacked capacity to choose due to the mental disorder or whether it could include responding to an irrational fear. The Court of Appeal allowed an appeal against the conviction, but the House of Lords allowed the Crown's appeal, upholding the conviction. It was held that the s. 30 offence could include cases of an irrational fear and that the lack of capacity could be person or situation specific. The question was

---

[95] [2009] UKHL 42.

whether the complainant was capable of choosing to agree to the touching at the time of the particular acts.[96]

Baroness Hale's speech includes some interesting comments on the old law, s. 7 Sexual Offence Act 1956, which made it an offence for a man to have extramarital sexual intercourse with a 'defective' (any woman who suffered from 'a state of arrested or incomplete development of mind which includes severe impairment of intelligence and social functioning'). Of this offence Baroness Hale stated:

This approach was both under- and over-inclusive. It included some severely handicapped women and men who might be quite capable of making a genuine choice about their sexual partners and would not be harmed by their sexual relationships. It denied them the sexual fulfilment which most people take for granted these days, simply on the basis of a status or diagnosis. On the other hand, it did not include people with other mental disorders which might well mean that they lacked the capacity to make a genuine choice about their sexual relationships.

She explained that the offence was drafted in broad terms so as to cover a case where their mental disorder means they are unable to make an autonomous choice, even though they may not lack an understanding of the information. There could be compulsions or phobias which impact on a person, and rob them of autonomy, without affecting their understanding. She also emphasized that the question was whether there was consent to the actual touching in question. Even though at other times the complainant in this case could have consented or refused, at the time of the act in this case she was not able to exercise free will.

While the decision is broadly welcome, in acknowledging that mental disorders can impact on a person's sexual autonomy, it must be questioned why it is necessary to have these offences. Section 74 of the Act, dealing with consent generally, states that consent means that 'a person consents if he agrees by choice, and has the freedom and capacity to make that choice'. A person with a mental disorder which causes the kind of difficulties mentioned in their Lordships' judgment (lack of understanding, delusions, compulsions, or phobias) should readily lead the jury to conclude that such a person lacks the necessary freedom or capacity to consent to sexual relations for the purposes of rape or sexual assault.

In her judgment Lady Hale gives two reasons for why s. 30 may be helpful to prosecutors. The first is because 'the prosecution has only to prove the inability to refuse rather than that the complainant actually did not consent'.[97]

---

[96] [2009] UKSC 42, para. 3.   [97] Ibid., para. 32.

However, that argument assumes that it does not follow from proof of an inability to refuse that there was a lack of consent. Given that the definition of consent under s. 74 requires an agreement 'by choice', that must be questionable.

The second relates to the *mens rea*. As Lady Hale points out, it is not necessary for s. 30 to show that the defendant did not reasonably believe the victim did not consent, as it is for rape; it only needs to be shown that the defendant knew the complainant had a mental disorder and therefore is likely to be unable to refuse. However, that assumes that a defendant with that state of mind could reasonably believe the victim consented and thereby not have the *mens rea* for rape. Surely it would be very surprising for a jury to conclude that although a defendant knew the complainant had a mental disorder and was unlikely to be able to refuse (in the particular circumstance), he reasonably believed the complainant consented.

Perhaps the truth is that juries find it difficult to determine whether a victim with mental disorders was consenting. A jury may feel more confident about convicting for a specific offence relating to mental disorder than they would for rape or sexual assault. The existence of these offences perhaps tells us more about the prejudicial attitudes that can exist about the sexuality of those with mental disorders than having a sound moral basis.

Criminal Justice and Courts Act 2015

In response to the public outcry at the maltreatment of patients at various hospitals, especially of older people, the government introduced an offence in the Criminal Justice and Courts Act 2015, s. 20:

(1) It is an offence for an individual who has the care of another individual by virtue of being a care worker to ill-treat or wilfully to neglect that individual.

(2) An individual guilty of an offence under this section is liable—
   (a) on conviction on indictment, to imprisonment for a term not exceeding 5 years or a fine (or both);
   (b) on summary conviction, to imprisonment for a term not exceeding 12 months or a fine (or both).

(3) 'Care worker' means an individual who, as paid work, provides—
   (a) health care for an adult or child, other than excluded health care, or
   (b) social care for an adult, including an individual who, as paid work, supervises or manages individuals providing such care or is a director or similar officer of an organisation which provides such care.

(4) An individual does something as 'paid work' if he or she receives or is entitled to payment for doing it other than—
   (a) payment in respect of the individual's reasonable expenses,

(b) payment to which the individual is entitled as a foster parent,

(c) a benefit under social security legislation, or

(d) a payment made under arrangements under section 2 of the Employment and Training Act 1973 (arrangements to assist people to select, train for, obtain and retain employment).

(5) 'Health care' includes—

(a) all forms of health care provided for individuals, including health care relating to physical health or mental health and health care provided for or in connection with the protection or improvement of public health, and

(b) procedures that are similar to forms of medical or surgical care but are not provided in connection with a medical condition, and 'excluded health care' has the meaning given in Schedule 4.

(6) 'Social care' includes all forms of personal care and other practical assistance provided for individuals who are in need of such care or assistance by reason of age, illness, disability, pregnancy, childbirth, dependence on alcohol or drugs or any other similar circumstances.

(7) References in this section to a person providing health care or social care do not include a person whose provision of such care is merely incidental to the carrying out of other activities by the person.

(8) In this section—

'adult' means an individual aged 18 or over;

'child' means an individual aged under 18;

'foster parent' means—

(a) a local authority foster parent within the meaning of the Children Act 1989,

(b) a person with whom a child has been placed by a voluntary organisation under section 59(1)(a) of that Act, or

(c) a private foster parent within the meaning of section 53 of the Safeguarding Vulnerable Groups Act 2006

A similar offence for care providers can be found in s. 21:

(1) A care provider commits an offence if—

(a) an individual who has the care of another individual by virtue of being part of the care provider's arrangements ill-treats or wilfully neglects that individual,

(b) the care provider's activities are managed or organised in a way which amounts to a gross breach of a relevant duty of care owed by the care provider to the individual who is ill-treated or neglected, and

(c) in the absence of the breach, the ill-treatment or wilful neglect would not have occurred or would have been less likely to occur.

(2) 'Care provider' means—

(a) a body corporate or unincorporated association which provides or arranges for the provision of—

(i) health care for an adult or child, other than excluded health care, or

(ii) social care for an adult, or

(b) an individual who provides such care and employs, or has otherwise made arrangements with, other persons to assist him or her in providing such care, subject to section 22.

(3) An individual is 'part of a care provider's arrangements' where the individual—
   (a) is not the care provider, but
   (b) provides health care or social care as part of health care or social care provided or arranged for by the care provider, including where the individual is not the care provider but supervises or manages individuals providing health care or social care as described in paragraph (b) or is a director or similar officer of an organisation which provides health care or social care as described there.

(4) A 'relevant duty of care' means—
   (a) a duty owed under the law of negligence, or
   (b) a duty that would be owed under the law of negligence but for a provision contained in an Act, or an instrument made under an Act, under which liability is imposed in place of liability under that law, but only to the extent that the duty is owed in connection with providing, or arranging for the provision of, health care or social care.

(5) For the purposes of this section, there is to be disregarded any rule of the common law that has the effect of—
   (a) preventing a duty of care from being owed by one person to another by reason of the fact that they are jointly engaged in unlawful conduct, or
   (b) preventing a duty of care being owed to a person by reason of that person's acceptance of a risk of harm.

(6) A breach of a duty of care by a care provider is a 'gross' breach if the conduct alleged to amount to the breach falls far below what can reasonably be expected of the care provider in the circumstances.

(7) In this section—
   (a) references to a person providing health care or social care do not include a person whose provision of such care is merely incidental to the carrying out of other activities by the person, and
   (b) references to a person arranging for the provision of such care do not include a person who makes arrangements under which the provision of such care is merely incidental to the carrying out of other activities.

(8) References in this section to providing or arranging for the provision of health care or social care do not include making payments under—
   (a) regulations under section 57 of the Health and Social Care Act 2001 (direct payments for community services and carers);
   (b) section 12A of the National Health Act 2006 (direct payments for health care);
   (c) section 31 or 32 of the Care Act 2014 (direct payments for care and support);
   (d) regulations under section 50 of the Social Services and Well-being (Wales) Act 2014 (anaw 4) (direct payments to meet an adult's needs).

(9) In this section—
    'Act' includes an Act or Measure of the National Assembly for Wales;
    'adult', 'child', 'excluded health care', 'health care' and 'social care' have the
        same meaning as in section 2.

Several points can be made about this offence. First, it is notable that this extends the protection for patients detained under the Mental Health Act 1983 and those lacking capacity to all patients who are being cared for by a care worker. That covers both social and health care. However, the offence is limited to paid workers. It would not apply, therefore, to a relative who is looking after someone on an informal basis. Second, it is important to note that it is restricted to cases of wilful neglect or ill-treatment. It therefore excludes those who through exhaustion or inexperience do not realize they have omitted to provide appropriate care. Third, the s. 21 is a welcome acknowledgement that the blame for neglect of care extends to those in management positions.

Hate offences against vulnerable adults

We do not currently have an offence specifically targeted at hatred of vulnerable adults. There are offences which are designed to acknowledge that an offence took place that was aggravated by virtue of the fact it demonstrated racial or religious hatred.[98] Do we need the same for offences against vulnerable adults?

Supporters of the need for such an offence may highlight cases where it seems a vulnerable adult was targeted by offenders for abuse. An example is Steve Hoskin, who moved to St Austell. Soon after arriving and having the first home of his own, he was befriended by a group of local youths.[99] He was in his late thirties but had severe learning difficulties. The youths exploited him and took control of his money and flat. They treated him as a slave, requiring him to call them 'sir' and 'madam', and dragged him around his flat on a dog's lead. On July 5, 2006 they set up a kangaroo court and sentenced him to death 'for being a paedophile'. They forced him to swallow painkillers and marked him to a viaduct, finally stamping on his fingers until he dropped to his death. Social workers had been involved in his case, but said they were unaware of what happened. Plenty of other horrific examples can be found.[100]

---

[98] Crime and Disorder Act 1998, ss 28–32.
[99] S. Morris, 'Tortured, Drugged and Killed, A Month After the Care Visits Were Stopped', The Guardian, Saturday, August 4, 2007.
[100] N. Chakraborti and J. Garland, 'Reconceptualzing Hate Crime Victimization Through the Lens of Vulnerability and Difference', (2012) 16 *Theoretical Criminology* 499.

Surely everyone would agree that a case such as the one just described would be regarded as a particularly serious offence. However, it is not clear that the hate crime model is entirely appropriate. According to Perry:[101]

Hate crime ... involves acts of violence and intimidation, usually directed towards already stigmatised and marginalised groups. As such, it is a mechanism of power and oppression, intended to reaffirm the precarious hierarchies that characterise a given social order. It attempts to re-create simultaneously the threatened (real or imagined) hegemony of the perpetrator's group and the 'appropriate' subordinate identity of the victim's group. It is a means of marking both the Self and the Other in such a way as to re-establish their 'proper' relative positions, as given and reproduced by broader ideologies and patterns of social and political inequality.

The issue then is whether there is a definable group of vulnerable people who are the target of hatred by some.[102] The justification for the specific hate crime offence lies on the impact on the members of the group when one of them is singled out for assault. As has been argued:

Beyond the impact of the individual hate, hate crime is a powerful poison in society. It emphasises and sensitises feelings of difference rather than focusing on what is shared in common. It breeds mistrust and suspicion, alienation and envy. It promotes isolation and exclusion and sets up barriers to communication.[103]

I would suggest that the group 'vulnerable people' is so diverse—and, as argued in Chapter 2, could cover everyone—that it lacks the appropriate group identity which provides the especial added wrong that hate offences require. It may be that a particular sub-group of vulnerable people could satisfy this group identity. A good case can be made for an offence of disability hate crime[104] or old age hate crime.

Conclusion

This chapter has explored the interaction of the criminal law and vulnerable adults. The very existence of the criminal law acknowledges that we are vulnerable to harms at the hands of others and need protection from it. Yet this chapter has sought to identify some troubling aspects of the way the criminal law responds to vulnerability.

---

[101] B. Perry, *In the Name of Hate* (Abingdon, Routledge 2001), 10.   [102] Ibid.

[103] Metropolitan Police, *Identifying and Combating Hate Crime* (Metropolitan Police, 2000), 21.

[104] A. Roulstone, P. Thomas, and S. Balderston, 'Between Hate and Vulnerability: Unpacking the British Criminal Justice System's Construction of Disablist Hate Crime', (2011) 26 *Disability & Society* 351.

First, the chapter has promoted a broad understanding of the concept of exploitation. It has argued that the law should recognize our universal vulnerability and the interdependence that we all experience. The law is entitled as a result to require a minimum degree of good faith in our dealings with each other. This is needed to recognize the importance of these relationships for our community. This good faith requires parties to ensure they do not take advantage of another's vulnerabilities in an unfair way by using dishonesty, deceit, or gaining through the ignorance of others. When one person deals with another they must, before doing an act which would otherwise be wrongful, ensure the other has been able to make an assessment that the act would benefit them.

Second, the chapter has argued that we should be wary of the way that offences designed to protect vulnerable adults can end up with other vulnerable people being prosecuted. Looking at the offences of gross negligence manslaughter and familial homicide it has been suggested that sometimes it would be better to focus on the responsibility of public authorities to care for vulnerable adults than prosecute individual carers.

Third, the chapter has looked at the offences which are designed specifically to protect vulnerable adults. These tend to provide patchwork protection. Particular groups are identified in particular contexts (e.g. those with mental disorders, detained under the Mental Health Act 1983), with the obligations focused on particular people (e.g. paid care workers). Such a piecemeal approach means that inevitably victims fall through the cracks. We need a more general offence of wilful neglect or mistreatment that can apply to anyone.

8

Contract Law and Vulnerability

Introduction

Contract law provides a fascinating example of how the law responds to vulnerability. The core principle underpinning classical contract law is freedom of contract. The law's primary role is to give effect to the agreement reached by the parties, whatever view others may have about its fairness. As we shall see shortly, that is based on a presumption that each party is able to look after their own interests. This is not to say that the law of contract is unaware of vulnerable contractors. Indeed it offers a fine example of how the law responds to vulnerable people, as we shall see. One might go further and suggest that, in fact, the very existence of contract law is an acknowledgement of our vulnerability. As mentioned in Chapter 2 we are deeply dependent on the assistance of others for a wide range of services. But that means we need to be able to rely on others. Contracts, it might be argued, provide a mechanism for providing reassurance our needs will be met. Michael Pratt explains: 'Our capacity to bind ourselves contractually enables us to cooperate with those on whose promises we would not otherwise rely ... including the untrustworthy and, more importantly, the unfamiliar.'[1] So seen, contract law is a way of protecting ourselves from the vulnerability of losing out as a result of the unreliability of others. Before exploring a little more the way the law responds to contractors who are seen as particularly vulnerable, more needs to be said about one of the foundational principles of contract law: freedom of contract.

---

[1] M. Pratt, 'Promises, Contracts and Voluntary Obligations', (2007) 56 *Law and Philosophy* 531, 572.

The principle of freedom of contract

As already indicated, the principle of freedom of contract is seen as at the heart of contract law. In *Printing and Numerical Registering Co. v Sampson* Sir George Jessel MR stated:

... if there is one thing which more than any other public policy requires it is that men of full age and competent understanding shall have the utmost liberty of contracting, and that their contracts when entered into freely and voluntarily shall be held sacred and shall be enforced by courts of justice.

The principle is premised on the ideal of the self-sufficient, informed, autonomous businessman who should be free to make his business deals for himself. It elevates protection of individual liberty over the heavy hand of government control.[2] It is not for the courts or the government to interfere in contractual freedom by seeking to declare that the terms of a particular contract are unfair or inappropriate for the parties.[3] This is closely tied to the principle of autonomy: a person should have their choices respected, as long as they have capacity. That includes respecting the choice of a person who decides to bind themselves under a contract. This was emphasized in *Radmacher v Granatino*[4] where the Supreme Court held that effect should be given to a pre-marriage contract in determining how property should be allocated on divorce, holding:

The reason why the court should give weight to a nuptial agreement is that there should be respect for individual autonomy. The court should accord respect to the decision of a married couple as to the manner in which their financial affairs should be regulated. It would be paternalistic and patronising to override their agreement simply on the basis that the court knows best.

Pre-marriage contracts are a striking example of the significance of freedom of contract. One might have thought of marriage as an example of a public institution in which there was a public interest in its content. The fact that even in relation to marriage 'autonomy' is seen as an essential value is striking.[5]

---

[2] R. Craswell, *Freedom of Contract* (Program in Law and Economics Working Paper No. 33, 1995).

[3] L. Boldeman, *The Cult of the Market: Economic Fundamentalism and its Discontents* (ANU Press 2011).

[4] [2010] UKSC 427, para. 78.

[5] For a critique see J. Herring, *Relational Autonomy and Family Law* (Berlin, Springer 2014).

Giving effect to a contract is said not only to reflect the parties' autonomy but also reflects ethical obligations. As Professor Goodhart states: '[T]he moral basis of contract is that the promisor has by his promise created a reasonable expectation that it will be kept.'[6] You should not be able to escape from your promise by arguing you made a bad choice or that the contract was unfair.[7]

The principle has also been supported in economic terms by emphasizing the importance of the free market. In short, the free market means that people are offered a range of options and they will be able to select the best for themselves. As Lord Bramwell put it in *The Manchester, Sheffield, and Lincolnshire Railway Co. v Brown*:[8] '... the fact that it has been voluntarily entered into by them is the strongest possible proof that it is a reasonable agreement ...' The argument is that if the parties have chosen to enter the agreement they, presumably, have taken the view that it is a fair agreement for them, in which case it is not for anyone else to interfere in their choice.

This last point might be supported by the fact that for many items the value cannot be objectively assessed. An artwork, a concert ticket, or even a house may be given hugely different values by different people, depending on the individual assessment of the would-be purchaser. As economists are keen to say, something is worth what people are willing to pay for it.[9] This is, in part, why the law tends to be reluctant to determine whether the terms of a contract are unfair or not. Even if it wanted to, the court could not readily determine what a fair price for an item is or what reduction in price would be appropriate for a harsh term in the contract. This means that in general contract law focuses on the unfairness of the bargaining process that led to the making of the contract, rather than the unfairness of the terms of the contract itself.[10]

A further point commonly raised in favour of the principle of freedom of contract is the importance of certainty. Moseneke DCJ explains:

The notion of contractual autonomy belongs to a larger worldview and ideology. It flows from classical liberal notions of liberty and the neoliberal penchant for free, self-regulating and self-correcting markets driven by individual entrepreneurs who thrive on freedom of choice and freedom to strike handsome bargains. The law

---

[6] A. Goodhart, *English Law and the Moral Law* (London, Stevens and Sons 1953).

[7] G. Hadfield, 'The Dilemma or Choice: A Feminist Perspective on the Limits of Freedom of Contract', (1996) 33 *Osgoode Hall Law Journal* 337.

[8] (1882–83) LR 8 App Cas 703.

[9] H. Neap and T. Celik, 'Value of a Product: A Definition', (1999) *International Journal of Value-Based Management* 181.

[10] J. Cartwright, *Unequal Bargaining* (Oxford, Clarendon Press 1991).

of contract is meant to facilitate the securing of market needs. It is meant to be a value-neutral set of muscular but predictable rules that curb uncertainty whilst inspiring confidence in the market place. For that reason, rules of contract ordinarily permit little or no judicial discretion.[11]

Certainty is, of course, a benefit to those who would be harmed if the law was less certain, and allowed contracts to be set aside if they were unfair to a more vulnerable party. Inevitably, that means the doctrine favours the stronger contractor. The law allows contracts to reflect power, or the lack of power.[12]

The central argument of this chapter will be that contract law starts with the norm of an independent autonomous man. The norm is of contractors who are at 'arm's length'[13] and are 'self-motivated, self-assertive and agree to self-imposed obligations'.[14] Individual intentions are the focus of the court's assessment, rather than the context of the agreement or the values underpinning the relationship between the parties. The focus is on the moment of the agreement (was there an offer and an acceptance?) rather than the broader context of the negotiations.[15] This, then, is part of a broader critique of the law that it focuses on separateness and individual autonomy, rather than values of connection and relationship.[16]

It is true that contract law provides exceptions for those who are vulnerable. John Cartwright states: 'Parties are free to bargain; and to bargain well or badly. But if one party by his words or conduct, or by abusing a positon of strength which he holds *vis a vis* the other party, disturbs the balance of negotiations, the disadvantaged party should have appropriate remedies.'[17] This seems an eminently sensible approach, at first. But notice the assumption that the parties are on an equal footing. There is a disturbance to the 'balance' of the negotiations only in one of the set kinds of behaviour. Only then will the law become concerned about an inequality of bargaining. These, however, are seen as departures from the norm, which need a good justification.[18] A person seeking to use one of these devices will need to persuade the court that their case falls within the established exceptions. The inherent lack of bargaining power between the parties is not acknowledged.

---

[11] D. Moseneke, 'Transformative Constitutionalism: Its Implications for the Law of Contract', (2009) 20 *Stellenbosch Law Review* 9.

[12] L. Mulcahy, *Contract Law in Perspective* (Abingdon, Routledge 2008), 28.

[13] S. Thompson, *Prenuptial Agreements and the Presumption of Free Choice* (London, Bloomsbury 2015), 133.

[14] Ibid., 133.   [15] Ibid., 132.

[16] P. Tidwell and P. Linzer, 'The Flesh Coloured Band Aid—Contracts, Feminism, Dialogue and Norms', (1991) 28 *Houston Law Review* 791.

[17] J. Cartwright, *Unequal Bargaining* (Oxford, Clarendon Press 1991).

[18] L. Mulcahy, *Contract Law in Perspective* (Abingdon, Routledge 2008), 39.

I will now explore the cases where the law does acknowledge the vulnerability of the contracting party. My argument is not that contract law is blind to vulnerability, but that it fails to tackle it sufficiently. It is, of course, not the purpose of this chapter to provide a detailed discussion of the law, but rather to enable a discussion of how vulnerability is understood and responded to in contract law. The chapter will conclude with a new vision of contract law which starts with the norm of a vulnerable contractor and imagines what such a law looks like.

Misrepresentation

Summary of the law

The starting point in relation to representations in contract law is the well-known principle of caveat emptor: let the buyer beware. A seller is not expected to disclose the truth about what they are selling; it is for the buyer to find it out. The primary rule for the seller is that they must not make an untrue or misleading statement.[19] If they choose to make a statement or perform some conduct (e.g. disguising a defect) which is untrue or a misleading half-truth, that will be misrepresentation.[20] Where they have made a misrepresentation which has been relied upon by the other and induced the other to enter into a contract, then the contact can be rescinded or damages can be ordered.[21]

Only certain kinds of misrepresentation are covered by the doctrine. It must be a statement of existing fact. Vague puffs, ambiguous statements, or sales talk will not be covered.[22] The terminology of 'fertile and improvable' to describe a piece of land was held to be too vague.[23] However, the more precise the statement, the more likely it is to be a statement of fact. Even then the statement might be regarded as a matter of belief rather than fact, if the person making the statement could not be known to have specific knowledge about what they were selling. An expert selling an item or a person who knows an item well is more likely to be representing a statement of fact or at least be representing that they used their expertise to make the statement.[24] Someone with no expertise making a claim about the item may be more likely to be seen as expressing an opinion.

---

[19] J. Buchanan, 'In Defense of Caveat Emptor', (1970) 38 *University of Chicago Law Review* 64.
[20] *Smith v Hughes* (1871) LR 6 QB 587.
[21] Sometimes both these remedies are available together.
[22] J. Cartwright, *Unequal Bargaining* (Oxford, Clarendon Press 1991).
[23] *Dimmock v Hallett* (1866) LR 2 Ch App 21.   [24] *Brown v Raphael* [1958] Ch 636.

A statement of future intention will not be treated as a representation unless at the time they make the representation he had no intention of fulfilling the promise. So if A says to B 'I will sell you my house and I intend to give the money to charity' then that will not be a misrepresentation, even if A uses the money on a lavish holiday, unless at the time when the words were spoken A had no intention to give the money to charity. As one judge put it: a statement about one's state of mind 'is as much a fact as the state of his digestion'.[25]

Discussion

A number of points about the law's approach to misrepresentation will be brought out. First, caveat emptor places the burden of finding out information about an item on the person purchasing it. This may seem reasonable in that only the purchaser knows what is important to them about an item and they can ask questions about the matters that particularly trouble them. However, that assumes a contractor with the abilities to make these enquiries. Caveat emptor is unfavourable to a 'vulnerable adult', if they lack the skills and knowledge to find out information or what to ask. Indeed one might wonder whether this vulnerability is very common. Do many people purchasing a computer, car, or mortgage plan really know the sensible questions to ask, beyond does it work? It might be added that vulnerable people may benefit from the rule that when they are selling they are not required to provide detailed information about the product.

Second, the law in the caveat emptor rule promotes a model of contract: one where each party is expected to look after their own interests. Honesty and good faith are not encouraged; indeed, they are positively discouraged because any disclosure can become a misrepresentation if it is found misleading. Much better in English law to be the quiet surly type than the brash bold salesperson! However, as mentioned earlier this promotes and favours a certain kind of contract: the powerful, knowledgeable, articulate, and persistent contractor. That is, not many people.

Third, there are exceptions to the caveat emptor rule. The most notable are certain contracts *uberrimae fidei* ('of the utmost good faith'). The most significant of these are found in the area of insurance, although they also apply in cases of a fiduciary relationship, such as a trustee dealing with a beneficiary. The justification for the insurance exception is that a company offering insurance needs to know all relevant information before assessing

---

[25] *Edington v Fitzmaurice* (1885) 29 Ch D 459, 482.

a risk and that is not information it can discover through its own efforts, while the person seeking insurance can readily provide the necessary facts.[26] While that is understandable, that seems true in many situations. If I am buying a television the manufacturer is in a far better position than I to know what the television can do. The detailed knowledge about the television's construction and its reliability will readily be at the hands of the manufacturer but not the purchaser. Perhaps it is not cynical to suggest caveat emptor always applies to consumers dealing with commercial enterprises, but not the other way round. Generally companies do not need to know anything about their consumers, just that they have money to spend. Insurance is one of the few cases where companies do require information and there the caveat emptor principle is held not to apply.

To some extent this problem is dealt with by implied terms, in particular those found under the Sale of Goods Act 1979, requiring that the goods correspond with their description, be of satisfactory quality, and be reasonably fit for the purpose disclosed by the buyer.[27] As Jonathan Morgan puts it, 'These duties give sellers the incentive to draw defects to the buyer's attention. Considering the provisions more generally there is little room for sellers to palm off goods with undisclosed defects, since they will generally not comply with these implied terms.'[28] Nevertheless this relies on the purchaser proving a breach of the implied term, which may be harder than proving a failure to disclose an error.

Notably civil law systems do include a requirement to make disclosure of all relevant information about the product, without causing undue difficulty.[29] Hugh Beale[30] has suggested a model where a party is required to speak if it knows the other was making a mistake when, had they known the truth, they would not have entered into the contract. He excludes an estimate of value in the proposal. He admits that it is problematic because there is plenty of room for what 'good faith' requires and what mistakes each party is expected to know about. Nevertheless such a system has proved workable in civilian systems.

John Cartwright writes:

A party cannot walk away from a contract by simply saying that he did not intend to be bound. If he has communicated inaccurately his intentions, it is the other party, who actually and reasonably thought that a particular agreement was being made,

---

[26] *Carter v Boehm* (1766) 3 Burr 1905.
[27] Sections 13 and 14, Sale of Goods Act 1979.
[28] J. Morgan, *Contract Law Great Debates* (Basingstoke, Palgrave 2015), 163.
[29] H. Beale, *Mistake and Non Disclosure of Fact* (Oxford, Oxford University Press 2012).
[30] Ibid.

who is allowed to assert his understanding at the expense of the first party. There is therefore a responsibility on a negotiating party to ensure that he communicates accurately his intentions in relation to the obligations to be created by the contract.[31]

This is the epitome of good sense under the standard model of contract. But notice, there is no reason for the responsibilities to be put in this way. We could put the responsibility to correct one contracting partner's mistakes, to take reasonable steps to inform them, and to recognize the muddle and errors to which humans are so typically prone.

At the root of the issue is a debate over the extent to which one party is responsible towards the other. As Friedmann points out, if one party is aware the other is entering a contract under undue influence, it does not matter who is doing the undue influence: the weaker party is entitled to have the contract rescinded.[32] Might we say the same thing about a mistake? Should the law allow A to take B's money when A knows A would not be handing over the money if B knew the truth? Is there not a basic duty of good faith that requires two parties entering into a contractual relationship to ensure they do not take advantage of the other's vulnerability? That should require one party to correct the mistake of the other, or at least stop doing business with them.

I would suggest that this debate turns on whose interests, what kind of people's interests, are protected by such a rule. The current approach of the law on misrepresentation works in favour of those with the skill, time, and money to find out the information they need from others or ensure the contracts include appropriate warranties. But it works against the interests of those who do not have the capacity or skills to uncover information about an item. In short, it works against the interests of the more vulnerable contractor and promotes values connected to independence. A rule that required disclosure of relevant information and did not allow one party to take advantage of another's ignorance would acknowledge our universal vulnerability and promote relational values.

Mistake

Summary of the law

There are two main categories of cases in which issues around mistake have arisen. The first concerns where the parties both make the same mistake

---

[31] J. Cartwright, *Unequal Bargaining* (Oxford, Clarendon Press 1991), 224.
[32] D. Friedmann, 'The Objective Principle and Mistake and Involuntariness in Contract and Restitution', (2003) 119 *Law Quarterly Review* 68.

(e.g. A contracts with B to sell her cow,[33] both A and B think the cow is alive, in fact the cow has died). In such a case if the mistake is over a fundamental matter the contract can be declared void. These cases do not really raise particular issues over vulnerable contractors. There is no sense in these cases of one person taking advantage of another. They will not be considered further.

The second category of mistake cases is where one person is mistaken, but the other is not. So A agrees to sell B a painting for £30 million. B believes it is an original Picasso, while A knows it is not. Essentially in such cases the focus of the law is on whether or not the mistake relates to the subject matter. So if A says 'would you like to buy my dog Rover for £40' and B, mishearing, says 'yes I will buy your dog Clover for £40' there is no contract simply because the offer and the acceptance did not 'match'. They were not in agreement over the subject. However, that approach operates only where there is a mistake as to the subject matter, not as to merely the quality of the item.[34] That distinction is not always easy to draw. Going back to the example of the Picasso, one might argue that whether or not the painting is by Picasso or a copy is a disagreement over the subject matter. However, that is not beyond doubt and it might be said to be a mistake as to quality, the subject matter being the particular canvas.[35]

That last issue may be resolved in some cases by considering whether or not the seller was contractually promising (warrantying) that the item had a particular quality. So, if it could be shown that A was promising that the picture was an original Picasso, as opposed to selling the picture 'as seen' or 'as a possible Picasso', then a straightforward breach of contract claim could be brought. But in the absence of these devices, in a straightforward case where A is selling B an item which B believes has a certain quality, there can be no claim. Importantly, that is true even where B knows that A is mistaken.

A similar approach is taken in relation to mistakes as to the person. If A makes an offer by e-mail to B, but mistypes the e-mail address, sending it to C, C cannot accept the offer.[36] There is simply no match between the offer and the acceptance. However, this only applies in relation to mistakes as to identity; it does not apply to mistakes as to characteristics or qualities of the person. So, an offer to B, who A believes to be a trustworthy person but is in fact a rogue, that will not negate the contract.[37]

---

[33] *Bell v Lever Brothers* [1932] AC 161.

[34] *Raffles v Wichelhaus* (1864) 2 Hand C 906.

[35] For a helpful discussion of the law see J. Morgan, *Contract Law Great Debates* (Palgrave, Macmillan 2015).

[36] *Cundy v Lindsay* (1878) 3 AC 459.   [37] *Lewis v Averay* [1972] 1 QB 198.

Discussion

The explanation for the law's general approach is set out by Blackburn J in *Smith v Hughes*:[38]

If, whatever a man's real intention may be, he so conducts himself that a reasonable man would believe that he was assenting to the terms proposed by the other party, and that other party upon that belief enters into the contract with him, the man thus conducting himself would be equally bound as if he had intended to agree to the other party's terms.

It is notable that this approach looks at the issue from the point of view of the non-mistaken party. It would be unfair to them if the contract were set aside if they had been led to reasonably believe the other party was agreeing to enter the contract. Indeed, seen from that point of view the rule seems fair. As Cartwright argues in the quote mentioned earlier, it might be said that one should not mislead one's contracting party as to one's intention. However, one could also put the argument from the other perspective. If a party was mistaken about what was, for them, a crucial fact, should they be bound by a contract they have chosen not to enter, even in a case when they were not to blame for the mistake?

There is in the law some recognition of the fact that humans are prone to make mistakes. Parties who make a common mistake are not bound by their contracts. The law seeks to protect those who are mistaken when their contracting partner tries to take advantage of that mistake. The *Smith v Hughes* approach does not apply in cases where the non-mistaken party is aware of the other's mistake. However, the law's recognition of the possibility of a mistake is somewhat limited.

First, the difficult cases are those where one party is mistaken through no fault of their own and the other party is unaware they have made the mistake. Should the contract be upheld? In a sense this is a case where there are two innocent parties. It is again notable that the law, by upholding the contract in such a case, favours the more knowledgeable, better skilled party over vulnerable contractors who are more likely to make mistakes. The values of certainty and reliability are given more weight than protection of vulnerable people being bound by contracts they did not intend to enter.

Second, the law on identity mistakes. As we have seen, this does not apply to mistakes over characteristics, only mistakes as to identity. This can be a somewhat artificial distinction. It is not hard to think of cases where a person's characteristics may be more important to the other party than their

---

[38] [1871] LR 6 QB 597, 607.

identity. A food bank providing food for those in dire need will be less concerned about the names of those seeking food than whether they are in need. Indeed they would not care too much if the person they thought was Susan was in fact Jayne. However, they would care if it turned out Susan was not poor as she claimed, but was in fact well off.

There is here an assumption that contracts are about commercial dealings at arm's length. Then, of course, the precise identity of the other party is relatively unimportant: if your primary goal is to make money, you do not care too much who gives you the money, as long as they have it. However, for contracts in the more personal sphere the characteristic of the party is likely to be far more important, because a person may not be motivated solely by financial gain, but by non-commercial considerations. In such a case the characteristics of the contracting party may be very important. A good example is *Ingram v Little*[39] involving three older women who lived together and were selling their car. They dealt with a Mr P. Hutchinson, whom they believed was a reliable man, but in fact turned out to be someone else and a rogue. The contract was found void on the much questioned ground that the presumption one deals with the person face to face who is the person one contracts with was rebutted on the basis they checked his name in the telephone directory. The case still upholds the standard principle that only mistakes as to identity and not characteristics can lead to a contract being void. Yet, the standard reasoning overlooks the point that often private sellers of this nature do care about the kind of person who buys their car or house. The older women in this case seemed to want to be sure their beloved car was going to a careful owner. They probably cared little about whether his name was Mr Hutchinson or Mr Jones, they just wanted to know their car was going to someone who would look after it as well as they had. The case shows the law's assumption that people care only about financial matters is false. Real people, not the people in contract law's imagination, are sentimental and not entirely driven by rationale. Contract law should acknowledge that.

The signature rule and 'non est factum'

Summary of the law

To avoid some of the difficulties just mentioned most important contracts are put into writing and then signed. There can then be few disagreements over who the parties to the contract are or what the subject matter is if it

---

[39] [1961] 1 QB 31.

is all there in black and white. Generally it is taken that once a person has signed the contract then they are bound by its terms. They cannot, absent a misrepresentation, claim not to have been aware of the terms of the contract or not intended to have signed them. *L'Estrange v F Graucob Ltd*[40] established this as the 'signature rule'. It applies to those who have not read the contract before signing it or to those who speak no English, as long as they are aware that what they are doing is signing a contract.

A notable departure from the signature rule applies to those who can plead 'non est factum'.[41] This states that if a person is illiterate or has some impairment then they can claim that the 'mind of the signer did not accompany the signature'[42] and so they are not bound by it. The following rules have been developed over the doctrine:

- It can only be used by those who are illiterate or those who have no real understanding of the document due to 'defective education, illness or innate capacity'.[43] It has been suggested it can also apply to those who have been tricked into signing the document, if they can be seen as in some sense vulnerable.[44]

- It is not available to a person who has been careless.[45] For example, an illiterate person who does not ask for the contract to be read to them but just signs it may not be able to rely on non est factum. Similarly the person who speaks no English, but does not ask for a translation of the document, cannot complain if they failed to appreciate what was in their contract.

- The documents signed must be different from the one believed to be signed in a radical or essential way.[46] The non est factum doctrine is not available to someone who simply fails to appreciate some of the detailed provisions in the contract.

Discussion

The signature rule clearly favours the principles of certainty. Get your customers to sign the contract and you do not need to worry about making sure they understand the terms of the contract: they are bound by it. With that in mind the non est factum rule is a striking example of where the principle of certainty is set aside in favour of protection of vulnerable contractors. However, there are some concerns about the doctrine.

---

[40] [1934] 2 KB 394.   [41] It is not my deed.
[42] *Foster v Mackinnon* (1869) LR 4 CP 704, 711.
[43] *Saunders v Anglian Building Society Ltd* [1971] AC 1004.   [44] Ibid., 1025.
[45] Ibid., 1023.   [46] Ibid., 1023

First, it seems to rely on a narrow, perhaps clichéd, notion of vulnerability: the old, the disabled, and the illiterate. It is true that there are some suggestions in the literature that a more modern notion of vulnerability is likely to be adopted if the doctrine is considered by a modern court. Even so it is unlikely to extend beyond the notion that a person has a 'defective' education, health, or capacity.[47]

Second, the doctrine takes no account of the innate vulnerability that any of us can face. Patrick Atiyah brings out well the falsehood at the heart of the signature rule:[48]

No matter how much sanctity one is prepared to allow to genuine bargains and agreements it surely flies in the face of all reality to treat written or printed contracts as though they themselves have been gone through clause by clause, word by word, and thoroughly accepted and understood by both parties.

Although the signature rule tends to be taken for granted in contract law, there is no reason why it must. A good example of an alternative approach is the much discussed Canadian case of *Tilden Rent-A-Car Co. v Clendenning*.[49] In brief this concerned a man who hired a car at an airport and signed a long standard form contract, including, unusually, a clause saying that no payment would be made if the driver had drunk any alcohol at all at the time of the accident. Dubin J held:

In modern commercial practice, many standard form printed documents are signed without being read or understood. In many cases the parties seeking to rely upon the terms of the contract know or ought to know that the signature of a party to the contract does not represent the true intention of the signer, and that the party signing is unaware of the stringent and onerous provisions which the standard form contains. Under such circumstances, I am of the opinion that the party seeking to rely on such terms should not be able to do so in the absence of first having taken reasonable measures to draw such terms to the attention of the other party, and, in the absence of such reasonable measures, it is not necessary for the party denying knowledge of such terms to prove either fraud, misrepresentation or non est factum.

In this case we see some recognition that all of us, except perhaps a lawyer acting as a professional advisor, are vulnerable in the face of a lengthy, complex standard form contract. We do not have the energy, time, skills, or knowledge to read through the lengthy forms regularly presented in a wide range of contexts. Most people simply sign the form or click on the box on the internet. Providers realize that consumers will not read these and do not expect them to do so. Indeed, the length and complexity of standard form

---

[47] Ibid.   [48] P. Atiyah, *Essays on Contract* (Oxford, Clarendon Press 1986), 366.
[49] (1978) 83 DLR (3d) 400.

contracts might be designed to put off even the most intrepid consumer willing to start reading the fine print. The ruling in *Clendinning* that particularly unusual clauses need to be drawn to the attention of the signing party is at least a partial acknowledgement of that. English law has yet to take a *Clendinning* approach. That case offers an example of how all of us, however apparently well-educated and skilled, are vulnerable when faced with lengthy documentation when we strongly desire a rapid provision of a service. A contract law that is based on the image of the self-contained, time rich, and knowledgeable consumer is a law based on a fiction.

Rectification

Summary of the law

Rectification is used where a written contract fails to record what the two parties actually agreed.[50] In such a case the document can be amended (rectified) so that it accords with the intention of both parties.[51] That is a relatively uncontroversial doctrine and typically used where there has been a typographical error in recording what was agreed.

Rectification can also be used where it fails to accord with the intentions of only one party, but only where there was fraud, or knowledge of the mistake, or one party wilfully shut his eyes to the mistake and took advantage of it.[52] In *Commission for the New Towns v Cooper (Great Britain) Ltd*[53] three kinds of knowledge were said to be covered by the doctrine:

(1) actual knowledge;
(2) wilfully shutting one's eyes to the obvious; and
(3) wilfully and recklessly failing to make such inquiries as an honest and reasonable person would make.

There has been some dispute on the level of knowledge required, in particular whether it covers the third category of cases.[54]

Buckley LJ in *Thomas Bates Ltd v Wyndham's (Lingerie) Ltd*[55] suggested that inequity was at the heart of the doctrine. Interestingly he seemed to see the unilateral mistake doctrine as essentially a version of the mutual mistake doctrine. It was just that the knowledgeable party could not resist a claim for

---

[50] *Faraday v Tamworth Union* (1916) 86 LJ Ch 436.
[51] *Swainland Builders Limited v Freehold Proprieties Limited* [2002] ECLR 71, 74.
[52] *Commission for the New Towns v Cooper* [1995] Ch 259.   [53] Ibid.,, 280, 292.
[54] *Daventry DC v Daventry Housing* [2011] EWCA Civ 1153 held that the law was unclear.
[55] [1981] 1 WLR 505, 515H–516B.

mutual mistake rectification if they were aware the other party was mistaken and did not draw the mistake to the other party's knowledge. They were prevented from saying that in fact they did understand the term in the way it was written. In *George Wimpy UL Limited v V I Construction Limited*[56] Sedley LJ suggested that a test of 'honourable and reasonable conduct' could be used. Unfortunately he did not explain whether this was intended to be a broader concept than the current law (that there might be cases where rectification was appropriate even though there had not been a failure to disclose an error) or narrower (that there may be some cases where it was honourable and reasonable not to disclose). As Sedley LJ did not explain the difference it may be that he was not intending a specific change in the law, but rather a test which better captures the key issues.

Discussion

In unilateral mistake rectification we do see some welcome acknowledgement of exploitation. One party is prevented from taking advantage of the mistake of another. However, even here it seems what concerns the law is a positive taking advantage of the vulnerability of the other. This is still short of a concept of a kind of duty of care towards one's fellow contractor. It is particularly welcome that the law has referred to the idea of 'honourable and reasonable conduct'. There is here some acknowledgement that entering into a contract with another creates a contract and that includes some base levels of obligations, at least not to exploit them.

Duress

Summary of the law

In order to rely on duress it is necessary to show that illegitimate pressure was applied by way of threats and that they caused a person to enter into a contract. The threats can be of physical violence to the person or to the goods of the person. In more recent years the courts have expanded the concept to include 'economic duress'. That is a challenge to the economic interests. An illegitimate threat to withdraw credit or not perform a contract can, therefore, form the basis of an economic duress threat. Where a contract is entered into under duress it is voidable. This entitles the person to terminate the contract, but not necessarily obtain damage.

---

[56] [2005] EWCA Civ 77, paras 56–7.

Threat to the person or property

Duress of the person applies where a person is threatened with death or physical injury. Duress to the property covers cases where there is a threat to damage or destroy the property of another.[57] These are relatively uncontroversial claims. Few people would accept that someone who forced another to enter a contract through threats to perform crimes should be permitted to enforce the contract. Notably it only needs to be shown that the threat was a cause of the person entering the contract[58] for the contract to be voidable.

Economic duress

Economic duress involves a threat to do something that will harm the economic interests of the other party.[59] The threat must be illegitimate. That means it must either be legally wrongful or what is threatened is wrongful.[60] This does not require the threat to be unlawful.[61] For example, a threat to break a contract can amount to an illegitimate threat in an extreme case. However, not every threat to break a contract will amount to illegitimate pressure.[62] Mere commercial pressures[63] or threats to exercise contractual rights[64] will not generally be illegitimate, but there is no rule they cannot be. In short, while a threat to do an unlawful act is likely to be illegitimate, is does not necessarily follow that it is. Similarly a threat to do a lawful act is unlikely to be legitimate, but it can be.[65] In cases where the act is lawful the question will be whether or not the threat was made in good faith.

The law's reluctance to find lawful acts being illegitimate was explained in *CTN. Cash & Carry Ltd v Gallaher Ltd.*[66] It was explained that allowing lawful acts to constitute duress:

> would introduce a substantial and undesirable element of uncertainty in the commercial bargaining process. Moreover, it will often enable bona fide settled accounts to be reopened when parties to commercial dealings fall out. The aim of our commercial law ought to be to encourage fair dealing between parties. But it is a mistake for the law to set its sights too highly when the critical inquiry is not whether the conduct is lawful but whether it is morally or socially unacceptable. That is the inquiry in which we are engaged. In my view there are policy considerations

---

[57] *The Alev* [1989] 1 Lloyd's Rep 138.   [58] *Barton v Armstrong* [1976] AC 104.
[59] *The Sibeon and Siborte* [1976] 1 Lloyd's Rep 293.
[60] *The Universal Sentinel* [1983] 1 AC 366,
[61] *Progress Bulk Carriers v Tube City IMS LCC* [2012] EWHC 273 (Comm).
[62] *Kolmar Group AG v Traxpo Enterprises* [2012] EWHC 113 (Comm).
[63] *Pao On v Lau Yiu Long* [1979] UKPC 2.
[64] *CTN Cash and Carry v Gallagher* [1994] 4 All ER 714.
[65] See *Borrelli v Ting* [2010] Bus LR 1718.   [66] [1994] 4 All ER 714, 718–19.

which militate against ruling that the defendants obtained payment of the disputed in-voice by duress.

Interestingly Steyn LJ did note that differences could arise between commercial cases and 'protected relationships'. He thought it would be rare in a commercial context for lawful act duress to operate. By implication it would be less rare in cases involving individuals, especially in a close relationship.

The notion of illegitimacy was explored further in *DSND Subsea v Petroleum Geo-Services*:[67]

In determining whether there has been illegitimate pressure, the court takes into account a range of factors. These include whether there has been an actual or threatened breach of contract; whether the person allegedly exerting the pressure has acted in good or bad faith; whether the victim had any realistic practical alternative but to submit to the pressure; whether the victim protested at the time and whether he affirmed and sought to rely on the contract. These are all relevant factors. Illegitimate pressure must be distinguished from the rough and tumble of the pressures of normal commercial bargaining.[68]

It is notable the weight that is placed on 'good faith' in this approach, an issue I shall return to shortly.

Causation

The threat must cause the weaker party to enter the contract. At one time it was suggested that the threat had to 'overbear' the will of the threatened party, but this was always a problematic concept.[69] A person with a gun to their head who is told to sign a contract may be able to exercise a choice. It is not as if their hand is forced to act. It is rather that the choice is made in circumstances in which it is not one which is a legally effective choice. In *Pao On v Lau Yiu Long*[70] Lord Scarman said it was material to enquire:

whether the person alleged to have been coerced did or did not protest; whether, at the time he was allegedly coerced into making the contract, he did or did not have an alternative course open to him, such as an adequate legal remedy; whether he was independently advised; and whether after entering the contract he took steps to avoid it.[71]

All those matters were said to be relevant in determining whether the victim had acted voluntarily or not. In *Progress Bulk Carriers v Tube City IMS*[72] Cook J suggested it was sufficient if it was shown the illegitimate pressure caused

---

[67] [2000] BLR 530; approved *Carillon Construction Ltd v Feliz* [2001] BLR 1, para. 24.
[68] Ibid., para. 131.   [69] *Universe Tankships v ITF* [1983] 1 AC 366, 383–7.
[70] *Pao On v Lau Yiu Long* [1979] UKPC 2.   [71] Ibid., 18.
[72] [2012] EWHC 273 (Comm).

the pressured party to enter the contract. In *Huyton v Cremer*,[73] Mance J (as he then was) suggested the pressure would have to be a significant cause in persuading the party to enter the contract.

Discussion

There are several points which are interesting about the notion of duress in contract law from a vulnerability perspective.

First, there is an acknowledgement that autonomy is not a straightforward concept. The fact a person has signed a contract does not indicate that this was a full exercise of autonomy. As we saw in Chapter 4, the concepts of autonomy and consent are not the same thing. The difficulty contract law faces in this area is twofold. The first is the balance between certainty and protection of autonomy. The clearer the law is about what kind of threats might or might not render a contract invalid, the greater the certainty is. A party knows what threats to avoid in trying to 'negotiate' the best deal they can. However, the more certain the law, the more room the stronger party has to find threats that fall the right side of the line and have the contract enforced even though the other party had not autonomously agreed to enter the contract. This is, no doubt, precisely why the courts have been so reluctant to accept that lawful conduct can amount to an illegitimate threat.

The second issue is the extent to which the issue is looked at from the point of view of the stronger party. It is notable that the primary focus of the law is on the nature of the threat, rather than the effect of the threat on the weaker party. If someone is pressurized in such a way that they do not autonomously enter a contract, they are bound by the contract, unless the threat was illegitimate. Again the perspective from which the issue is addressed is the 'stronger' party, not the vulnerable one. The current approach favours those who have the power to exercise pressure on the others (particularly when that power can be used in a way not covered by current contract law doctrine) and not the vulnerable who are more susceptible to pressure. The court assumes a particular kind of 'bad behaviour' which is illegitimate: the use of explicit threats. This concept helps hide a host of other wrongdoing which is not seen as relevant for the law on duress: manipulation of the markets, advertising targeted at vulnerable groups, high pressure selling techniques, and the like.

A third point of interest is that the law draws a distinction between commercial contracts and others. It acknowledges that the kinds of pressures that

---

[73] *Huyton S v Cremer GMBH* [1999] 1 Lloyd's Rep 620.

may be appropriate in 'rough' commercial dealings are different from other kinds of contract. A positive interpretation of this is that it acknowledges that the key question in this area is what norms are to be used to regulate dealings between contractors. If that is the question then the answer may vary depending on the different settings. That may be a helpful approach, although it may require a more sophisticated analysis than one based on the sharp distinction between commercial and non-commercial contracts.

Undue influence

Summary of the law

Lord Nicholls in the *Etridge* case explained the essence of undue influence:

Undue influence consists of the abuse of a relationship of trust and confidence. Leaving aside cases of improper pressure, coercion or threats, where equity follows the common law doctrine of duress, undue influence arises 'out of the relationship between two persons where one has acquired over another a measure of influence, or ascendancy, of which the ascendant person then takes unfair advantage'.[74]

So, while cases of duress are based on coercion or threats, undue influence involves one party using the influence they have over the other, in a way which may not involve explicit threats or pressure.

A contract is voidable if one party entered it under the undue influence of another. Given the nature of undue influence the courts have recognized that it is not always possible to provide direct evidence of one party putting the other under undue influence. There may be cases where a secret tape recording of a pressuring conversation can be produced, but in many cases that will not be available. The courts have therefore accepted that undue influence can be presumed from the circumstances.

There are two elements that need to be proved to generate a presumption of undue influence. The first is that the relationship is of the kind where undue influence could be exercised. The second is that the transaction calls for an explanation.

The relationship

The relationship must be of the kind in which undue influence can be exercised. This is classically where one party reposes trust and confidence in the other. This may be proved from the facts of the case, for example where there

---

[74] *Royal Bank of Scotland v Etridge (No 2)* [2002] 2 AC 77 (per Lord Nicholls), para. 8.

is evidence that one person had influence over another.[75] If there is no such evidence then the law acknowledges certain categories of relationships where it will be presumed that the relationship is one of potential undue influence. These include:

- Parent and child[76]
- Trustee and beneficiary[77]
- Solicitor and client[78]

Spouses and cohabitants will not fall into this category,[79] although, of course, a spouse might seek to show that in their particular relationship they were dominated by the other.[80] Indeed it may be easier for a spouse or partner to show their relationship was unequal than people in a less close relationship. There have been a series of cases where it has been shown that a husband dominated his wife and pressurized her into guaranteeing his loans.[81] The court will take into account matters such as who made decisions over the finances, the financial knowledge of the parties, and their characters in deciding whether such cases involve unequal relationships.[82]

The key question in deciding whether the relationship was of the kind where undue influence could be exercised is whether one party has acquired a 'measure of influence or ascendancy', as it was put in *Evans v Lloyd*.[83] It is important to appreciate that this does not suggest there was any impropriety. As Mummery LJ went on to say in *Niersmans v Pesticcio*:[84] 'A transaction may be set aside by the court, even though the actions and conduct of the person who benefits from it could not be criticized as wrongful ...'

Transaction calls for an explanation

The court will consider the transaction in the light of the relationship between the parties and ask whether the gift is a normal transaction within that relationship or whether it would 'raise an eyebrow'. Is the transaction one which, in a much quoted dicta in *Allcard v Skinner*, is 'not to be reasonably accounted for on the grounds of friendship, relationship, charity or other

---

[75] *O'Sullivan v Management Agency and Music Ltd* [1985] QB 428.
[76] *Bullock v Lloyd's Bank* [1995] Ch 317.   [77] *Ellis v Barker* (1871) LR 7 Ch App 104.
[78] *Wright v Carter* [1903] 1 Ch 27.   [79] *Barclays v O'Brien* [1994] 1 AC 180.
[80] *Smith v Cooper* [2010] EWCA Civ 722.
[81] *Royal Bank of Scotland v Etridge* (*No 2*) [2002] 2 AC 77.
[82] *Smith v Cooper* [2010] EWCA Civ 722.   [83] [2013] EWHC 1725 (Ch).
[84] [2004] EWCA Civ 372, at para. 20.

ordinary motives on which ordinary men act'?[85] So, for example, if a client gave a solicitor a box of chocolates at Christmas, that would probably be seen as entirely understandable and so no presumption of undue influence would arise. If the client gave their solicitor a valuable antique at Christmas, that would seem surprising and would generate the presumption.

It is the combination of these first two features which justifies the presumption of undue influence: if the relationship was one where one party was dominant over the other and the transaction is unusual then it seems a reasonable presumption (barring any further evidence) that the transaction was the result of undue influence. As Lord Nicholls[86] in *Etridge* stated:

> Proof that the complainant placed trust and confidence in the other party in relation to the management of the complainant's financial affairs, coupled with a transaction which calls for explanation, will normally be sufficient, failing satisfactory evidence to the contrary, to discharge the burden of proof. On proof of these two matters the stage is set for the court to infer that, in the absence of a satisfactory explanation, the transaction can only have been procured by undue influence. In other words, proof of these two facts is prima facie evidence that the defendant abused the influence he acquired in the parties' relationship. He preferred his own interests. He did not behave fairly to the other. So the evidential burden then shifts to him. It is for him to produce evidence to counter the inference which otherwise should be drawn.

Rebuttal

It is important to remember that the presumption of undue influence created by the two facts just mentioned (the nature of the relationship and the nature of the transaction) is rebuttable. To use the example above, there may be a perfectly good reason why the client gave their solicitor an antique, if the client was the solicitor's mother, for example. So the presumption can be rebutted by the stronger party if they can show that the transaction was a free exercise of the will of the other party as a result of full, free, and informed thought.[87]

Perhaps the most common way to rebut the presumption is to demonstrate that the 'weaker party' received independent and competent advice.[88] This is important because it enables the stronger party to receive reassurance that the transaction will not be set aside on undue influence. If they are aware the facts may give rise to a presumption of undue influence, by ensuring the

---

[85] (1887) 36 Ch D 145.   [86] [2002] 2 AC 77, para. 14.
[87] *Hackett v CPS* [2011] EWHC 1170; *Presticcio v Hurst* [2004] EWCA Civ 372.
[88] *Presticcio v Hurst* [2004] EWCA Civ 372.

other party has independent advice, they can rest assured the transaction will not be questioned on that basis. This has been an important feature of a series of cases involving banks who are receiving guarantees from a spouse or partner of a creditor. By ensuring that the partner receives independent advice they can be secure that the guarantee will be effective.

Interestingly the 'independent advice' avenue can work the other way. If a dominant party enters into an unusual transaction with a weaker party and does not encourage them to receive independent advice, that might be seen as reinforcing the idea the transaction was indeed the result of undue influence, especially if the dominant party is a professional and should have known of the need for independent advice.

The rebuttal must do more than simply demonstrate that there was an explanation for the transaction. It must show there was no undue influence and the weaker party exercised their free will in entering into it.[89] In *Hammond v Osborn*[90] Ward LJ adopted as a 'useful guide' the following words from *Snell's Equity*: 'In order to rebut the presumption it is not sufficient to show that the complainant understood what he was doing and intended to do it. The problem is not lack of understanding but lack of independence.' The extent of the loss to the weaker party may also be a relevant factor in deciding whether the presumption was rebutted. As Lord Nicholls put it, 'the greater the disadvantage to the vulnerable person, the more cogent must be the explanation before the presumption will be regarded as rebutted'.[91]

Discussion

There is clearly an overlap between cases of duress and undue influence. Both involve one party seeking to influence the decision of the other. The distinction is best understood as one where duress is about threats, while undue influence is about the abuse of a relationship.[92] The development of the law on undue influence from a vulnerability perspective is highly welcome. It shows an acknowledgment that we make decisions in a relational context. While our universal vulnerability means we need relationships within which to make decisions, those relationships can be misused by others to our disadvantage. The law of undue influence has developed with a degree of

---

[89] *Smith v Cooper* [2010] EWCA Civ 722.   [90] [2002] EWCA Civ 885, para. 25.

[91] *Royal Bank of Scotland v Etridge* (*No 2*) [2002] 2 AC 77, para. 24.

[92] M. Chen-Wishart, 'Beyond Influence: Beyond Impaired Consent and Wrongdoing Towards a Relational Analysis' in A. Burrows and A. Roger, *Mapping the Law* (Oxford, Oxford University Press 2006).

sophistication to acknowledge the different ways in which a relationship can undermine autonomy.

A lively theoretical debate surrounding the law is whether the heart of the undue influence is the lack of genuine consent on the behalf of the weaker party or the wrongful conduct of the defendant. The competing models indicate a central contrast for this chapter. The 'abuse' model indicates that the contract cannot be enforced if the stronger party has engaged in some kind of bad conduct, impropriety, or wrongdoing. By contrast the 'lack of consent' model emphasizes the lack of free and full consent of the weaker party. In distinguishing these views it is worth asking who is favoured by each approach. I would argue the 'abuse' model favours stronger parties. It gives them the reassurance that as long as they avoid any improper conduct of the kind listed in the textbooks the contract will not be set aside. It limits their responsibility to simply ensuring that they themselves do engage in wrongdoing. In particular they avoid threats, misrepresentation, and pressure. The abuse model would be favoured by the weaker party. They will not be bound by a contract which they did not freely enter into, even if that is not the result of identifiable wrong conduct of the stronger party. In effect, it puts the added responsibility on a stronger party of ensuring the weaker party has sufficient capacity to enter the contract.

Mindy Chen-Wishart[93] points out that the difference between the two versions is not as significant as it first appears. The difference is really about what is identified as the source of the claimant's impaired consent to enter the contract: the other party's behaviour or any factor.

One of the concerns Chen-Wishart has about the current approach to undue influence is that the case law and some academic writing seems to regard the fact someone is in a relationship which could be used to influence them as problematic. Birks and Chin suggest that victims of undue influence are 'impaired in their judgmental capacity … arising from their morbid dependence on another'. They suggest that her autonomy is 'sub-standard' or 'impaired to an exceptional degree'. This, however, assumes that there is something wrong in entering relationships of interdependency, while, as argued in Chapter 1, in fact that is almost inevitable. Indeed as argued there, our relationships are a pre-condition to autonomy, not a challenge to it.

As Chen-Wishart[94] points out, the fact that one party is dependent on the other party should not per se be seen as abnormal:

There is nothing wrong (pathological) with the claimant's trust in, dependence on, or allegiance to a defendant with whom she shares a caring relationship (a

---

[93] Ibid.   [94] Ibid.

relationship of influence). Trust, dependence, or allegiance is constitutive of close relationships, which, in turn, facilitate human flourishing and characterize a good life. To uphold the integrity of such valuable relationships, the law requires the defendant to have due regard for the *substantive and procedural norms implicit in the relationship of influence* he shares with the claimant when he transacts with her.

It is suggested this helpfully identifies the key issue for this chapter: what are the responsibilities of a person dealing with a 'vulnerable contractor'? Both sides to the argument may agree that undue influence or duress are cases where the stronger party has failed to live up to their responsibilities towards the weaker party and as a result the weaker party has entered into the contract. The issue is what those responsibilities are. Are they simply to avoid positive improper behaviour (the abuse model) or do they compel the stronger party to take positive steps to ensure effective consent and only proceed if they are convinced there is effective consent (the consent model)?

In *Etridge* Lord Nicholls noted that influence can occur even where the stronger party stands by:

[T]he influence one person has over another provides scope for misuse without any specific overt acts of persuasion. The relationship between two individuals may be such that, without more, one of them is disposed to agree a course of action proposed by the other. Typically this occurs when one person places trust in another to look after his affairs and interests, and the latter betrays this trust *by preferring his own interests*. He abuses the influence he has acquired.[95]

This is a welcome acknowledgement that a relationship can generate a responsibility towards the other that is not restricted to not abusing the other. It can require positive acts to ensure the other does not unfairly lose out under the relationship.

Peter Birks and Yin Nyuk Chin[96] suggest a clear mark can be drawn between duress and undue influence and indeed suggest that in cases where there is actual undue influence proved this should be seen as duress. The difficulty with this view is that what constitutes a threat may only be understandable in the context of the relationship. In a particular context and relationship words may become a threat; or the strength of the words may only be understood as they form part of a broader pattern of controlling conduct.[97]

---

[95] *Royal Bank of Scotland v Etridge (No 2)* [2002] 2 AC 77, para. 8.
[96] P. Birks and C. Yin, 'On the Nature of Undue Influence' in J. Beatson and D Friedman (eds), *Good Faith and Fault in Contract Law* (Oxford, Oxford University Press 1997).
[97] *Bank of Scotland v Bennett* [1998] EWCA Civ 1965.

As Chen Wishart suggests, the key features should be 'the defendant's *failure to safeguard the claimant's interests* in view of their relationship'.[98] Within a close relationship, she suggests:

[T]he defendant must *either* protect the claimant's welfare interest (if he does, there would be no improvidence to raise the inference of undue influence) *or*, successfully emancipate the claimant to protect her own welfare interest (if he does, he can rebut any inference of undue influence).

This can show that in rebutting the undue influence it is necessary to show that either the claimant did have an acceptable basis for the transaction (i.e. it did, broadly understood, promote the well-being of the claimant); or the claimant did exercise her own judgement. The difficulty with this last point is that it may be questioned whether anyone is able to exercise their own judgement. Rick Bigwood[99] suggests that this is why we need to find some positive wrongdoing on the stronger party's part:

What is objectionable about exploitation is that a defendant chooses, freely and knowingly, to benefit from the relative position of power resulting from such vulnerability, and that the defendant's gain—in this context, the right to a contract—results from the exercise of that power.

This, however, seems to fail to appreciate the way that relationships can be misused to exercise power over another, in a way which may well not involve some positive act which can amount to an exercise of power.

Perhaps the least satisfactory aspect of the undue influence doctrine is the suggestion that the presumption of undue influence can be rebutted by the provision of independent advice. This seems to assume that people make their decisions as rational, logic-driven, commercially minded people. The example of the wife who guarantees her husband's business loans which has much troubled the courts is a telling one. Surely it cannot sensibly be suggested that a meeting with a lawyer informing her of the legal terms of the guarantee is meaning that the pressure she is under within the relationship is dissipated.[100] Certainly the provision of legal advice as the way of rebutting undue influence, or notice of it, is convenient for banks, but can hardly be said to be a genuine attempt to ensure people are not improperly manipulated through relationships into contracts.

---

[98] M. Chen-Wishart, 'Beyond Influence', (n. 95).

[99] R. Bigwood, 'Undue Influence: "Impaired Consent" or "Wicked Exploitation"?', (1995) 16 *Oxford Journal of Legal Studies* 503.

[100] A. Belcher, 'A Feminist Perspective on Contract Theories from Law and Economics', (2000) 8 *Feminist Legal Studies* 29.

Unconscionable bargains

Summary of the law

The courts are willing to set aside a contract where there is an unconscionable bargain. The phrase is a broad one and covers cases where one party has exploited a weakness of the other. It seems that the category 'unconscionable bargain' is to be used only if the case does not fall within the category of duress or undue influence.[101] In *Fry v Lane*[102] Kay J stated the key principle underpinning the doctrine: '[W]here a purchase is made from a poor and ignorant man at a considerable undervalue, the vendor having no independent advice, a Court of Equity will set aside the transaction.' A more modern formulation can be found in *Alec Lobb (Garages) Ltd v Total Oil GB Ltd*[103] where Peter Millett QC, sitting as a deputy judge of the High Court, stated:

[I]f the cases are examined, it will be seem that three elements have almost invariably been present before the court has interfered ... Second, the weakness of the one party has been exploited by the other in some *morally culpable* manner: see, for example, *Clark v Malpas* ... where a poor and illiterate man was induced to enter into a transaction of an unusual nature, without proper independent advice, and in great haste.

Subsequent case law has moved beyond the notions of poverty and ignorance to 'special disadvantage'. That has been held to include 'less highly educated',[104] 'member of the lower income group',[105] drunkenness, mental impairment, and necessity.[106] It may be that whether a person is at a special disadvantage will depend on the complexity of the transaction.[107]

A good case can be made for saying that the overarching requirement is that there is 'unconscionability'.[108] That cannot be reduced to a set formula, but will involve looking at the status of the weaker party, the distribution of the gains and losses in the contract, the form of the negotiations, and so on. It will require more than simply proving the content of the contract was unfair.[109] There needs to be some form of unconscionable

---

[101] J. Devenny and A. Chandler, 'Unconscionability and the Taxonomy of Undue Influence', (2007) 8 *Journal of Business Law* 541.
[102] (1888) 40 Ch D 312.　　[103] [1984] EWCA Civ 2.
[104] *Cresswell v Potter* [1978] 1 WLR 255.　　[105] Ibid.
[106] J. Devenny and A. Chandler, 'Unconscionability', (n. 104).
[107] *Howell Evans v Lloyd* [2013] EWHC 1725 (Ch).
[108] *Cresswell v Potter* [1978] 1 WLR 255.
[109] *Boustany v Pigott* [1993] EGCS 85.

conduct,[110] that is some kind of unfair advantage being taken.[111] In *Multiservice Bookbinding Ltd v Marden*[112] Browne-Wilkinson J emphasized that point:

The classic example of an unconscionable bargain is where advantage has been taken of a young, inexperienced or ignorant person to introduce a term which no sensible well-advised person or party would have accepted. But I do not think the categories of unconscionable bargains are limited: the court can and should intervene where a bargain has been procured by unfair means.

Discussion

It is in the area of unconscionable bargains that we get closest to the idea promoted in this chapter that there is a special responsibility on contracting parties to look for the vulnerability of the other party and ensure they do not suffer as a result of it. As Lord Denning put it in *Lloyds Bank v Bundy*,[113] 'it is not right that the strong should be allowed to push the weak to the wall'.

There is still some way for the doctrine to develop if it is to go as far as I would like to see it. First, it is generally assumed the doctrine only applies where the stronger party acts positively to take advantage of the other party in a way which is morally culpable.[114] David Capper[115] argues that the doctrine requires that one party consciously intends to take advantage of the weaker. This seems to allow people to too easily take advantage of another's vulnerable state, short of actively manipulating or oppressing them.

Second, there is a limit on the kinds of vulnerability included within in the doctrine. Sharon Thompson suggests 'an unconscionable bargain might also be found in cases where the special disadvantage to or impairment of one party leads to the other receiving a passive benefit from the transaction'.[116] Even this formulation of the doctrine, which is broader than many, is limited to 'special' disadvantages or impairments. As argued in Chapter 2, this overlooks the disadvantages and impairments to which we are all prone.

---

[110] D. Capper, 'The Unconscionable Bargain in the Common Law World', (2010) 126 *Law Quarterly Review* 403.

[111] *Fineland Investments Ltd v Pritchard* [2011] EWHC 113 (Ch).

[112] [1979] Ch 84, 110.   [113] [1975] QB 326.

[114] *Boustany v Pigott* [1993] EGCS 85.

[115] D. Capper, 'The Unconscionable Bargain', (n. 113).

[116] S. Thompson, *Prenuptial Agreements and the Presumption of Free Choice* (London, Bloomsbury 2015), 125.

Statutory protections

Summary of the law

Despite the pre-eminence given to the principle of 'freedom of contract' in the academic writing the practice of English contract law is profoundly impacted on by statutory regulation on the details of contracts in a host of areas. Freedom of contract in insurance law, labour law, landlord–tenant law, and products liability law (to give but a few examples) are severely restricted by statutory regulation. This is not the place to go into the details of these regulations, save to note that the statutory regulation is typically designed to protect vulnerable contractors.

Regulation can involve different techniques. Sometimes these take the form of procedural techniques. For example they may require a party to be given a 'cooling off' period after the contracts have been signed during which they are free to exit the contract,[117] or that the more vulnerable contractor be given certain information before they enter a contract.[118] More dramatically the regulation may render certain clauses compulsory or at least set minimum standards for certain terms. For example, the minimum wage legislation prohibits the payment of less than a certain sum per hour for different categories of people. In sales of goods to consumer contracts, statute automatically implies in terms relating to the quality of the goods. Regulations can also allow a public authority such as the Office of Fair Trading to promote good consumer practices and to challenge unfair clauses in contracts. The two best known pieces of legislation which impact on the content of contracts are the Unfair Contract Terms Act 1977 and the Unfair Terms in Consumer Contracts Regulations 1999, SI 1999/2083. These will be very briefly summarized.

Unfair Contract Terms Act 1977

This legislation applies to terms covering 'business liability'. That is where there is a contract creating liability for someone acting in the course of their business who enters a contract with a consumer. The Act primarily focuses on the clauses which exclude or restrict their duties (exclusion clauses). It therefore cannot be used to challenge terms which define the parties' obligations (e.g. which fix the price or describe the goods to be supplied). In can be used to challenge terms which restrict the business party's duty under

---

[117] For example the Consumer Credit Act 1974, ss 67, 68.
[118] Consumer Protection (Distance Selling) Regulations, SI 2000/2334.

negligence liability or limit their obligations under statutorily implied terms into a contract. The Act renders some clauses ineffective automatically and some clauses only invalid if they are not reasonable.

An example of a term which is automatically invalid includes a term which excludes or restricts a person's business liability for death or personal injury from negligence.[119] An example of a term subject to a reasonableness test is a term which seeks to exclude or restrict liability for negligence for losses other than for death or personal injury.[120] The test for reasonableness is determined at the time of entering the contract.[121] This is important because it means the reasonableness test applies to the term itself, rather than considering whether it was reasonable to exclude liability for the breach which actually occurred.[122]

Unfair Terms in Consumer Contracts Regulations 1999

These regulations[123] are in broader terms than the 1977 Act.[124] In particular they are not restricted to exclusion clauses. However, there are limitations. They only apply to contracts between a commercial seller and a consumer[125] and do not apply to contracts if their terms have been individually negotiated.[126] If the term is found unfair it 'shall not be binding on the consumer'.[127] A consumer is defined[128] as a person who acts outside his trade, business, or profession. A term is unfair if it is 'contrary to the requirement of good faith' (meaning there is not 'fair and open dealing' and 'causes a significant imbalance between the parties rights and obligations arising under the contract, to the detriment of the consumer').[129] This appears to be a very open test providing a broad discretion. The court is required to take account of 'the nature of the goods and services for which the contract was concluded' and 'all the circumstances attending the conclusion of the contract' and 'all the other terms of the contract'. Andrew Burrows[130] suggests these mean the facts the goods were second-hand or that the consumer had examined the goods could be taken into account. Schedule 2 also lists many

---

[119] Section 2(1).   [120] Section 2(2).   [121] Section 11.

[122] The statute provides a list of factors which are taken into account in assessing reasonableness (Sch 2).

[123] They give effect to the EC Council Directive (EEC) 93/13 OJ L95/29.

[124] There is nothing to stop a consumer seeking to rely on both the 1999 Regulations and the 1977 Act.

[125] Regulation 3.

[126] They will not be individually negotiated if drafted in advance and the consumer has not influenced the substance of the term (reg 5). The burden of showing the term is negotiated is on the seller or supplier.

[127] Regulation 8.   [128] Regulation 3.   [129] Regulation 5.

[130] A. Burrows, 'Contract: In General' in A. Burrows (ed.), *English Private Law* (Oxford, Oxford University Press 2013), 8.122.

examples of terms which 'may be regarded as unfair'. These are taken as 'indicative and non-exhaustive'.[131] Some of these relate to the contents of the term (e.g. '(a) excluding or limiting the legal liability of a seller or supplier in the event of the death of a consumer or personal injury to the latter resulting from an act or omission of that seller or supplier') and others to the form of the negotiations ('(i) irrevocably binding the consumer to terms with which he had no real opportunity of becoming acquainted before the conclusion of the contract'). None of these specifically relate to any vulnerability of the contractor, although one might expect the court to take vulnerability into account in determining fairness.

A significant restriction on the coverage of the Regulations is that they do not apply '(a) to the definition of the main subject matter of the contract, or (b) to the adequacy of the price or remuneration, as against the goods or services supplied in exchange'.[132] The only exception is that interference may be possible if those terms are not 'in plain intelligible language'.[133] This makes it clear that the Regulations are not designed to ensure a reasonable price is charged or that the goods are of an appropriate quality. One explanation for this limitation is that these are the terms which the consumer is most likely to ensure they understand: what they are buying and how much it costs. Seen in that light, the regulations are designed to deal with the 'small print'; terms of the contract which a consumer may well not notice.

In *Director General of Fair Trading v First National Bank*[134] the House of Lords indicated it would give a narrow interpretation to these restrictions because otherwise terms limiting liability could too easily be expressed as concerned with the 'price of the contract'. However in *Office of Fair Trading v Abbey National*[135] the Supreme Court backtracked on this a little by saying that the regulations did not apply to the 'essential price' or to 'any monetary price or remuneration payable under the contract'. However they added that the restriction only means these terms cannot be challenged in terms of their 'price/quality' ratio: that is, essentially a claim the consumer has paid too much for the item. This decision limits the impact of regulation of loans where the terms primarily deal with what money is paid under the contract in different circumstances.

Discussion

Lord Brightman in *Hart v O'Connor* noted there are different ways a contract may be unfair:

---

[131] Regulation 5(5).   [132] Regulation 6.   [133] Regulation 6.
[134] [2001] UKHL 52.   [135] [2009] UKSC 6.

If a contract is stigmatised as 'unfair', it may be unfair in one of two ways. It may be unfair by reason of the unfair manner in which it was brought into existence; a contract induced by undue influence is unfair in this sense … It may also, in some contexts, be described (accurately or inaccurately) as 'unfair' by reason of the fact that the terms of the contract are more favourable to one party than to the other.[136]

The unfair contract terms regulations are significant because they deal with the second kind of unfairness. They involve a recognition that consumers are not really in a position to bargain with businesses in most contexts. The model of a negotiated contract which the parties choose to enter into is a false one in the case of consumers buying products from businesses. Content-based regulation is the only effective option in such a case to protect consumers.

It is noticeable in these regulations that vulnerability does not feature a great deal. Clauses are struck down on the basis that they are unfair or unreasonable in an abstract way, with little consideration of the impact of these on a particular individual consumer. In part this is a recognition that we are generally talking about standard term contracts which businesses create and expect to apply to all consumers, whatever their individual characteristics. The law might reasonably expect businesses to ensure that their contracts are fair or reasonable in general and cannot be expected to tailor their contracts to the needs of each consumer's unique characteristics. That seems inevitable, but what the courts could do, in considering the reasonableness or fairness of a term is to recall that a wide range of consumers will be dealing with these businesses and a term should be regarded as unfair, even if it would only be unfair to a section of consumers (e.g. more vulnerable consumers).

By contrast EU law seems more open to providing especial protection for vulnerable consumers. For example, the Unfair Commercial Practices Directive[137] draws a distinction between 'average' and 'particularly vulnerable consumers' in relation to the regulation of commercial practices. Article 5(3) of the Directive therefore awards special protection to 'a clearly identifiable group of consumers who are particularly vulnerable' to a certain commercial practice or product. Vulnerability for the purpose of the Directive may arise out of the consumers' 'mental or physical infirmity, age or credulity'. Commercial practices which are likely to 'materially distort the economic behaviour' of such specifically 'vulnerable' consumers will be assessed from the perspective of the average member of that group. However, the obligations only arise if the seller could be 'reasonably expected to foresee' the consumer's

---

[136] [1985] UKPC 1.
[137] Directive 2005/29 concerning unfair business-to-consumer commercial practices in the internal market and amending Council Directive 84/450, Directives 97/7, 98/27, 2002/65, and Regulation 2006/2004 (Unfair Commercial Practices Directive) [2005] OJ L149/22.

'vulnerability'. Another example is the Consumer Rights Directive[138] which deals with 'distance and off-premises contracts'. In relation to the requirement that there be clear and comprehensible information given to the consumer before the contract is completed, it states that the trader 'should take into account the specific needs of consumers who are particularly vulnerable because of their mental, physical or psychological infirmity, age or credulity in a way which the trader could reasonably be expected to foresee'.[139] Although there are these specific regulations dealing with vulnerability, more often the courts proceed using the norm of a standard contractor. Stephen Weatherill argues that, despite the specific regulations, generally in EU contract law 'vulnerable consumers are sacrificed to the interests of self-reliant consumers in deregulation, market integration and wider choices'.[140] This is shown by the fact that, as Lisa Waddington[141] notes:

> It seems that the EU legislator and the Court generally regard requirements to provide additional protection to 'vulnerable' consumers as barriers to market access and market integration ... The legislator and Court seem to believe that allowing for greater levels of protection for 'vulnerable consumers', and thereby requiring that producers, suppliers and sellers differentiate between types of consumers, and treat them in accordance with their specific needs and abilities, would undermine this 'full harmonisation'. In such circumstances the needs of 'vulnerable consumers' come second place to the needs of the market.

It is noticeable that in the debates around EU regulation of contracts much more attention is given to vulnerable contractors than is given in UK law. A report of the European Parliament Committee on the Internal Market and Consumer Protection[142] suggests that vulnerability can be both 'endogenous' and 'exogenous'. By 'endogenous' it is meant that the consumer's vulnerability is the result of factors inherent to the consumer or their situations (e.g. a mental impairment). These may be temporary (being a child) or permanent (e.g. a disability). There can also be 'exogenous' factors such as a lack of education or knowledge. These are not inherent in the individual. The report emphasizes that the impact of these factors may vary depending on the

---

[138] Directive 2011/83 on consumer rights, amending Directive 93/13 and Directive 1999/44 and repealing Directive 85/577 and Directive 97/7 (Consumer Rights Directive) [2011] OJ L304/64.

[139] Recital 34.

[140] S. Weatherill, 'Recent Case Law Concerning the Free Movement of Goods', (1999) 36 *Common Market Law Review* 51, 58.

[141] L. Waddington, 'Vulnerable and Confused: The Protection of "Vulnerable" Consumers Under EU Law', (2013) *European Law Review* 757.

[142] Committee on the Internal Market and Consumer Protection, *Report on a Strategy for Strengthening the Rights of Vulnerable Consumers* (2012).

product and context. To similar effect the *European Parliament Committee on the Internal Market and Consumer Protection*[143]argues that 'the concept of vulnerable consumers should also include consumers in a situation of vulnerability, meaning consumers who are placed in a state of temporary powerlessness resulting from a gap between their individual state and characteristics on the one hand, and their external environment on the other hand'.[144] These are broad and sensitive understandings of vulnerability, and it is that kind of analysis that is sadly lacking from orthodox UK contract law.

Traditionally substantive fairness provisions are seen as contrary to autonomy. They are the state or the law imposing standards of proprietary for contact, rather than allowing the parties to determine what is fair for themselves. However, I would suggest that in fact substantive fairness provisions need not be seen as inconsistent with autonomy, especially in the consumer context.[145] When most people sign the contract for electricity provision or click on the 'I agree' button for a download, the consumer is accepting the standard terms, which they do not read, but assume to be reasonable or fair. Ensuring that the terms are reasonable and fair is ensuring the contract meets the expectations of the parties.[146] That is the very opposite of undermining autonomy. Further, while it is sometimes said that protecting substantive fairness undermines uncertainty in that it cannot be predicted what a court might or might not determine unfair, in fact it promotes certainty in reassuring consumers that the contract will be in within the boundaries of what is fair and that unexpected clauses will be struck down.[147]

A vulnerability based contract law

Contract law is generally based on the norm of the average consumer who is seen as 'reasonably well informed, observant and circumspect'. Contracting parties are assumed to be knowledgeable, able to stand up for themselves, and, absent some improper behaviour, on an equal footing to bargain for themselves.[148] The values that are promoted by contract law are those of self-interest, promoting free-markets, self-sufficiency, and profit maximization.

---

[143] Ibid.   [144] Ibid., *finding D*, pp. 6–7.
[145] S. Smith, 'Contracting Under Pressure: A Theory of Duress', [1997] *Cambridge Law Journal* 343.
[146] C. Thomas, 'What Role Should Substantive Fairness Have in the English Law of Contact? An Overview of the Law', (2010) *Cambridge Student Law Review* 177.
[147] Ibid.   [148] L. Waddington, 'Vulnerable and Confused', (n. 144).

We could have a very different kind of contract law if we start with the notion of universal vulnerability set out in Chapter 2. If we are all vulnerable, then we start with a contracting party who is ignorant about many things, is open to emotional and physical pressures, who is best with the norms of human life, and short on time and energy to read mountains of paperwork. We could see contracts as designed to promote those things that are central to a good human life: mutuality, relationships, and interdependence. We approach our contracting partners as those we want to have a fair relationship with. People who are more than a source of profit. As fellow vulnerable people who need to be looked out for.

Such a vision of contract law would expect and require the parties to take reasonable steps to ensure that the other party is not mistaken about any significant matter of the contract. That they are aware of the important terms of the contract. The law would seek to ensure that the terms of the contract were in line with a fair balancing of rights and responsibilities under the contract. The law would be alert to the misuse of relationships to obtain an advantage for one party over another.

The fiction of the typical contractor which is at the heart of orthodox contract law was well demonstrated in the most recent edition of the European Commission's Consumer Conditions Scoreboard, which argued:

[T]he portrait of the European consumers that emerges from the consumer surveys does not fit easily with the notion of the *'average consumer'* defined by European case law as someone who is 'reasonably well-informed, and reasonably observant and circumspect'. The scoreboard finds that consumers' knowledge and understanding of fundamental consumer rights is fairly poor. Only 13% of respondents were able to answer all three questions correctly (regarding guarantees, cooling-off periods and unsolicited selling), compared to 12% who did not give a single correct answer.[149]

The average consumer understands little about the nature of the contracts they are entering into or even basic information about the goods they are purchasing.[150] We need a contract law which recognizes this and is based on the vulnerable contractor as a norm.[151]

We need also to rethink the notion of undue influence. Being in a relationship with another person does carry with it obligations and responsibilities. Being in a relationship where the other person can influence you is not

---

[149] Committee on the Internal Market and Consumer Protection, *Report on a Strategy for Strengthening the Rights of Vulnerable Consumers* (2012), 5.

[150] C. Brennan and M. Coppack, 'Consumer Empowerment: Global Context, UK Strategies and Vulnerable Consumers', (2008) 32 *International Journal of Consumers Studies* 306, 306.

[151] F. Morgan, D. Schuler, and J. Stoltma, 'A Framework for Examining the Legal Status of Vulnerable Consumers', (1995) 14 *Journal of Public Policy and Marketing* 267.

a bad thing, it is a normal thing. The problem is that the law has failed to give due weight to the responsibilities that relationships bring with them. As Chen-Wishart has argued, when the law is considering what might impact on the free consent of a contractor, it imagines someone who is detached and independent.[152] She notes that leading work on contract law describes 'pressure, emotional blackmail or bullying' as 'relatively innocuous'. Only threats to our person or property count for 'super-detached man'. Yet relationships of this kind are necessary and inevitable, as argued in Chapter 2.

We should come to a contract imagining our vulnerable contractor within a network of relationships. So understood the focus in contract law should move away from a 'snapshot' approach to consent, to looking at whether there was an offer and acceptance at a particular moment in time which fixes henceforth the obligations between the parties. We need to look at the relationship between the two parties and the agreement in the context of that.[153] This means the 'signature rule' is highly problematic. It looks simply at one moment in time and fails to take into account the broader context within which the decision was made. As Joseph Raz has argued:

The purpose of contract law should be not to enforce promises, but to protect both the practice of undertaking voluntary obligations and the individuals who rely on that practice ... One protects the practice of undertaking voluntary obligations by preventing its erosion—by making good any harm caused by its use or abuse.[154]

Yet, these obligations cannot necessarily be fixed at one point in time (the offer and acceptance), but can change as performance of the contract is undertaken and must be read in the light of the overall relationships between the parties. As the relationship develops new obligations may be taken on and expectations created. These may well, over time, have little to do with the agreement that was created at the start of the relationship.

Not only that, but the formation of responsibilities arising from a relationship may not neatly fit into a traditional contract law analysis. As Tidwell and Linzer have argued:

From the perspective of women, the cornerstone contract doctrine of consent often seems contrived. The homemaker, the PTA mom, the rising executive's wife, the errand runner, the 'assistant', the secretary, and the teacher, even the female lawyer, doctor and accountant, know that obligations arise as mysteriously and frequently

---

[152] M. Chen-Wishart, 'Undue Influence: Vindicating Relationships of Influence', (2009) 56 *Current Legal Problems* 231.
[153] R. Auchmuty, 'Men Behaving Badly: An Analysis of English Undue Influence Cases', (2002) 11 *Social and Legal Studies* 257.
[154] J. Raz, *The Morality of Freedom* (Oxford University Press) 161.

as dust. Obligations float in through the central air ducts, the loudspeaker, the light fixtures. To speak of consent, of carefully negotiated words on paper, of clearly defined and presented duties is to speak of a world made and inhabited by men.

The role, then, of contract law is to enable people to enter into relationships and agreements free from exploitation. They can put their trust and confidence in another, as is needed for relationships to flourish, but not be concerned that the trust or confidence will be misused, or know that if it is the law will recognize this for the wrong it is and ensure there is legal protection. Their relational values will be acknowledged and respected, whether or not they fall into a traditional offer and acceptance analysis.

There is much in this approach which is sympathetic to relational contract theory. Robert Gordon argues:

Parties [to relational contracts] treat their contracts more like marriages than like one night stands. Obligations grow out of the commitment that they have made to one another, and the conventions that the trading community establishes for such commitments; they are not frozen at the initial moment of commitment, but change as circumstances change; the object of contracting is not ... to allocate risks, but to signify a commitment to co-operate. In bad times the parties are expected to lend one another mutual support, rather than standing on their rights; each will treat the other's insistence on literal performance as wilful obstructionism ... and the sanction for egregiously bad behaviour is always ... refusal to deal again.[155]

A critique of this kind of approach may well be that the obligations undertaken by the parties are unclear and the extent of the remedies unclear. However, this is precisely the point. Many relationships will involve obligations and responsibilities that cannot be defined in advance. Take, for example, someone taking on care of their elderly parent. It is not possible, often, to define a moment when that responsibility was taken on. It would not be possible to set down in advance precisely what the work required would be or what would be a fair recompense for it and any resulting losses. Indeed it would cause the parties grave distress to expect them to do so. In such a case it is only possible at the end of the relationship to ascertain how the benefits and burdens of the relationship played out. What would be a fair payment for the care provided? Intimate work of that kind cannot be assessed in advance in terms of pounds per hour and can only be assessed in retrospect when the relationship has come to an end. So, yes, it is uncertain; uncertain because it has to be.[156] In such cases, and generally in

---

[155] R. W. Gordon, 'Macaulay, Macneil, and the Discovery of Solidarity and Power in Contract Law', (1985) *Wisconsin Law Review* 565, 569.

[156] R. Mackenzie, 'Private Risk, Trust, Money and Handling the Proceeds of Corruption: Steps Towards an Ecology of Financial Systems Design' in B. Rider (ed.), *Corruption: The Enemy Within* (Amersterdam, Kluwer Law 1997).

contracts I would argue, the values of certainty, predictability, and abstract rules do not govern the case well. Rules that ensure fairness, that are sensitive to the context of the relationship, and that reflect the values of the parties are far more desirable.[157]

Concern about this kind of relational approach has been voiced by Dori Kimel.[158] For him there is a 'value of personal detachment', that is, of 'doing certain things with others not only outside the context of already-existing relationships, but also without a commitment to the future prospect of such relationships'.[159] In short, he argues, the value of contracts is that you can be legally bound by someone, without having to enter a long term, emotionally laden relationship with them. This, however, takes a rather narrow view of relationships. The relational approach is requiring a reading of the contract in terms of the nature of the relationship between the parties. That might be a 'cold' relationship and that can be certainly acknowledged under a relational approach. Contract law need not require contractors to be friendly or even personal. However, it can require that, at least, the parties look out for the vulnerabilities each other have and share.[160] This is fully acknowledged by Macneil,[161] the leading relational contract theorist, who thinks a relational approach would draw a difference between a discrete transaction and a contract dealing with an ongoing relationship.

Conclusion

Contract law is based on a very striking norm of what a contractor is like and the promotion of a particular set of values. The typical contractor around which contract law is built is the man driven by rationality, who is intelligent, powerful, and able to stand up for himself. He is a man who likes to drive a hard bargain and get as much as he can from his contracting partner. His only real fear in terms of being taken advantage of in a contract is that another will use lies or threats against him.

---

[157] P. Tidwell and P. Linzer, 'The Flesh Coloured Band Aid—Contracts, Feminism, Dialogue and Norms', (1991) 28 *Houston Law Review* 791; M. Frug, 'Re-reading Contracts: A Feminist Analysis of a Contracts Casebook', (1985) 34 *American Universities Law Review* 34.

[158] D. Kimel, 'The Choice Paradigm for Theory of Contract: Reflections on the Relational Model', (2007) 27 *Oxford Journal of Legal Studies* 233.

[159] D. Kimel, *From Promise to Contract* (Oxford, Hart 2003), 55–66.

[160] R. Stone, 'Unconscionability, Exploitation, and Hypocrisy', (2014) 22 *Journal of Political Philosophy* 27.

[161] I. Macneil, *The New Social Contract* (New Haven, Yale University Press 1980).

It could all be very different. We could have a contract law built around a vulnerable contractor: one who knows very little about what they are purchasing, who lacks the expertise to read complex legal documents, who is driven by emotional pressures as much as rational thought, and who enters contract without the time, energy, or ability to understand all the issues involved. We might have a contract law that seeks to promote relationships where there is a fair sharing of the losses and gains. Where a contractor can rest assured that the law will regulate the contract and only give effect to those clauses which are fair. Where contracting parties are encouraged to recognize each other's vulnerability and act in good faith towards each other, providing them with the information they need, doing what they can to ensure the other is not mistaken, or entering a clearly unfair bargain. Where the values promoted are honesty, mutuality, and interdependence. Where contracts must be understood as part of the ongoing relationship between the parties and where they gain their meaning and value from those relationships.

This vulnerability centred contract law would, I suggest, be a far better version than the one we have at the moment. Sadly, we are a long way from it.

9

Concluding Thoughts

In this chapter I want to bring together some key themes in the preceding chapters and to correct some possible misapprehensions.

Rethinking the norm

A consistent theme of this book has been the need to rethink the norm of personhood around which the law is based. The law is based on a norm of a person who is self-sufficient, able to meet their own needs, self-seeking, and able to make decisions for themselves. With that image of the self it is not surprising that the law emphasizes the rights of autonomy and privacy which underpin much of the law. It explains why the principle of freedom of contract, is seen as underpinning contract law. That is why autonomy has risen to such a hallowed place in medical law and ethics.[1] It is why the law found it so difficult to recognize or value caring.[2]

This book has advocated starting with the norm being vulnerable people in an interconnected network of relationships. As Catriona Mackenzie, Wendy Rogers, and Susan Dodds explain:

Human life is conditioned by vulnerability. By virtue of our embodiment human beings have bodily and material needs; are exposed to physical illness, injury, disability, and death; and depend on the care of others for extended periods during our lives. As social and affective beings we are emotionally and psychologically vulnerable to others in myriad ways ... As sociopolitical beings, we are vulnerable to exploitation, manipulation, oppression, political violence and rights abuses.[3]

---

[1] C. Foster, *Choosing Life, Choosing Death, The Tyranny of Autonomy in Medical Ethics and Law* (Oxford, Hart 2009).

[2] J. Herring, *Caring and the Law* (Oxford, Hart 2013).

[3] C. Mackenzie, W. Rogers, and S. Dodds, 'Introduction' in C. Mackenzie, W. Rogers, and S. Dodds (eds), *Vulnerability* (Oxford, Oxford University Press 2014), 3.

That is why it is argued contract law should be based on a model where contracting parties should look out for the other party, where good faith should be required, where exploitation of the other party is penalized. As it is, contract law in its basic form is designed to enable the stronger party to obtain as much as they can from the other, to encourage parties not to disclose information, and to promote a short-term view of contracting relationships.

In relation to criminal law, the book has urged a re-centring of exploitation. A recognition of our mutual vulnerability imposes an obligation to look out for each other and respect our vulnerabilities. Where, therefore, a person is going to commit a wrong against another, but is relying on their consent, it is not enough simply to obtain a 'yes' from that other. There must be sensitivity to the situation the person is in and a giving of space and time and room to enable them to make the decision. A law of rape, for example, which can allow a person to have sex with another knowing they are fearful, mistaken, or confused, fails to show adequate respect for our vulnerabilities.[4]

Breaking down the boundaries

The law loves its categorizations and the drawing of boundaries. We are boxed in as the competent, the vulnerable, and the self. Yes these boxes, like the concepts they represent, are porous. The notion we can be separated into the competent and the incompetent was shown to be profoundly false in Chapter 3. The labelling of groups as vulnerable disguises the vulnerability of all of us.

There is, perhaps, an inevitability in the law drawing categories. That way we can ensure that like cases can be treated alike. But the legal categorizations often fail to do this. The business person purchasing office equipment is not 'like' the consumer purchasing some food. Examining the detail of the lives and relationships of individuals is not considering irrelevant matters, but looking carefully at why someone might or might not be expected to comply with a legal standard, or how they are different from the legal norm underpinning the rule.

Recognizing our vulnerabilities means acknowledging that each of us are profoundly dependent on others and on a range of social provisions. The extent to which we can, or even should, comply with legal norms (or the cost of complying with them) very much depends on the particular circumstances the individual is in. It requires a softness in legal categorization, a sensitivity

---

[4] See Chapter 7 for further discussion.

to the individual's circumstances which are all too often lacking in our current legal system.

Most significantly, recognizing our vulnerability means rethinking the self. We are not hermetically sealed billiard balls whose interests, rights, and responsibilities can be considered in isolation. That is not true in terms of biology,[5] sociology,[6] or philosophy.[7] The boundaries between selves quickly break down in the real world, where the questions of what are my interests, my rights, and my responsibilities break down in the relational complexity of the real world, where relationships are the key currency, rather than the self.

This means a rejection of the negative assumptions about the nature of vulnerability. As Jo Bridgeman writes: 'Humans are vulnerable ... because we care, love, are intimately connected to others.'[8]

De-centring autonomy

Charles Foster claims, with a little exaggeration, 'Modern debates in medical ethics are often very boring. Whatever the subject, there is usually little debate about the governing principle: everyone assumes that it is "autonomy" and only autonomy.'[9] A similar point could be made about much of the law, and indeed politics, where the buzzword is choice and allowing people to make decisions for themselves, and protecting those decisions. Even in the area of provision of care, the Care Act 2014 emphasizes the importance of allowing people to pursue their goals and set their agendas for service provision.

A vulnerability approach questions the pre-eminence given to autonomy in two ways. First, it questions whether any of us can be autonomous in a rich sense. We rarely have a sufficiently full knowledge of the facts, a clear picture of our values, the commitment to follow our values, and the absence of external pressure needed to be fully autonomous. That is not to say our wishes do not deserve respect, but we should acknowledge them as products of a flawed process.

Second, most people see their decisions in terms of relationships with others. They are not simply decisions about how to live their lives. It is a decision

---

[5] J. Herring and P.-L. Chau, 'My Body, Your Body, Our Bodies', (2007) 15 *Medical Law Review* 274.

[6] P. Donati, *Relational Sociology* (Abingdon, Routledge 2011).

[7] C. Foster and J. Herring, *Altruism, Welfare and the Law* (Berlin, Springer 2015).

[8] J. Bridgeman, 'Vulnerabilities, Care and Family Law' in J. Wallbank and J. Herring (eds), *Vulnerabilities, Care and Family Law* (Abingdon, Routledge 2014), 201.

[9] C. Foster, *Choosing Life, Choosing Death, The Tyranny of Autonomy in Medical Ethics and Law* (Oxford, Hart 2009), 3.

marked in the context of our obligations to others, which will impact on others; and is typically made with others. This relational understanding of autonomy requires a reworking of many of the traditional aspects of the concept.

Rethinking responsibilities

If we are all vulnerable and all dependent on others for the meeting of our needs, responsibilities become of central importance for the law. The caring relationships which we live in, meeting all our needs, are the lifeblood for us and our communities. These relationships must be promoted and respected. A central part of good caring relationships is that one person can rely on the other. Caring only when it is convenient is not the highest kind of care. In genuine caring relationships, it is important to recognize that if one person enters a caring relationship with someone, others may not then offer care for that person. They may assume that any needs are met within that relationship. The parties in the relationship may not seek care from others, relying on each other to meet their needs.[10]

There are dangers in talking of the responsibilities of care. It may be that an individual is facing competing caring responsibilities and may not be able to meet all of them. Further, I am talking here about genuinely caring relationships. Where they have become abusive the responsibilities fall away.

While there may be especial responsibilities in care in some relationships, in others there is at least a responsibility not to exploit the other person you are dealing with; to acknowledge the human traits of ignorance, compulsivity, and irrationality, and not to use those to one's own advantage; to try in our dealings with each other to find arrangements that take into account both parties' interests and a fair distribution of gains and losses. This is not simply some kind of moralistic claim that 'we should be nice to one another'. It is an acknowledgement that our universal vulnerability means we need each other. Co-operation works better than each individual seeking to gain for themselves. It is therefore essential to our survival, and not enforcing a platitude.

The dangers of vulnerability

It is important to emphasize the dangers of the language of vulnerability. Indeed in this book we have seen plenty of examples of the language of

---

[10] J. Herring, *Caring and the Law*, (n. 2), ch 2.

vulnerability being used to the disadvantage of various groups and individuals. The dangers arise because of the current law's norm of us being competent autonomous individuals. Vulnerability is used to describe a particular individual or group as lacking what we look for. It is not surprising the concept is seen as 'oppressive, controlling, and exclusive'.[11]

This carries three particular dangers.

First, it opens that group to invasive and paternalistic interventions which we would not accept for others. The label 'vulnerable' is used to indicate the group are unable to look after themselves and may even pose a risk to others. It leads us ('the non-vulnerable') to assume we know what is best for them ('the vulnerable'). This is completely contrary to the approach based on universal vulnerability highlighted in this book.

Second, those interventions are often designed to help the people escape from vulnerability and become 'independent' and 'self-sufficient'. The goal is to move the 'vulnerable people' to a safe place and equip them to stand up for themselves. This too is contrary to the universal vulnerability approach which does not see vulnerability as something to escape from, but an inherent part of life. We flourish through being dependent on others and our caring relationships.

Third, the current approach in the law tends to suggest that there are vulnerable groups, but the rest of us are not vulnerable. So as long as you are not dealing with someone in a designated vulnerable group you can treat them as having full capacity and autonomy. This too is rejected by universal vulnerability.

Can the law do it all?

In other writing I have been accused of seeing the law as a 'knight in shining armour'.[12] This book may be seen as making the same error. However, I do not claim that simply by changing the law 'all will be well'. Indeed there are serious dangers in seeking to develop a law based on a paradigm of vulnerability, if political and social forces promote individualism and self-sufficiency.[13] I have written this book as a lawyer, but believe these arguments could readily transmit into other areas of public life too. Indeed that is being done in other fields of study: from politicians arguing for public policy centred on

---

[11] K. Brown, 'Vulnerability: Handle with Care', (2011) 5 *Ethics and Social Welfare* 313, 315.
[12] H. Reece, 'Book Review: Caring and the Law', (2014) 23 *Social and Legal Studies* 278.
[13] N. Kohn, 'Vulnerability Theory and the Role of Government', (2014) *Yale Journal of Law & Feminism* 1.

vulnerability[14] to theologians arguing we need a rethinking of a 'vulnerable god'.[15] Nor do I deny the great dangers that can arise from an improper use of vulnerability. Refocusing the law on the norm of vulnerability is only part of the response, and law on its own can do little. But recognizing that human-kind are vulnerable, interconnected, and relational beings is to recognize us as we are. That cannot be a bad place for the law to start.

---

[14] See the work of the Vulnerability and the Human Condition Initiative: <http://web.gs.emory.edu/vulnerability/Affiliated%20Faculty/Global%20Affiliated%20Faculty.html>

[15] W. Placher, *Narratives of a Vulnerable God* (Edinburgh, John Knox Press 1994).

Index

Printed and bound by CPI Group (UK) Ltd, Croydon, CR0 4YY